Lesbian Film Guide

Lesbian Film Guide

Alison Darren

CASSELL
London and New York

Cassell
Wellington House, 125 Strand, London WC2R 0BB
370 Lexington Avenue, New York, NY 10017-6550

First published 2000

© Alison Darren 2000

All rights reserved. No part of this publication may be reproduced or transmitted in any form or by any means, electronic or mechanical, including photocopying, recording or any information storage or retrieval system, without permission in writing from the publishers.

British Library Cataloguing-in-Publication Data
A catalogue record for this book is available from the British Library.

ISBN 0-304-33376-X

Library of Congress Cataloging-in-Publication Data
Darren, Alison
 Lesbian film guide / Alison Darren.
  p. cm.
 Includes indexes.
 ISBN 0-304-33376-X (pbk.)
  1. Lesbians in motion pictures. 2. Motion pictures catalogs.
 I. Title.
 PN1995.9.L48D37 1999
 791.43'65206643–dc21   99-43640
                                                                    CIP

Typeset by BookEns Ltd, Royston, Herts.
Printed and bound in Great Britain by Biddles Limited,
Guildford and King's Lynn

Contents

List of Illustrations	vi
Preface	vii
Acknowledgements	viii
How to Use This Guide	ix
Introduction	1
The Films	7
Index of Directors	229
Index of Countries of Origin	235
Index of Actors	237

Illustrations

The Bitter Tears of Petra von Kant   26
Born in Flames   29
Claire of the Moon   47
Crush   53
Desperate Remedies   59
From Russia with Love   80
Fun   82
Goldfinger   92
Great Moments in Aviation   95
I Shot Andy Warhol   107
Isle of Lesbos   112
It's in the Water   114
I've Heard the Mermaids Singing   115
Late Bloomers   128
Lust for a Vampire   137
Nineteen Nineteen   151
Nocturne   153
Novembermoon   154
Olivia   156
Salmonberries   181
Sister My Sister   199
Les Voleurs   215
When Night Is Falling   218

Preface

This book is a guide to films to watch out for. It represents a selection of films containing some of the strangest, saddest, most infuriating, nauseating, entertaining, gorgeous, murderous, pathetic and fabulous lesbians on screen, put there by some of the most brilliant, incompetent, homophobic, switched-on, clever, idiotic and thoughtful directors in the world.

Of course, there are more films with relevant themes or characters in existence than are written about here. The problem is, they're almost impossible to get hold of. So in this guide you will find reviews of films that are available for viewing, either at the cinema or on television and video. You will find reviews for all the most important feature films made with a lesbian audience in mind, films created for a mainstream audience but with a lesbian theme or significant lesbian character, and films that have only minor lesbian characters but which may be of interest from a historical point of view. Since few people agree on the quality of films, the reviews try to give a *flavour* of what you are in for, rather than either a complete condemnation or unreserved ovation. Even the most badly made or most homophobic films can be of interest on occasion, and I have tried to indicate the saving graces where they exist.

Acknowledgements

Searching for lesbian images in films requires a tenacity and patience similar to a life of devotion, and unfortunately not everyone whose assistance I sought believed that this project was worthwhile or indeed tasteful. Others, however, were more than helpful. Here are their names: Simon Morris, Nasreen Memon, Cherry Smyth, Alison Strauss, Lorraine Bromley, Carol Coombes, Giorgina De Santo, Jane Ivey and Megan Olden.

Most of all, though, thanks go to Sarah Graham. Without her long-suffering support this guide would not have been written.

How to Use This Guide

The films are listed under their most familiar title, followed in some cases by the original foreign-language title, or a well-known English-language alternative. Separate entries for these alternative titles will lead the reader to the main entry.

The arrangement is alphabetical by word, so that *Go Fish* precedes *The Goddess*. Definite and indefinite articles in any language are ignored, but prepositions appear under the appropriate letter.

Each entry consists of a credit listing, a short plot summary in italics and the main review. The use of bold small capitals for a film title (e.g., **THE MAIDS**), either in the main review or under *See also*, indicates there is a main entry for that film in the *Guide*. Films not discussed in the *Guide* are given in italics.

There are just two abbreviations used: GB refers to Great Britain and Northern Ireland, while US refers to the United States of America.

Three indexes allow the reader to search for films by director or country of origin, and to trace an actor's appearances in different films.

for

Sarah Graham

Introduction

TV AND ALL THAT

Today's lesbian youth may be rather bewildered by the lack of positive images on the big screen. Equally, they may find it hard to believe that there was ever a lack of positive images on the small screen. In late 1994 and through most of 1995 it was possible to switch on your television set any weekday and see some lesbian or other in a soap or drama. Not only were these images overwhelmingly positive but they were all, to a woman, attractive, intelligent and assertive. The first, and most enduring, soap character came in the form of Zoe, *Emmerdale*'s country vet (Leah Bracknell). Initially closeted, she seemed doomed to live alone, until a good-looking business woman happened by. Thereafter Zoe has been at the centre of a seemingly endless stream of lesbian intrigue, while simultaneously providing the only consistent TV lesbian character on British television (if not the world). Meanwhile, *EastEnders* offered us Binny and Della, two young, ambitious working-class girls, one white, one black, both looking for a way to get up and get out (having both found it they left the series in May 1995).

For a while, though, all eyes were on *Brookside* and *the* TV lesbian, the beautiful, smart and feisty Beth Jordache played by Anna Friel. It was the Jordache character who over a period of two years caused more controversy about lesbian images on TV than all the others put together. Real kissing(!), with first her mainly straight best friend (Nicola Stephenson), then an older woman with whom she had an affair, then a college girl. The tabloids went mad with excitement, often previewing the kisses in their papers with grainy black-and-white photos taken from TV screens. Their condemnation, moral outrage and thrilled disgust ensured massive ratings and the lipstick lesbian 'phenomenon' was widely discussed.

As if the soaps were not offering enough to the previously starved lesbian viewer, the satirical TV news sitcom *Drop the Dead Donkey* gave us Helen, the efficient dyke mother who had come out to everyone except her parents. Then there was the regular lesbian character in the supremely intelligent police drama *Between the Lines*. This characterization was subtle at first, with merely a hint about the detective's (played by Siobhan Redmond) sexuality. By the third series she was shown living openly with her girlfriend. Relatively explicit sex scenes were shown, a sequence of which was used in the opening titles. The comedy *You Rang M'Lord?* gave us the wonderful Cissy (Catherine Rabett replete with monocle and a series of beautifully tailored suits). Cissy was the eldest daughter of the household, who, as well as being close friends to many lovely women, was also the champion of the workers and behaved with integrity and style.

A one-off drama, *A Village Affair*, was transmitted in spring 1995. This concerned the dilemma of a young mother played by Sophie Ward, in an apparently happy marriage, who found herself falling in love with another woman (Kerry Fox). The programme was repeated in 1997 in the wake of Sophie's real-life coming-out, an event greeted with bewilderment and disbelief by the tabloids.

Then, suddenly, it seemed to be over. Almost all the lesbian regulars disappeared from the screens as fast as you could say lesbian chic. Only reliable Zoe remained, causing the occasional stir down on the farm.

For a short time it went very quiet indeed. Then, gradually, one or two lesbians began to emerge here and there. One notable example was the drama *Close Relations*, which distinguished itself by having a fairly dislikable couple, played by Kate Buffery and Kelly Hunter, engage in very explicit sex scenes. A more enjoyable and more positive lesbian couple (plus child) turned up frequently in the comedy series *Friends*. Most recently *Xena: Warrior Princess* sensationally bridged the gap between entertainment for straight and lesbian viewers with an often breathtakingly explicit subtext. The Amazon Princess (Lucy Lawless) and her faithful sidekick Gabrielle (Renee O'Connor) kicked ass one minute and stared meaningfully at each other the next, a physical relationship frequently implied.

All the while, lesbians were watching an imported American sitcom that wasn't gay at all. It featured a likable, wacky bookstore owner who never seemed able to find a date ...

While *Ellen* was searching for the closet door, and preparing to present the world with the biggest coming-out we had ever seen, back on the big screen things were pretty much as they always had been. The odd scattering of images here and there but nothing to compare with the plethora of mid-1990s TV. Of course, things were improving, but the process was painfully slow. Lesbians had to rely on a handful of independent films, made by lesbian directors, to see themselves as they would like to be seen.

WHAT IS SHE LIKE?

Most people would agree that, to put it mildly, lesbians have been *inadequately* served by the cinema. Misrepresented and misunderstood, the images we have seen – when they have existed at all – have presented a sad gallery of interesting losers, victims, killers, neurotics, drug addicts, prostitutes and so on. We have been ridiculed, feared and pitied. Our fate has included humiliation, rape, miraculous conversion to heterosexuality or, if not, death.

According to mainstream cinema, and Hollywood particularly, a lesbian is likely to display one or more questionable – and often contradictory – personality traits. She might be sadistic, ruthless, antisocial, perverse, lacking in maternal instinct, predatory, anti-male, lecherous and sick. She may also exhibit characteristics such as repression and inadequacy. She might fear men and yet desire to be 'saved'. Her situation is likely to be lonely, tragic or desperate. She might be caught in the throes of unrequited love, especially with a heterosexual woman, or else display an inability to express herself physically. She is very likely to carry an ice-pick with her wherever she goes. It hasn't been the best of times.

IN THE BACK ROW

When a woman has been issued with a lesbian identity in film, the situation is still so rare that the audience always wants to know 'Why is this woman gay? What purpose does it serve the film to have her be this way? What's the point to it?' Even we ask the questions. We expect an explanation for this difference, and that its significance will become clear to us at some stage. We cannot believe she would be there simply for herself.

Until recently the most common reasons for including a lesbian character in a film have been sexual titillation or as a temporary threat to heterosexuality. Usefully, too, a lesbian has acted as an effective standard by which 'normal' women could measure themselves,

INTRODUCTION

helping them to ensure they met society's definition of what a heterosexual woman should be like. Once these functions were fulfilled the lesbian character was most often simply dispatched from the film and the audience was usually pleased to see her go.

SO IS SHE OR ISN'T SHE?

When an actress plays gay in a film, why are we so desperate to know whether she might be a lesbian in real life? We can drive ourselves into a frenzy of conjecture, searching endlessly for clues in her private life, scanning interviews for a single word that might 'give it away'. In this, we very much resemble straight people, who are largely wondering the same thing.

Like all cinema-goers we project reality onto the screen. We have an urgent need to suspend disbelief and become involved. In the same way that heterosexuals have placed themselves in the screen with their object of desire for a hundred years, we too have the same longing to be in *that scene* with *that woman*, whoever she might be.

However, straight people generally take a dim view of the possibility that an actress might be gay in real life. It is still, even now, vital to be heterosexual in Hollywood, and thus 'available' to the maximum audience. A career as a leading woman can be jeopardized if the audience suspects that in her love scenes with men she is 'only acting'.

So, when a famous actress plays lesbian, she will find herself in the middle of a remarkably subtle inquisition, in which she is invited to confirm her essential straightness. Notice how many interviews include the assumption that 'It must have been *so difficult* to play *those scenes*'.

That said, some of the greatest actresses in the world have been (accurately) suspected of Sapphic leanings, including Greta Garbo, Barbara Stanwyck, Marlene Dietrich and Joan Crawford. None of these women came out in the sense that we understand it today, but rumours persisted at the time, and were rejected or ignored to varying degrees by those involved. Only Marlene Dietrich seemed able to operate relatively open relationships with women without damaging her career. Others chose to say nothing. However, their positions as lesbian icons became rock-solid even in the face of studio-arranged marriages and carefully orchestrated mock heterosexual affairs.

Not a great deal has changed in modern times. Speculation is rife about certain stars, none more celestial than Jodie Foster, but we may have to wait a long time – understandably perhaps – before these women are prepared to risk their careers for the sake of openness.

IT'S NOT ALL BAD NEWS

Things are changing. We may still crave a lesbian version of *Sleepless in Seattle* or, more likely, *Terminator 2*, but this being rather improbable in the short term we have long since learned to make do. We have always idolized the independent woman, and hypothesized that her sexuality is surely open to question. We have looked to Ripley to save us from the Alien, hoping that she might go out for a drink with us afterwards. Soon this may no longer be necessary. Since the beginning of the 1980s lesbian images in feature films have been improving, in terms of both numbers and quality. For the first time in film history, films are being made with a lesbian audience in mind.

However, as every film director knows (often to their cost), there are no sterner critics on the planet than lesbians judging lesbian films. Lesbian directors themselves are often crippled by the burden of producing a winning film that is all things to all people. There is an unspoken understanding that every new lesbian film is expected to be – at last – *the* lesbian film, an expectation that places an intolerable pressure on even the most accomplished directors, let alone first-timers. Despite this, the mantle of direction is being assumed by women burning to produce a great lesbian film for us all, even when hampered by low budgets, lack of support and general inexperience. The results may not always be to our liking, but be a little charitable! Films are hard, hard work. They take huge amounts of money to produce, enormous patience and determination, and are often the result of years of preparation and groundwork. It's still early days for lesbian film-making and there is much more to come.

We are now starting to see lesbians on screen whom we would actually like to meet in real life. In 1984 the wartime drama *Novembermoon* featured a wonderful lesbian love story, and in 1985 the world saw its first wholehearted lesbian romance in Donna Deitch's superb *Desert Hearts*. While Hollywood continued to churn out (admittedly entertaining) psychopathic serial killers in lesbian form – *Basic Instinct* being the supreme example – independent film-makers like Rose Troche and Guinevere Turner were coming up with low-budget winners like *Go Fish*. Canadian Patricia Rozema offered us the brilliant, heartbreaking comedy *I've Heard the Mermaids Singing* and the equally clever and quixotic *When Night Is Falling*. Suddenly we are

INTRODUCTION

seeing women with attractive personalities who demonstrate positive qualities! From the hilarious *It's in the Water* to the sleek and sexy *Bound*, at last we have images of women we wouldn't mind taking home to meet our mother! Finally, at long last, we're moving on.

The Films

Les Abysses 1962

Director: Nico Papatakis. Country: France. Screenplay: Jean Vauthier. Production company: Lenox Films. Duration: 96 mins, black and white

Cast: Francine Berge (Michele), Colette Berge (Marie-Louise), Pascale de Boysson (Elizabeth), Paul Bonifas (M. Lapeyre), Colette Regis (Mme Lapeyre)

Story based on an actual case in France that inspired Jean Genet to write The Maids. *Two sisters are employed as servants in the home of Monsieur, Madame and their daughter Elizabeth. Gradually the maids rebel against their repression until in a terrible outburst they exact a violent revenge on their masters.*

Michele and Marie-Louise, the two young sisters at the centre of the drama, are presented as deranged from the first moment we see them. Although we pity their circumstances, we fear more for their unlucky masters than we do for the odd siblings. The strange girls contrive to torment the householders in small ways at first – tearing down bits of wallpaper and breaking roof tiles. But confrontation starts soon afterwards when the maids are not scared to answer back to their initially bemused employers. The young daughter of the house treats Marie-Louise with kindness, but this is by turns welcomed or ridiculed. Eventually the violence escalates out of control as feelings are given furious expression and all the individuals apply extraordinary measures of mental and physical cruelty upon each other. Exceedingly violent for the time.

As far as lesbianism is concerned, in real life the sisters were involved in a fully sexual incestuous relationship but we see little evidence of that here. Instead there is just the odd physical embrace and the merest hint of something more.

AFTERNOON BREEZES

See also: other versions of the same story, **SISTER MY SISTER** and **THE MAIDS**.

Afternoon Breezes (Kazetachi No Gogo) 1980

Director: Hitoshi Yazaki. Country: Japan. Production company: Shunichi Nagasaki. Duration: 106 mins, black and white

Cast: Setsuko Aya (Natsuko), Naomi Ito, Hiroshi Sugita, Mari Atake

Tokyo. Natsuko is a nursery school teacher. Mitsu is a hairdresser. They share a flat, but for Natsuko the relationship is more than just friendship, for she is desperately in love with the man-chasing Mitsu.

Remarkable feature by Japanese director Hitoshi Yazaki, who was just twenty-four when he made this debut. His view of Natsuko's hopeless crush on her heterosexual friend is a sombre and doomed account of unrequited love. Natsuko is portrayed as selfish, childish and obsessive. Although the strategies she devises to try to win her friend over are blunt and unsophisticated (she tries to persuade Mitsu's womanizing boyfriend to stray by offering herself as bait), one cannot help but feel twinges of pity at her predicament and her longing. She is strongly contrasted with Mitsu, who is similarly selfish but with a different motivation – she wants a man to marry and is searching for a good provider.

Mitsu is, of course, oblivious to Natsuko's growing obsession with her and sees nothing odd in the gestures and gifts of love with which she is presented. An expensive and thoughtful birthday present – a necklace – is received casually (compared to Mitsu's boyfriend's careless present of perfume samples, which are received with flirtatious gratitude). Later Natsuko gives her beloved Mitsu a lighter, which she in turn passes on to her boyfriend without a thought. These, and other achingly sad observations of the endless small hurts suffered by those caught up in unrequited love, are the main strength of the film. However, filmed in black and white, and with several sequences in real time, *Afternoon Breezes* is a touch ponderous and suffers greatly from its low budget. Nevertheless, the extraordinary performance by Setsuko Aya as the immature, lovelorn Natsuko is something to wonder at.

Alien: Resurrection   1997

Director: Jean-Pierre Jeunet. Country: US. Screenplay: Joss Whedon. Production company: Twentieth Century Fox. Duration: 105 mins, colour

Cast: Sigourney Weaver (Ripley 8), Winona Ryder (Call), Dominique Pinon (Vriess), Ron Perlman (Johner), Gary Dourdan (Christie), Michael Wincott (Elgyn), Kim Flowers (Hillard)

> Somewhere in deep space on board a United Systems Military starship, aliens are being harvested by unethical humans for future use. A band of pirates lands on the spaceship with the cargo commissioned by the military – frozen humans who will act as hosts for new baby aliens. But among the pirates is Call, a freedom fighter who – unknown to everyone – intends to sabotage the operation. In the meantime the aliens break free from their prison and the pirates find they have a real fight on their hands. Only one person seems able to help them, a strange woman known as Ripley 8 . . .

At the end of *Alien 3* Ellen Ripley threw herself suicidally into a melting-pot to ensure she did not give birth to the alien that was growing inside her. Now she's back, cloned from blood taken from her body just before her untimely death. Ripley is the subject of an experiment by unscrupulous persons to extract the Alien from her body. But two hundred years on she's not quite the woman we used to know. Alien DNA has found its way into her bloodstream and now Ripley 8 (there were seven unsuccessful cloning attempts before she was created) demonstrates some remarkable qualities, including extraordinary muscular dexterity and acid for blood. She has also lost much of the compassion that drove her to fight for the lives of others in the previous films. Now she really couldn't care less.

An excellent Alien movie, a real return to form after the wretched and morbid *Alien 3*. Now the fabulous Ripley, both mind and body fantastic, must battle something that is in many senses a part of her. Like all of the Alien films, on one level this is still simply a brilliantly clever sci-fi slasher movie and none the worse for it. But if it's psychological subtexts you want, *Alien: Resurrection* is the film for you. Questions about humanity, the nature of what it is to be human, about cloning, progeny and life itself are there if you want them. And in the final reel comes one of the saddest, most unexpectedly moving climaxes ever to end a movie.

Of course, there is no lesbianism as such in *Alien: Resurrection*. But there is something, definitely *something*, going on between Ripley 8 and Call. When the two first meet it is in Ripley 8's cell where she is sleeping. Call is wielding a knife with the intention of releasing Ripley from her 'mostly human, partly alien' state. Ripley 8 wakes and, unperturbed, observes the elfin girl kneeling over her. 'So are you going to kill me ... or what?' she asks, with an almost kinky amusement. Or what indeed. The two do not fight but instead join forces (inasmuch as Ripley 8 will align herself with anything). A little later Call is injured in her abdomen. Ripley 8 puts her fingers into the wound and ... well it's not exactly **DESERT HEARTS** but your stomach might still drop a little watching it.

It is fascinating (though hardly surprising) that only at this point – in the fourth Alien film and when Ripley is definitely no longer herself – that the vaguest possibility of lesbianism is allowed to enter the proceedings. Right from the beginning of the series Flight Officer Ellen Ripley – the greatest movie heroine ever and an iconic presence for so many lesbians – was always implicitly heterosexual (although uninvolved in a relationship with a man for the first two films). But Ripley 8 is a bit of an alien, and therefore able to be distinctly odd in other ways – a flirtation with lesbianism is not unexpected ...

Sigourney Weaver is, as ever, sensational in the role which has been hers alone for twenty years. Winona Ryder makes a delicate, winsome Call, a girl partner for the impossibly grown-up Ripley 8. It is interesting to note that Winona was a big fan of Sigourney in her teen years and had a picture of Ripley above her bed. Well, didn't we all? ...

All over Me   1996

Director: Alex Sichel. Country: US. Screenplay: Sylvia Sichel. Production company: Medusa Pictures. Duration: 90 mins, colour

Cast: Alison Folland (Claude), Tara Subkoff (Ellen), Cole Hauser (Mark), Wilson Cruz (Jesse), Ann Dowd (Anne), Leisha Hailey (Lucy), Pat Briggs (Luke)

Hell's Kitchen, New York, in the present day, and life is not easy for teenager Claude. Left largely to look after herself by an uncaring mother, her time is spent working in the local pizza restaurant or hanging out with best friend Ellen. Claude is in love with Ellen, but she in turn has rough drug-dealer boyfriend Mark in tow. Claude watches helplessly as Ellen slides towards addiction.

Powerful low-budget coming-of-age drama distinguished by extraordinary performances from the two young leads. If you didn't get enough teenage angst when you were there yourself, here is a chance to catch up and relive the moments you've tried so hard to forget. Remember being fifteen, clumsy, gauche and with nothing to say? Feeling the pain of seeing your beloved best friend in the arms of the most unsuitable boy around? Not forgetting, of course, having to listen to her tell you about the wonderful sex they're having? It's all here, perfectly realized, against a backdrop of dirty New York streets and violent homophobia. Still, although Claude may not have much idea of what she wants from her life, she knows for sure she's a lesbian. Very positively, Ellen's rejection does not stop Claude's interest in girls, and soon she takes tentative steps towards someone else. But the timbre of the movie can be gauged by the Patti Smith poster on Claude's wall. You know what you're in for.

Note: Alison Folland also features in the brilliant Gus Van Sant black comedy *To Die For* (1995). Alison plays Lydia, grungy teen acolyte infatuated with Nicole Kidman's ambitious cable TV weather girl Suzanne Stone. In the story the enamoured adolescent indirectly helps ruthless Stone kill her husband. When the going gets tough Suzanne accuses the hapless girl of having 'lesbian tendencies'.

See also: **ONLY THE BRAVE** for more teenage blues.

Anne Trister   1986

Director: Lea Pool. Country: Canada. Screenplay: Marcel Beaulieu and Lea Pool. Production company: Films Vision 4/National Film Board of Canada. Duration: 115 mins, colour

Cast: Albane Guilhe (Anne), Louise Marleau (Alix), Lucie Laurier (Sarah), Guy Thauvette (Thomas), Hugues Quester (Pierre), Nuvit Ozdogru (Simon), Kim Yaroshevskaya (Mother)

Anne is a young Jewish painter living in Switzerland. Grief-stricken after her father dies, she leaves behind her boyfriend Pierre and returns to Montreal to stay with her older friend Alix. Time passes and, in an outpouring of creative despondency, Anne paints a giant mural. She also finds she has fallen in love with Alix.

Slow and reflective, *Anne Trister* is a drama of delicate sensibilities and refinement. We are taken on a journey – conducted at a stately pace – through Anne's emotional development as she progresses from grieving daughter to recovered adult woman. Anne's distress at losing her father opens the proceedings, and the burial in the Israeli desert is a beautiful sequence. The return to Quebec moves the plot along, and we know the trip will prove to be a turning-point for Anne in several respects. Alix obligingly offers her a place to live while she sorts herself out, despite the fact that this causes friction with Alix's lover Thomas.

Alix is a child psychiatrist who, in the course of her daily work is attempting to help Sarah, a disturbed child. The film draws a parallel between the child and Anne, and the demanding emotional attachments both form with Alix. Meanwhile Anne's huge abstract painting becomes the core of the film, with the artistic process strikingly reflecting Anne's development and recovery.

The lesbian theme is slight and really of only minor consequence. Of the two women, Alix appears the most likely lesbian figure but it is Anne who is most interested and makes the first move – a gentle kiss in the studio from which Alix withdraws. Things advance a little but not very far. Strangely, the evolving relationship between the two women seems rather uninteresting. A blankness of emotion, rather than an urgent feeling of love or desire, prevails, and both women seem to be 'trying on' the idea of a lesbian relationship rather than being emotionally drawn into it. Anne decides that she no longer loves her boyfriend, but she wants much more from Alix than Alix is willing or able to give. The film ends with them separating as friends. A chronicle of an artist's progress rather than a lesbian love story.

Another Way (Egymásra Nézve) 1982

Director: Karoly Makk. Country: Hungary. Screenplay: Erzsebet Galgoczi and Karoly Makk (based on the book *Torvenyen Belul* by Erzsebet Galgoczi). Production company: Dialog Studio. Duration: 109 mins, colour, subtitled

Cast: Jadwiga Jankowska-Cieslak (Eva), Grazyna Szapolowska (Livia), Josef Kroner (Editor), Gabor Reviczky (Fiala)

Hungary 1958. Two journalists, Eva and Livia, work on a newspaper called The Truth. *Eva, an idealist, falls for the married, more conventional Livia. The two begin a precarious flirtation which eventually develops into a relationship. Livia's husband begins to suspect what is happening, while Eva faces growing problems at work. The two decide to flee the country.*

Karoly Makk's film is based on an autobiographical book written by the 'Eva' character, and with the exception of the ending, the story is very much a true account of real events. *Another Way* has two subjects, one is the lesbian relationship, the other is the political upheaval going on two years after the revolution in Hungary. By turns sombre and uplifting, with a beautiful, mournful jazz score, *Another Way* coveys the astonishing degree of courage required to face the authorities both in terms of expressing a sexual preference and the need for political freedom.

Polish actress Jadwiga Jankowska-Cieslak plays Eva with a veracity that earned her Best Actress at the Cannes Film Festival (incidently, Grazyna Szapolowska is also Polish – no Hungarian actresses could be found to fill the roles). Eva's need for emotional and professional integrity causes her to risk everything by pursuing the woman she loves and at the same time challenging her editor over the lies printed in the newspaper as required by the state. This is living dangerously by anyone's estimation, and in that context Livia's initial reluctance to involve herself with Eva is understandable. Both women are shown in a realistic light, which is less than flattering on occasions. Eva is surprisingly brutal when dealing with a former lover who turns up at her door needing help. Livia is shown to be selfish and ultimately too weak to cope with the problems she faces. In terms of her appearance, she is rather glamorous and well dressed with blond coiffured hair. Eva, by comparison, has a pragmatic approach to her clothing: she wears her hair short and plain, and wears inexpensive clothes (money doesn't go so far without a husband supporting you). Neither are heart-warming characters but their predicament is enough to ensure audience involvement. Unexpectedly, there are one or two amusing exchanges, including a conversation between Eva and a bewildered police chief who does not understand lesbianism. 'When you look at me,' he asks, completely confused, 'don't you see me as a man?' 'Of course,' replies Eva. 'You *are* a man, aren't you?'

Makk had some difficulty getting the film made, for reasons of sexuality and politics equally. He once remarked that when the Hungarian authorities saw the film they were 'not exactly charmed'. Nevertheless, the film was released all over the world, and to much acclaim.

Antonia's Line   1995

Director: Marleen Gorris. Country: Netherlands, Belgium and GB. Screenplay: Marleen Gorris. Production company: Antonia's Line International. Duration: 102 mins, colour

Cast: Willeke van Ammelrooy (Antonia), Els Dottermans (Danielle), Dora van der Groen (Allegonde), Veerle van Overloop (Thérèse), Mil Seghers (Kromme Vinger), Jan Decleir (Boer Bas), Elsie de Brauw (Lara), Reinout Bussemaker (Simon)

At the age of eighty-five Antonia decides she has reached her last day on earth. She uses the time to reflect on her life. She thinks back to the end of World War II, and the forty years that have followed.

Wonderful, moving, funny, gritty and sometimes whimsical drama following the fortunes of a number of idiosyncratic characters living in a small village in Holland. The chronicle sees Antonia return home after the war to make a life for herself on a farm as part of a small, patriarchal community. She has a daughter, Danielle, and the two make a home despite difficult and sometimes brutal conditions. Antonia herself is pragmatic and just. She protects innocents from the bullying (sometimes worse) of the less pleasant members of the village. Thus the put-upon, the social misfits and the badly treated flock to her, and her extended family becomes a place of safety for the dispossessed.

Danielle, meanwhile, grows up and decides she wants a child without the benefit of a husband. Unsurprised, Antonia locates a suitable sperm donor and soon Thérèse is born, a little girl so intelligent she is pronounced a prodigy. As Thérèse grows up Danielle provides her with a tutor, Lara. This proves a turning point for Danielle, who falls in love with Lara. In an amusing sequence the women meet in the family kitchen, and as their interest in each other grows, a sensuous discussion about artichokes develops, leaving the young child annoyed and forgotten between them. Danielle and Lara form a close and loving relationship which lasts, it is implied, all of their lives.

Excellent performances all round and a fluid directing style ensure that the saga never palls or becomes confusing. The lesbian relationship may be simply part of the general mêlée, but it is warmly presented and endorsed throughout. Lovely.

See also: **MRS DALLOWAY** by the same director.

L'Araignée de Satin: see under **THE SATIN SPIDER**

At First Sight (Coup de Foudre; Entre Nous)   1983

Director: Diane Kurys. Country: France. Screenplay: Diane Kurys and Alain Le Henry (based on the book by Olivier Cohen and Diane Kurys). Production company: Partners Productions. Duration: 111 mins, colour

Cast: Miou-Miou (Madeleine), Isabelle Huppert (Lena), Guy Marchand (Michel), Jean-Pierre Bacri (Costa), Patrick Bauchau (Carlier), Robin Renucci (Raymond)

True story of the lifelong friendship between two women set in France after World War II. The lesbian frustration quotient reaches an all-time high in this film, so beautifully told but with an ambiguous relationship at its core that will leave you longing for something more explicit. The story is based on director Diane Kury's mother, Lena, and her close friend Madeleine, with whom she sets up a business.

The two women meet by chance at a school function and, to the strains of 'I Wonder Who's Kissing Her Now', they find they are immediately attracted to each other. Although they have both made marriages of convenience, the similarity stops there. Lena, a quiet housewife with a solid, caring husband, is contrasted with artist Madeleine, whose actor partner is forever attempting silly get-rich-quick schemes to make money. Set against the backdrop of 1950s Lyon, the film moves along splendidly, demonstrating the devotion between the two women but suggesting, at all times, that there is nothing physical going on. Instead the emotional intensity of passionate feeling is expressed by Lena's husband Michel, who suspects he is losing his wife and tearfully pleads with her to give Madeleine up. To no avail, however, and the women leave their husbands to set up a dress shop together. The dedication between the two is undeniable, yet the emotional feelings they share are so understated as to render the relationship most perplexing. They refer to each other throughout the film in the formal 'vous' form, rather than the informal (and therefore more appropriate) 'tu', as if they wish to draw a firm line between them. However, there are moments of delicacy, warmth, tenderness, contentment, and – oh so briefly – a whisper of eroticism. It's a lovely film, and a postscript from Diane Kurys at the end dedicates it to both her parents and Madeleine.

Bar Girls   1994

Director: Marita Giovanni. Country: US. Screenplay: Lauran Hoffman. Production company: Lavender Circle Mob/Lauran Hoffman. Duration: 95 mins, colour

Cast: Nancy Allison Wolfe (Loretta), Liza D'Agostino (Rachel), Camilla Griggs (JR), Justine Slater (Veronica), Lisa Parker (Annie)

Very amusing comedy chronicling the life and loves of Loretta, and her search for Ms Right. Loretta frequents LA's Girl Bar where the current range of lesbians hang out – lipstick, leather, femme, butch, etc. One night she meets Rachel and the two begin dating. Before long the rogues' gallery of ex-lovers and potential future partners intervene and disrupt the happy couple with their jealousies and temptations. Will the relationship survive?

Described by the director as the 'next step after *Go Fish*', *Bar Girls* explores the idea that not all lesbians get along in a haze of lavender sisterhood and that promiscuity can cause as many problems as it solves. Made for just $600,000, *Bar Girls* is, on that level, an admirable achievement. Orion distributors picked the film up early on and it opened in America on 7 April 1995 in forty states. Mainstream appeal is centred around a strong, witty script and held together with a marvellous central performance by Nancy Allison Wolfe as Loretta. She carries most of the comedy via one-liners made all the better through her excellent timing and natural style. And if the film slows down or falls a little flat, Nancy is there to pull it up again.

As is her intention, Giovanni succeeds in creating a 'being out' rather than 'coming out' film, populated by some 'realistic' and often dislikable characters. Top of the list is the charismatically challenged JR, the dyke cop with no brain and no idea of foreplay, with whom Loretta finds herself compromised. But one of the best scenes involves Loretta's straight friend who takes a Sapphic turn over the green salad. Smart dialogue and insider knowledge of the West Coast la, la, lesbian scene make the experience fun, frivolous and knowing.

Note: Chastity Bono makes a fleeting appearance as one of the Bar's customers.

Barbarella   1967

Director: Roger Vadim. Country: France and Italy. Screenplay: Terry Southern (based on the book by Jean-Claude Forest). Production company: Marianne Productions. Duration: 98 mins, colour

Cast: Jane Fonda (Barbarella), John Phillip Law (Pygar), Anita Pallenberg (The Black Queen), Milo O'Shea (The Concierge), David Hemmings (Dilando)

Sent off to the planet Sorgo, Barbarella is required to display much derring-do in her bid to save the Universe from the evil deeds of the Black Queen and her people.

A very young Jane Fonda plays Barbarella in this amusing sci-fi flick set in the year 40,000. On her travels she encounters demonic children, a blind angel, numerous kinky machines and other horrors, all of which she experiences at first hand. This being a Roger Vadim film, Fonda spends most of her time with few or no clothes on, and indeed she opens the film performing a weightless, zero-gravity strip in the confines of her space capsule. Designed to cater to all, *Barbarella* inevitably contains a little lesbian offering, in this case in the form of the Black Queen who takes an immediate fancy to our heroine, though this is (surprise) not reciprocated. Still, remarkably for a lesbian baddie, the Queen is not killed in the end, and the duo even do a little bonding. Camp rather than Sapphic.

Bare Behind Bars (A Prisão)   1981

Director: Oswaldo De Oliveira. Country: Brazil. Screenplay: Oswaldo De Oliveira. Production company: Produçãos Cinematograficas Galante. Duration: 87 mins, colour, dubbed

Cast: Marie Stella Splendore, Martha Anderson, Danielle Ferriti, Neide Ribeiro, Sonia Regina, Marliane Gomes

Remarkably explicit women's prison soft-porn flick that has to be seen to be believed.

Somewhere in South America is a prison run by an omnipotent warden with a taste for sadism and sex. She uses the prison to operate a sex-slave business, providing nubile girls for local rich women. That's when she isn't seducing them herself, or else inflicting whippings and beatings on the more hapless inmates. However, she is not alone in her proclivities. *Everyone* is having sex with everyone else, whether it be in the corridors, the prison yard, the showers or even through the cell doors. Staff and inmates are equally involved, revelling as they do in the filthy conditions, the fights and the torture as well as the sex. Most fun of all is the hilarious morphine-addicted 'Nurse' who gives internal examinations regardless of the medical problem.

Sleazy and unremitting, this exploitation film is distinguished from the usual dross by its wit and lack of pretension. Nevertheless exploitation is still the name of the game. Don't say you haven't been warned.

Basic Instinct 1992

Director: Paul Verhoeven. Country: US. Screenplay: Joe Eszterhas. Production company: Carolco. Duration: 127 mins, colour

Cast: Michael Douglas (Nick Curran), Sharon Stone (Catherine Tramell), George Dzundza (Gus), Jeanne Tripplehorn (Dr Beth Garner), Denis Arndt (Lieutenant Walker), Leilani Sarelle (Roxy), Dorothy Malone (Hazel Dobkins)

Sensational exploitation movie in which rich author (Stone) is the prime suspect in a gruesome murder case. The investigator (Douglas) finds himself falling for her as he pursues a conviction.

Basic Instinct was a controversial film even before it was made. Word was out early that Hollywood was financing a savagely anti-lesbian movie, and as a result both writer and director were harangued constantly on set by various pro-lesbian and gay groups. Paul Verhoeven and Joe Eszterhas protested that their intentions were honourable, and courteously made one or two minor adjustments to the script. Secretly, though, they must have been delighted with the controversy and the resulting media coverage. *Basic Instinct* became an event as much as a film. It was never going to offer up positive images of lesbians, but then no one comes out of this film looking particularly admirable. On release, the same protest groups demonstrated outside of cinemas with banners saying 'Catherine did it!', hoping to scupper the audience figures by revealing the so-called surprise ending. As always, the resulting publicity only helped the box office, which was already well into overdrive due to the leg-crossing-no-knickers interrogation scene performed by Stone.

In fact Sharon Stone is mightily impressive as the bisexual serial killer with brains, beauty and considerable wealth at her disposal. Men count for nothing to her – unless they are good in bed – though she appears to care a little for her girlfriend in her own alluringly psychotic way. All this changes of course when the Right Man comes along. Michael Douglas – in his customary Everyman guise – plays the cop in hot pursuit who can't stop dropping his trousers whenever Stone gives him the nod. Although it is implied that the sex they have is nothing special to Catherine, Douglas wants more and is soon confronting her girlfriend – 'man to man' – as he puts it, to square off over their shared partner. Shortly afterwards Roxy is off the scene altogether and we are left with the two leads battling it out in a maze of false clues and wrong conclusions. Will he arrest her, will she kill him first? Well, this isn't *Jagged Edge* (1985) unfortunately, so the suspense is absent and the last few seconds of the film are genuinely hilarious.

Essentially, this is just pure flash trash. Troubling, certainly. But if you like Sharon Stone, just lie back and enjoy it.

See also: **SHOWGIRLS** by the same director, and **DIABOLIQUE** for more Sharon.

Becoming Colette 1991

Director: Danny Huston. Country: US, France and Germany. Screenplay: Ruth Graham. Production company: Bibo Film Productions. Duration: 93 mins, colour

Cast: Klaus Maria Brandauer (Willy), Mathilda May (Colette), Virginia Madsen (Polaire), Paul Rhys (Chapo)

The life and times of the young French writer. At a young age Colette marries the older, charismatic Willy. While leading a work-free life in Paris she decides to begin writing. When Willy sees the work he publishes it under his own name and becomes famous. Time passes and Colette grows tired of writing for her husband, particularly as he is now having adulterous affairs. She begins a lesbian affair with a friend which proves to be as supportive as it is sexual.

Romantic drama or European art movie? Just the former really, but with too many rude bits to allow it to pass as an ordinary TV film. The acting is good, particularly Mathilda May as Colette and Klaus Maria Brandauer as the roguish big bad husband. But this is strictly second-division drama. By far the best thing about it is the tender and sexy relationship between the two women (with soft-focus love scenes included), seen in stark contrast to the exploitative one Colette experiences with her husband. Nice and soapy.

Behind This Mask: see under IN A LONELY PLACE

Belle de Jour 1967

Director: Luis Buñuel. Country: France and Italy. Screenplay: Luis Buñuel and Jean-Claude Carrière (based on the novel by Joseph Kessel). Production company: Paris Film Productions. Duration: 100 mins, black and white

Cast: Catherine Deneuve (Séverine), Jean Sorel (Pierre), Michel Piccoli (Henri Husson), Genevieve Page (Mme Anaïs), Francisco Rabal (Hyppolite), Pierre Clémenti (Marcel)

Rich, middle-class housewife Séverine experiences sado-masochist fantasies and decides to become a prostitute by day in order to relieve her boredom. In the rather top-drawer brothel, she meets a strange array of characters and maybe falls in love with one of them. Nothing is certain.

Buñuel's brilliantly clever surreal comedy is a comment on the French bourgeoisie whom he always saw as hypocritical profligates. It contains just a minor lesbian character. Genevieve Page plays the brothel madam who displays more than a passing interest in her new recruit. Fairly unremarkable from the lesbian point of view, except that this stereotype is a precursor which occurs over and over in films too numerous to mention.

See also: **ÉCOUTE VOIR, THE HUNGER** and **LES VOLEURS** for Catherine Deneuve in various lesbian guises.

Belle Époque 1992

Director: Fernando Trueba. Country: Spain and France. Screenplay: Rafael Azcona. Production company: Fernando Trueba Film Production. Duration: 108 mins, subtitled

Cast: Fernando Fernán Gómez (Manolo), Jorge Sanz (Fernando), Maribel Verdú (Rocío), Ariadna Gil (Violeta), Miriam Díaz-Aroca (Clara), Penélope Cruz (Luz)

On the eve of the Spanish Civil War, a young soldier flees his responsibilities

and takes refuge in the home of an old man and his four daughters. Bewildered and good-natured, the soldier finds himself in love with each of the daughters, who in their turn have various reasons for sleeping with him.

The first daughter to mesmerize the soldier Fernando is Violeta. For reasons which are never quite explained, Violeta was raised as a boy until her first period. The result is a boyishly handsome young woman, clearly a lesbian and thought of – affectionately – as such by the entire family. Her mother advises her that marriage is not for her. 'You should find a nice girl who loves you and keeps house for you,' she says! However, Fernando is blissfully unaware of this covert understanding and is happily seduced by Violeta after a fancy-dress party – she dressed as a boy, he dressed as a girl. Violeta assumes the dominant role throughout and even blows a bugle at the essential moment ... The following day Fernando, completely smitten, approaches the father to ask for Violeta's hand. He is mystified. 'How can you marry a man?' he asks. Violeta meanwhile wants nothing more to do with the crestfallen soldier. Brilliantly joyous comedy which deservedly won a Best Foreign Film Oscar. Lesbianism treated with warmth and respect, although safely within the confines of an exceptionally unorthodox Spanish family.

Beyond the Valley of the Dolls   1970

Director: Russ Meyer. Country: US. Screenplay: Roger Ebert. Production company: Twentieth Century Fox. Duration: 109 mins (GB 106 mins)

Cast: Dolly Read (Kelly MacNamara), Cynthia Myers (Casey Anderson), Marcia McBroom (Petronella Danforth), John La Zar (Ronnie 'Z-Man' Barzell), Michael Blodgett (Lance Rocke), Erica Gavin (Roxanne)

Kelly leads an as-yet-undiscovered all-girl pop group. She hears that she has an inheritance waiting for her in Hollywood, so off she goes with the band. Once there, the girls are taken under the wing of swinging philanthropist 'Z-Man' Barzell. Can he help them to succeed and what will be the price if he does?

Director Russ Meyer's style of psychological sex drama – a genre he has made all his own – is fully realized in this blissfully trashy melodrama that is filled to the brim with sex, drugs and rock 'n' roll. The fab and groovy 1960s are where it's at, a time of twangy guitars and electric organs. The Carrie Nations pop group becomes the latest thing and 'Z-Man's' parties are the place to be. The 'chicks' succumb to the heady mixture of grass and free love (all pretty up-front stuff, where a typical pick-up line – from the lips of a woman – goes something like, 'You're a groovy boy. I'd like to strap you on sometime' ...).

Our lesbian is Casey, guitarist with the Carrie Nations. Casey is unaware of her sexuality at first, she only knows that she is not interested in men and finds their attentions a drag. At one of 'Z-Man's' parties Casey meets Roxanne and suddenly a warm glow fills her heart. It's not all straightforward though, and Casey has to endure various ups and downs – including an abortion – before the two get together. The love scene is rather sweet, however. It takes the form of a seduction (though Casey needs very little enticing), in which Roxanne (practised lesbian) makes all the right moves, while Casey (former straight woman) is rendered orgasmically rapturous. All the while the film's theme tune twinkles in the background.

Russ Meyer cannot bring himself to condemn the women for their Sapphic leanings, for he is a half-hearted moralist and, fortunately, no hypocrite. However, he is certainly a full-time philosopher, and thus at the end of the film the narrator advises us that 'theirs was not an evil relationship, though evil did come because of it'. Smashing stuff.

See also: **FASTER, PUSSYCAT, KILL! KILL!** and **VIXEN** by the same director. Erica Gavin appears in **CAGED HEAT** and **VIXEN** as the love-crazy heroine.

Les Biches (The Does) 1968

Director: Claude Chabrol. Country: France and Italy. Screenplay: Paul Gégauff and Claude Gaillard. Production company: Films La Boétie. Duration: 99 mins, colour

Cast: Stéphane Audran (Frédérique), Jacqueline Sassard (Why), Jean-Louis Trintignant (Paul Thomas), Nane Germon (Violetta), Henri Attal (Robegue), Dominique Verdi (Riais)

Rich Frédérique picks up poor street artist Why on a Paris street. A liaison develops and the muted romance continues on the Riviera. Shortly afterwards Why becomes attracted to a local architect Paul ...

Classic Chabrol, cool, calm and multi-layered, *Les Biches* appears to be *merely* a rather elegant story of bisexual intrigue, but below the surface is a clever, disturbing and funny tale of human nature, jealousy and revenge.

Stéphane Audran (Chabrol's wife at the time) is breathtakingly exquisite as the aristocratic woman who tempts a girl's affection with a 500-franc note. In her black fur-trimmed coat and matching hat worn at a jaunty angle, she is a picture of French perfection. She takes the girl back to her flat and a seduction is implied – just. Unfortunately, one of the many frustrations of this clever film is that the predatory lesbian is not quite predatory enough. It is never certain that the two women are involved in what one might call a 'fully sexual' relationship. This rationale is further compounded later in the film when Frédérique asks the increasingly charmless Why whether or not she likes making love. In response Why declares herself a virgin, implying either that she is not having sex with Frédérique, or that she is doing so but that it doesn't count in terms of virginity. Disappointing either way.

Down in off-season St Tropez Why becomes almost instantaneously keen on handsome Paul and overnight they become lovers. But as far as relationships go this is only the beginning, for Frédérique is not to be outdone or left out. As with most cinematic bisexual triangles, both women are involved with the same man (who has had to do little to inspire devotion beyond merely existing). What is different here is that the woman who is eventually the *loser* decides she will still replace her rival somehow.

Glorious playing by all three leads but particularly the wonderful Stéphane Audran, who won Best Actress at the 1968 Berlin Film Festival for her efforts.

Bilitis 1976

Director: David Hamilton. Country: France. Screenplay: Catherine Breillat. Production company: Films 21. Duration: 95 mins, colour

Cast: Patti D'Arbanville (Bilitis), Mona Kristensen (Melissa Hampton), Bernard Giraudeau (Lucas), Gilles Kohler (Pierre Hampton)

Bilitis spends her school holidays receiving a series of sexual awakenings at the hands of a school friend, a male photographer and her own stepmother.

The film for which the expression 'moving picture' might well have been invented. David Hamilton was a photographer of extraordinary popularity in the 1970s; his photos of nymph-like young nubiles were to be found everywhere, most especially on posters and greetings cards. Almost all the photographs featured girls in languorous repose and wearing very little, and many were coyly lesbian in subject, carefully set within a firmly pre-pubescent frame. It was really no surprise when Mr Hamilton decided to branch out into the world of cinema to further his art. Unsurprising too, perhaps, is the result, which resembles a series of beautiful, soft-focused photographs joined up to look like a movie.

Tasteful Sapphic encounters are everywhere in this film. It's all very youthful and innocent, though: girls and women are the stepping-stones to men, the gentle, sensuous prelude to more grown-up sex. Patti D'Arbanville is rather good as Bilitis, the confused adolescent who doesn't understand the adults' games, although the script does her no favours. The most romantic, and also the sexiest, encounter happens rather early on, when Bilitis sleeps with her school friend.

See also: **THE GETTING OF WISDOM, MAIDENS IN UNIFORM, OLIVIA, PICNIC AT HANGING ROCK** and **SECRET PLACES** for more schoolgirl crushes.

Bitter Moon (Lunes de Fiel)   1992

Director: Roman Polanski. Country: France and GB. Screenplay: Roman Polanski, Gérard Brach, John Brownjohn (based on the novel *Lunes de Fiel* by Pascal Bruckner). Production company: R. P. Productions. Duration: 139 mins, colour

Cast: Peter Coyote (Oscar), Emmanuelle Seigner (Mimi), Hugh Grant (Nigel), Kristin Scott-Thomas (Fiona), Luca Vellani (Dado)

On a cruise ship to Istanbul, uptight English couple Nigel and Fiona meet American Oscar and his French wife Mimi. Oscar spends most of the voyage giving the reluctantly interested Nigel an account of his complex relationship with the beautiful Mimi. It seems that while Nigel and Fiona have been experiencing seven contented, if uneventful, years of marriage, Oscar and Mimi have been engaged in a relationship of hate.

A fantastically awful film, *Bitter Moon* is a satirical melodrama *par excellence* masquerading as a multi-layered psychological drama. Worth seeing for a dozen reasons, not least of which is the uniformly excellent acting by all four main characters. Peter Coyote enjoys himself the most as the charismatically obnoxious Oscar, wheelchair-bound after an 'accident'. Kristin Scott-Thomas is very good too as the suppressed wife who finds, at the very last moment, a way to surprise her husband.

The early part of the film deals with the happy times Oscar and Mimi spend together, largely engaged in imaginative sexual adventures and seemingly insatiable. One day Oscar's interest in Mimi palls and he tries to be rid of her. The scenes of mental cruelty which follow are hard to watch, but Mimi is allowed a worthy revenge later on.

By the end of the film, and the story, which culminates on New Year's Eve, the lesbian frisson enters the proceedings. Fiona, fed up with her husband's interest in Mimi, and having already warned him that 'anything you can do I can do better', goes on to flirt with her in full view of the two men (and all the other passengers on board) before taking her back to a cabin (we don't see what happens, but we see them naked and asleep in a bunk a while later). A surprisingly restrained scene, given the heterosexual athleticism witnessed throughout the film, except when one remembers that the lesbian bit is there for the effect it has on the men, not for the gratification of the women. Will please Kristin Scott-Thomas fans, though.

The Bitter Tears of Petra von Kant (Die Bitteren Tränen der Petra von Kant) 1972

Director: Rainer Werner Fassbinder. Country: Germany. Screenplay: Rainer Werner Fassbinder (from his own play). Production company: Tango Film. Duration: 124 mins, colour

Cast: Margit Carstensen (Petra von Kant), Hanna Schygulla (Karin Thim), Irm Hermann (Marlene), Katrin Schaake (Sidonie), Eva Mattes (Gabriele von Kant), Gisela Fackeldey (Valerie von Kant)

Fashion designer Petra lives in her luxurious flat with Marlene, her maid/partner, who does not speak. Petra meets a young woman, Karin, to whom she is immediately attracted but who appears to be heterosexual. Petra seduces her with money and offers of work as a model. Karin acquiesces.

Sensationally stylish Fassbinder œuvre, taken from his own play and performed by a matchless cast. Set entirely in one room, the action may be somewhat static but the drama is high and the dialogue blade sharp. Power, passion, dominance and submission all play a part in this highly theatrical comedy/tragedy in which Petra, an astonishing creation, stars as the lead in her own drama. Her surroundings, a collection of mirrors, mannequins and murals, reflect one of the (many) themes of illusion, surface and appearance. Petra herself

DIE BITTEREN TRÄNEN DER PETRA VON KANT

All cried out. Margit Carstensen (r) stars in *The Bitter Tears of Petra von Kant*. Courtesy of Futura Film.

changes wigs according to the mood of the scene and every aspect of her life is the result of her own design. All conversation is carefully considered but the truth is rarely spoken. When Petra meets Karin, the spidery predator within emerges. Lust gets the better of her brilliant mind and Petra becomes both deluding and deluded. As Karin gradually reveals herself to be totally unsuitable for Petra by virtue of her background, education and interests, Petra simply chooses to ignore the warning signals and instead adapts the information to suit her own needs. Within an hour she is telling Karin that she loves her, wants to kiss her and asks her to move in (even by lesbian standards this is quick ...).

Back in 1972 the main problem with this film was that such a lesbian style-fest drama was the last type of movie lesbians actually wanted to see. Sophisticated and wickedly funny it may be, but at the time lesbians desperately needed some compassionate realism and were longing for romantic drama (it would be another thirteen years before **DESERT HEARTS** appeared). See it now, though, and be amazed.

Die Bitteren Tränen der Petra von Kant: see under **THE BITTER TEARS OF PETRA VON KANT**

Black Widow   1987

Director: Bob Rafelson. Country: US. Screenplay: Ronald Bass. Production company: Twentieth Century Fox. Duration: 102 mins, colour

Cast: Debra Winger (Alexandra Barnes), Theresa Russell (Catharine), Sami Frey (Paul Nuytten), Dennis Hopper (Ben Dumers), Nicol Williamson (William Macauley), Terry O'Quinn (Bruce), James Hong (Shin)

Alex works in the Justice Department analysing data. She notices that a series of wealthy men have died from the same cause and decides there is a link. The connection appears to be their wives, who may be the same person. Although she is alone in her theory, Alex's boss allows her to head off to Hawaii in pursuit of Catharine, the likely suspect.

First-rate thriller with fascinating themes concerning appearance and identity. It is also about obsession and attraction and this is where the lesbian frisson comes in.

When we first see Alex we know several things about her instantly: she has no life outside of her work, she dresses carelessly, eats junk food and is regarded by the rest of the team as one of the guys. Contrast this with the immaculate and feminine Catharine, whom we first see dispatching her husband by poisoning his brandy. Impeccably groomed, Catharine's appearance is everything to her, and she tailors it to meet the requirements of the man she wishes to trap.

As Alex hunts down her quarry the two meet in a hotel swimming pool where some of the residents are taking scuba-diving lessons. The two pair off and run through a mouth-to-mouth session. 'You're not taking this personally, are you?!' asks Alex, as their mouths meet. She doesn't, and to make sure *we* don't, within minutes we are introduced to a man the two will eventually share.

When Alex befriends Catharine in order to discover whether she is the killer, she begins to change aspects of herself – her clothes, her deportment – to match Catharine's. As the relationship develops, the audience begins to wonder whether Catharine will attempt to dispatch Alex in the same way as she had rid herself of her unfortunate husbands: namely, will she 'mate and kill'? They should have some sort of physical relationship, but of course they don't. Instead, at the point where Catharine would normally be seducing her potential next husband, she gives Alex an aggressive kiss, which is not reciprocated. And at the point where she would normally kill them, she opts for a non-fatal frame-up. So, in a way Catharine's normally psychotic *modus operandi* is watered down when it comes to dealing with another woman. Interesting.

See also: **FIVE EASY PIECES** by the same director.

Blood on Her Lips: see under **DAUGHTERS OF DARKNESS**

Born in Flames 1983

Director: Lizzie Borden. Country: US. Screenplay: Lizzie Borden. Production company: Lizzie Borden. Duration: 80 mins, colour

Cast: Honey (Honey), Jeanne Satterfield (Adelaide Norris), Adele Bertei (Isabel), Flo Kennedy (Zella Wylie)

Ten years after a peaceful socialist revolution in America, things still look pretty bad for women generally. As the economy worsens, the underground Women's Army tries to recruit black and white women from two pirate radio stations and the Socialist Party's newspaper to help fight the cause.

Interesting, fast-moving docudrama which raises controversial and difficult questions about society, feminism and the whole damn thing. New York is in the middle of a financial sex war where women are routinely sacked in favour of men, and where walking alone on the street is a very dangerous business. The state is increasingly exerting its control via intense surveillance, but it is the death of one of their leaders that galvanizes the Women's Army into direct action. Some polemical discussions between the protagonists prevent this being the action drama it might have been. However, although uneven in quality, *Born in Flames* proposes that women of different colours, backgrounds, sexualities and beliefs can unite as a dynamic force (however briefly). Confusing, hyperactive and revolutionary.

Note: Watch out for a rare acting appearance by director Katherine Bigelow (*Blue Steel*, *Strange Days*) as a newspaper editor.

Talk radio. Honey stars in *Born in Flames*. Courtesy of Cinenova.

The Boston Strangler   1968

Director: Richard Fleischer. Country: US. Screenplay: Edward Anhalt. Production company: Twentieth Century Fox. Duration: 109 mins, colour

Cast: Tony Curtis (Albert De Salvo), Henry Fonda (John S. Bottomly), George Kennedy (Phil DiNatale)

Documentary-style drama in which the case of the notorious Boston Strangler is examined. Tony Curtis gives an exemplary performance as Albert De Salvo, a plumber whose schizophrenic behaviour resulted in the deaths of at least thirteen women.

The lesbian part of the film involves two women, Ellen Ridgeway (Eve Collyer) and Alice Oakville (Gwyda Donhowe) who give the police a lead as to the identity of the strangler early in the investigation. An agent briefs a colleague that the two women are 'married', and indeed the two are portrayed as a close couple. Unfortunately the women's suspicions have fallen on a gay man with whom one of the women once had a relationship. The police are confused as to how this could be until the man later explains, 'She played the man's part, I the woman'.

See also: **RED SONJA** by the same director.

The Bostonians   1984

Director: James Ivory. Country: GB. Screenplay: Ruth Prawer Jhabvala (based on the novel by Henry James). Production company: Merchant Ivory Productions. Duration: 122 mins, colour

Cast: Vanessa Redgrave (Olive Chancellor), Christopher Reeve (Basil Ransome), Madeleine Potter (Verena Tarrant), Jessica Tandy (Miss Birdseye)

Henry James's satire – an attack on American suffragettes – sees Olive Chancellor engaged in a battle of wits against her cousin Basil Ransome, both fighting for the body and soul of the young and winsome Verena Tarrant.

Deeply depressing film of James's loathsome book – a deeply felt attack on the Boston feminist movement, which, although disguised as an amusing satire, was in fact a poisoned arrow aimed to discredit those he targeted. Brought to us by Jamesean specialists Ivory/Jhabvala/Merchant with no apparent understanding of their material (it couldn't have been deliberate surely?).

Boston, 1875. The emancipation of women is the subject and the struggle is on between dashingly handsome charmer Ransome and strident, humourless, intense feminist Olive Chancellor.

Ransome sees the movement as a pitiful attempt to prove women superior to men rather than equal, and thus dismisses the cause immediately. His chauvinism is half-heartedly mocked by a forgiving script. He slyly decides to fake an interest in the movement when he meets and is attracted to innocent young Verena Tarrant. Verena is a talented speaker, and she is being cultivated by Olive to be a leading light for the suffragettes. Verena and Olive link up intellectually, but for Olive the relationship is profoundly significant: 'Promise me not to marry,' she pleads.

Vanessa Redgrave as Olive is characterized as a clinging, cerebral female with barely suppressed lesbian tendencies. Mesmerized by Verena, she sees Ransome's intervention as deeply threatening, and becomes distraught and desperate. She has no weapons with which to fight him because she cannot express the depth of her feeling and has no claim to make. As the film moves inexorably towards the inevitable, Olive must simply stand by and watch. Her only argument (which is false) is to suggest to Verena that Ransome's interest in her is not personal; he just wants to undermine the cause. This doesn't wash, of course, and little by little Verena moves towards heterosexuality. Ransome, of course, has no doubt about his position: 'Can't I make you see how much more natural it is, not to say agreeable, to give yourself to a man instead of to a movement of some morbid old maid?' he asks.

Lesbianism as empty and pointless, so secondary to heterosexuality that the fight is over before it begins. Ransome asks Verena to marry him, give up public speaking and thereafter remain at home. Off she goes to do his bidding. Ah, normality!

See also: **JULIA, GREAT MOMENTS IN AVIATION** and **MRS DALLOWAY** for more Vanessa. James Ivory also directed **THE WILD PARTY**.

Bound 1996

Directors: The Wachowski Brothers. Country: US. Screenplay: The Wachowski Brothers. Production company: Dino De Laurentiis Company. Duration: 105 mins, colour

Cast: Jennifer Tilly (Violet), Gina Gershon (Corky), Joe Pantoliano (Caesar), John P. Ryan (Mickey), Christopher Meloni (Johnnie).

BOUND

Fresh out of the slammer, having spent five years behind bars for the 'redistribution of wealth', Corky is decorating an apartment for a criminal friend. Her neighbour is Violet, moll to Mafia man Caesar. Violet takes one look at Corky and wants her for herself. The two form a sexy alliance and when Caesar is given the job of looking after $2 million for the big boss, Violet suggests that they steal the money and leave Caesar in the frame. Smitten but suspicious Corky agrees and conceives a highly risky plan. Violet seems to be telling the truth, but is the seduction just bait for a double-cross?

From the first meeting in the elevator between Corky and Violet the flirt is on! The two gaze thoughtfully at each other and it is the ever so femme Violet, trailing into her apartment behind her man, who makes the first move. Before long the two are engaged in an incendiary physical encounter followed by a brief but explicit sex scene (famously filmed in one continuous movement to prevent the censors cutting anything). Immediately after the thrill of the sex, however, the film puts the plot into gear with an exceptionally violent torture scene which serves to underline the danger both women face should their affair be discovered.

Presumably it has always been a perilous business to sleep with a gangster's moll, but in this case Corky's additional predicament is knowing whether or not to trust her new lover. As the story twists and turns and fear changes loyalty into thoughts of betrayal, the audience is asked to guess whether or not sensational sex and burgeoning love is enough to be a tie that binds.

Lesbianism in *Bound* might be described as the novelty factor which makes the movie different and interesting compared to other, similar, films. It also renders it, to some degree, exploitative. However, it remains one of the most mainstream films to use a female couple as the lynch-pin of a story, albeit in that familiar lesbians-in-the-movies way in which both women are positioned firmly on the wrong side of the law. This doesn't stop them being attractive figures, of course, and the Wachowskis' intention is that we the audience should like these women and want them to get away with their plan. It is this that distinguishes the film from its predecessors in which the usual scenario meant that lesbian lovers would be 'justifiably' punished rather than encouraged to overcome the odds.

Gina Gershon as Corky is portrayed as the butch one, with her '63 Chevy, her plumbing skills(!), casual oil-stained clothes, boots and a sexy, louche swagger. In stark contrast, Jennifer Tilly is the ultra-femme girly with immaculate make-up, dresses which definitely fit where they touch, a whispery voice and an utterly inscrutable expression. It is she who makes all the running and seduces Corky. Interestingly, in contrast to (heterosexual) audiences' expectations of what femme girls do (and don't do), rather than hook Corky simply to service her own needs and then leaving her high and dry, it is Violet we see making love to Corky rather than the other way around.

To increase the accuracy of the film, the heterosexual Wachowski brothers enlisted the consultative support of writer and 'educator' Susie 'Sexpert' Bright to advise on the veracity of the sex scenes! Gina Gershon allegedly did some field research by visiting gay bars and trying out various chat-up lines (although Ms Gershon is no stranger to lesbian scenes – she played the bisexual predator Cristal in **SHOWGIRLS**).

Gina Gershon and Jennifer Tilly convey an amazingly intense sexual chemistry between them on screen. Both actresses are sensational in their roles, and bold too, in the way that the sex scene is handled. This may go some way to explaining why both women, particularly Jennifer Tilly, felt compelled to underline their own personal heterosexuality when interviewed about the film. Testament to the fact that, even now, out there in the real world you can play gay but please don't do it in real life. Not if you want a career.

See also: **SHOWGIRLS** for more Gina.

Bound and Gagged: A Love Story (Meantime) 1994

Director: Daniel Appleby. Country: US. Screenplay: Daniel Appleby. Production company: Cinescope Productions. Duration: 90 mins, colour

Cast: Ginger Lynn Allen (Leslie), Christopher Denton (Cliff), Elizabeth Saltarrelli (Elizabeth), Karen Black (Carla)

Elizabeth decides that her girlfriend Leslie should leave her abusive husband. However, Leslie hasn't the courage, or even much of an inclination, to do it, so Elizabeth kidnaps her and drives her across the country to see her friend Carla, an expert in de-programming people. Accompanying them on their journey is Cliff, a man tormented by thoughts of his estranged wife's adultery, who tries at frequent intervals to kill himself. In pursuit is Steve, Leslie's husband.

Compelling road-movie comedy centring around the increasingly weird behaviour of Elizabeth, who sees herself as Leslie's saviour and employs extreme methods to demonstrate her love. Unfortunately, although she has the best intentions in wishing to separate Leslie from her violent husband, her own dominant behaviour verges on bullying and Leslie is not at all amused. Surreal moments include friend Cliff's increasingly desperate, bizarre and completely ineffective attempts at suicide.

Sex scenes there are aplenty, although interestingly no lesbian ones. We know that Elizabeth and Leslie's relationship is sexual, but this is only mildly implied. A couple of kisses and a quick touching up of make-up after an encounter (nice subtlety ...), and that's all.

The fact that Elizabeth loses the plot halfway through the film need not reflect badly on lesbians generally. The other characters seem at least as crazy as she is, and she does, after all, come to her senses in the end. It's worth bearing in mind that the most stable person in the whole film is Leslie, who at least seems to be solidly bisexual. When Leslie finally escapes the clutches of all concerned she runs for the hills, and you can hardly blame her.

Boys on the Side 1995

Director: Herbert Ross. Country: US. Screenplay: Don Roos. Production company: New Regency/Hera Productions. Duration: 117 mins, colour

Cast: Whoopi Goldberg (Jane), Mary Louise Parker (Robin), Drew Barrymore (Holly), Matthew McConaughey (Abe)

An unlikely trio of women travel across America to escape their respective lives and find themselves on the run from the police.

Very strong mainstream road movie/comedy/drama in which the fabulous Whoopi Goldberg plays Jane, a straight-talking, talented but overlooked club singer. A dirty mouth but a heart of platinum, Jane is a character lesbians will recognize and probably identify with. She is the dependable type, one who knows the score, and will be around to pick up the pieces when others' lives fall apart. She also has some of the best lines. When she drops in on her young friend Holly early in the film, her obnoxious boyfriend Nick baits her with 'What's sex like without a dick?' 'I don't know,' comes the reply. 'You tell me.'

On the road, the three women share bits of their lives and aspirations with each other in a girly and unexpectedly touching way. Robin (Mary Louise Parker largely reprising her **FRIED GREEN TOMATOES AT THE WHISTLE STOP CAFÉ** role) is excellent as the

WASP woman with a mysterious illness and an extraordinarily conventional, pragmatic view of life. Initially unaware that Jane is gay, Robin is given the facts by Holly (Drew Barrymore, hilarious as a 'pretty young thing'), who explains that not only is Jane a lesbian but that she herself once had a fling with her. Holly advises Robin gravely that, as far as she can tell, lesbians tend to be 'very emotional ... and like uniforms'.

Lesbianism is treated rather delicately by the script (Jane is the only one who doesn't get laid, whereas heterosexuality is rampant). At one stage Jane unnecessarily tells Robin – without a trace of irony – 'You're safe with me', an echo from an earlier scene in which Holly reassures Robin that Jane won't 'try anything'. Implying what exactly? That most lesbians would 'try *something*' but that Jane is exceptionally different?

Jane is certainly characterized as controlled, managing even to subjugate the articulation of her own desires for the sake of the dignity of all concerned, which suggests that the film can cope best when lesbians are not visible sexually. There's a lot of suffering in silence here, which may be familiar stuff to lesbians who have fallen for straight women in their lives, but a little more go-getting on Jane's part wouldn't have hurt anyone. The tone of worthiness may pall with some, but Whoopi Goldberg has said that she is very proud of her work in this movie and there is no reason why she should feel any other way. One of the very, very few mainstream films with a lesbian lead who is neither psychotic or a victim (though of course she is denied happiness).

There is much to enjoy in *Boys on the Side*, including a terrific female-based soundtrack (Annie Lennox and Joan Armatrading, to name but two). All the leads are adorable, the acting is great and Hollywood production values just make you want more, more, more.

See also: **THE COLOR PURPLE** for more Whoopi, **POISON IVY** for Drew and **FRIED GREEN TOMATOES AT THE WHISTLE STOP CAFÉ** for Mary Louise Parker.

The Brady Bunch Movie 1995

Director: Betty Thomas. Country: US. Screenplay: Laurice Elehwany, Rick Copp, Bonnie Turner and Terry Turner. Production company: Paramount Pictures. Duration: 89 mins, colour

Cast: Shelley Long (Carol), Gary Cole (Mike), Michael McKean (Mr Dittmeyer), Jean Smart (Mrs Dittmeyer), Henriette Mantel (Alice),

THE BRADY BUNCH MOVIE

Christine Taylor (Marcia), Christopher Daniel Barnes (Greg), Alanna Ubach (Noreen)

The Brady family live in happy, comfy contentment in downtown Los Angeles, oblivious to modern living. One day a tax arrears bill arrives, giving the family a week to come up with $20,000. If they can't find the money the Brady home will fall into the hands of the scheming neighbour ...

Very enjoyable spoof on the incredibly popular primetime US TV series (you don't have to have seen it to enjoy the film). The Brady Bunch TV series peaked at a point in America's history when family values badly needed reinforcing (it was the time of the Vietnam War and the Nixon political scandal). In producing a film for the market of the cynical late 1990s, director Betty Thomas and her scriptwriters have come up with a brilliant strategy: they have modernized society but kept the Brady family exactly as they were back in the 1960s. Thus the homespun family values of TV land and a strong moral sense get the Bradys through modern life as we know it, unaware of its harsh realities.

One result of this oblivion is that perfect eldest daughter, Marcia, is blissfully unconscious of the effect she has on others. As she has no particular sexual interests beyond romantic desire, she fails to see that at college the boys lust after her – particularly bad boy Doug – and that she is also adored by her best friend Noreen, the young lesbian who secretly loves her. Noreen's character is thoroughly positive – the audience will recognize her predicament immediately and we are meant to sympathize with her. She is so besotted with 'the prettiest girl in the school', as she calls her, that she suffers agonies of frustration when 'sleeping over' in the same bed as the lovely Marcia. Her attentions go unnoticed, of course: Marcia would never be anything but a hundred per cent TV-land heterosexual.

However, far from being condemned to a lonely college life Noreen receives attention from an unexpected quarter. Towards the end of the film she behaves in a most heroic fashion, and at one point protects Marcia's reputation from the dreadful Doug. Unluckily this bit of heroism is attributed to someone else and Noreen loses Marcia to nice boy Charlie. Fortunately, the event is witnessed by Doug's used and abused former girlfriend, who takes a shine to Noreen herself! Great fun. Don't miss the closing credits, where Noreen's love for Marcia is briefly fulfilled.

The Butcher's Wife   1991

Director: Terry Hughes. Country: US. Screenplay: Ezra Litwik and Marjorie Schwartz. Production company: Paramount Pictures. Duration: 105 mins, colour

Cast: Demi Moore (Marina), Jeff Daniels (Alex), George Dzundza (Leo), Mary Steenburgen (Stella), Frances McDormand (Grace), Margaret Colin (Robyn)

Truly delightful, magical comedy in which Demi Moore stars as a clairvoyant whose predictions for those around her bring about hilarious consequences for all concerned.

One of the half-dozen people around whom the film revolves is Grace (the fabulous Frances McDormand in an earlyish role), a single lesbian who runs a clothing store. Portrayed as completely 'normal', she is fully integrated into society and has friends who all accept her sexuality without a second thought. Marina forecasts that Grace will soon find true love and indeed by the end of the film she is shown to be completely happy in a new relationship.

Butterfly Kiss   1995

Director: Michael Winterbottom. Country: GB. Screenplay: Frank Cottrell Boyce. Production company: Dan Films. Duration: 88 mins, colour

Cast: Amanda Plummer (Eunice), Saskia Reeves (Miriam), Paul Bown (Gary), Freda Dowie (Elsie)

Bleak story concerning Miriam, who works in a petrol station by day and takes care of a disabled relative at night, and Eunice, an unbalanced sociopath. When Eunice arrives at the petrol station looking for 'Judith' it is instead Miriam who joins her on a murderous journey around the empty, cold motorways of northern England.

Shattering drama in which a sense of doom and horror pervades from the outset. At the same time, *Butterfly Kiss* is a surprisingly profound and at times very moving film, as much about the boundaries of friendship and obsessive desire as murderous intent. Saskia Reeves is just wonderful as the desperately shy, lonely and emotionally deprived Miriam. How sad it is to hear her list the people who have ever kissed her – just three in her entire life. Amanda Plummer brings horrendous veracity to the role of disturbed and dangerous Eunice.

But far from being yet another worn-out tale of killer dykes on the rampage, *Butterfly Kiss* throws away the clichés and, hand on heart, insists that sexuality is not the issue. Yes, it's true the women become lovers and that for Miriam at least this develops into a tie that binds. But beyond a shocking seduction scene early on, this is a film concerned with wider issues than the gender of someone's bedfellow. Instead we are faced with a grave study of the search for emotional and spiritual satisfaction in a grey and unforgiving landscape. How far would you go to prove your love for someone? *Butterfly Kiss* provides a frightening answer.

Caged (Locked In) 1949

Director: John Cromwell. Country: US. Screenplay: Virginia Kellogg and Bernard C. Schoenfeld. Production company: Warner Brothers. Duration: 91 mins, black and white

Cast: Eleanor Parker (Marie Allen), Agnes Moorehead (Ruth Benton), Hope Emerson (Evelyn Harper), Ellen Corby (Emma)

Marie Allen is the new, frightened inmate in the state prison. She's there as an accessory to an armed $40 heist in which her husband has been killed, and, at nineteen years old, faces one to fifteen years.

Cromwell's revolutionary prison drama offers a dire warning on the brutalizing effects of cold, uncaring institutions which make things worse, not better, for those caught up in the system. Eleanor Parker is excellent as the young, desperately vulnerable girl, who, subject to the dehumanizing and relentless pressure of the jail, slowly hardens into the criminal she will become when she is eventually released. There are several lesbian characters scattered about, including Kitty, an inmate who generally runs things. 'When you've been in here too long you don't think of guys at all. You get out of the habit,' she tells Marie. Later, the debonair butch Elvira, Kitty's nemesis, is consigned to the prison. Elvira casts a glad eye over Marie too, and says of her, 'She's a cute trick.' Elvira wants to recruit Marie into her little gang but Marie is hardening up by this stage. 'If I said no to Kitty, I'm not going to say yes to you,' she says, presumably referring to a criminal lifestyle, although an alternative reading is there if you want it.

Lesbianism in this context is inevitably equated with criminal activity, or viewed as an unfortunate side-effect of prison and therefore the sort of thing that nice girls don't do, even when they've been corrupted. It's all part of the cesspit atmosphere, although the modern viewer might interpret some of the 'humiliations' slightly differently to the way they were intended: for example, Marie's short 'punishment' haircut renders her into the cutest baby-dyke you ever did see. Terrific stuff.

See also: **THE GODDESS** by the same director.

Caged Heat   1974

Director: Jonathan Demme. Country: US. Screenplay: Jonathan Demme. Production company: Artists Entertainment Complex. Duration: 83 mins, colour

Cast: Juanita Brown (Maggie), Roberta Collins (Belle Tyson), Erica Gavin (Jacqueline Wilson), Ella Reid (Pandora Williams), Lynda Gold (Crazy Annie), Warren Miller (Dr Randolph), Barbara Steele (McQueen)

Women in prison.

Extremely slim pickings in this very average exploitation movie. Although all the usual ingredients are there – women's prison, degradation, brutality and desperation for sex – Demme has unusually side-stepped the opportunity for gratuitous lesbianism. Instead we see, for a millisecond only, a couple holding hands in the yard, and equally briefly, some fairly innocuous back stroking. And that's all, folks. Perhaps Demme felt his first feature should be a cut above the usual Roger Corman flick, from whose stable this picture emerged, and thus deliberately avoided the obvious use of one or two dyke bed scenes to spice it up.

See also: **BEYOND THE VALLEY OF THE DOLLS** and **VIXEN** for more Erica Gavin.

Caged Women (Le Prede Umane)   1991

Director: Leandro Lucchetti. Country: Portugal. Screenplay: Leandro Lucchetti. Production company: Film 90. Duration: 65 mins, colour, dubbed

Cast: Pilar Orive, Isabel Libossart, Elena Wiedermann, Cristian Lorenz, Ronald Russo, Aldo Sambrell

Uninspired sex film in which an American woman, alone in a foreign

country, is framed for drug-trafficking and sent off to some godforsaken prison without a trial (sound familiar?). The hook in the plot which makes it different from the usual formula is the so-called 'hunting parties', in which a handful of unlucky inmates are released into the jungle in order to be hunted down by men.

Unfortunately, compared to other 'women in the slammer' flicks, this is a very tepid affair, having neither the camp humour of **CHAINED HEAT 2** or the wild abandon of **BARE BEHIND BARS**. Lesbian sex is depicted as both good and bad, depending on who's doing it. Good when it is performed by innocents who seek comfort in the arms of a woman (in the absence of a good man). Bad when it is performed by the assistant warden who forces herself on the hapless women and who is clearly doing it for real.

Sexist, idiotic and profoundly unrewarding.

Le Cahier Volé: see under THE STOLEN DIARY

Céline and Julie Go Boating (Céline et Julie Vont en Bateau; Phantom Ladies over Paris) 1974

Director: Jacques Rivette. Country: France. Screenplay: Eduardo de Gregorio and four others. Production company: Films du Losange. Duration: 192 mins, colour

Cast: Juliet Berto (Céline), Dominique Labourier (Julie), Bulle Ogier (Camille), Marie-France Pisier (Sophie), Barbet Schroeder (Olivier)

Two women, a librarian and a magician, meet each other in Paris and become friends. They begin living together and embark on a series of adventures involving a house peopled by characters who may or may not exist. Sweets chewed in the vicinity of the house allow the women to enter and participate in a drama happening within it.

Rivette's film, incomprehensibly regarded as important and profound, is in fact a staggeringly tedious art-flick in which the self-indulgence of the direction is breathtaking. There is no lesbianism as such (and in fact Céline tells her friends 'She's not a dyke, you know', when describing Julie to them), but back in 1974 a close friendship between women who were out there doing it for themselves was enough to have every lesbian/feminist trotting along to their local film society hoping against hope to see themselves represented on screen. No luck here, however. The endless repetitions of various scenes, as viewed by the different protagonists, do at least allow you to fall asleep, wake up an hour or so later and find you have not actually missed anything. The script was written by most of the cast and it would appear that they all wanted their pound of flesh as far as screen time is concerned. The only redeeming feature is the presence of the excellent Marie-France Pisier, who must have got lost on the way to another film set. For cineastes and insomniacs only.

Céline et Julie Vont en Bateau: see under **CÉLINE AND JULIE GO BOATING**

Chain Reaction: see under **SILKWOOD**

Chained Heat 2   1993

Director: Lloyd Simandl. Country: US. Screenplay: Chris Hyde. Production company: New Line Cinema. Duration: 99 mins, colour

Cast: Brigitte Nielsen (Magdar Kassar), Paul Koslo (Stanley Goff), Kimberley Kates (Alexandra Morrison), Kari Whitman (Suzanne Morrison), Lucie Benes (Tina Lukof)

Alex has cocaine planted on her during a trip to meet her sister Suzanne in Prague. She is arrested, tried and sentenced to ten years' imprisonment in Raisik Prison. The prison is also a brothel engaged in making porn films and drug-running. It is a 'model of free enterprise in the new East', the narrator tells us.

Superior exploitation movie made all the better by the presence of Brigitte Nielsen, who seems to enjoy appearing in these films as much as we enjoy seeing her. Resembling a man in drag at all times, Brigitte plays prison warden Magdar, who rules all before her with the help of sadistic butch number Rosa. Both greet the new arrivals with lascivious interest, including, in this case, our wrongly convicted heroine. Things get particularly interesting an hour in, when Alex shrewdly decides that the only way she will ever get out of prison is to seduce the warden. Brigitte, by sheer good fortune, has tired of Rosa and happens to be looking for a replacement.

The plot is not terribly important, though. Any excuse to get the women's clothes off is the name of the game. Prolonged shower scenes, bedroom scenes and lots of dressing and undressing occupy most of the screen time. In common with most prison films of this kind the inmates are generally innocent and good, the authorities corrupt and evil. Lesbianism is viewed as the perverse pleasure of the evil ones – the women forced to perform with them are either drugged and compliant or too scared to resist. Most of the perversity is implied rather than explicit – lots of heaving bosoms and black underwear, together with a bit of bondage and flagellation (off screen). Fun if you like that kind of thing.

See also: **RED SONJA** for more Brigitte.

Chasing Amy 1997

Director: Kevin Smith. Country: US. Screenplay: Kevin Smith. Production company: View Askew. Duration: 113 mins, colour

Cast: Ben Affleck (Holden McNeil), Joey Lauren Adams (Alyssa Jones), Jason Lee (Banky Edwards), Dwight Ewell (Hooper), Jason Mewes (Jay), Kevin Smith (Silent Bob)

Holden and Alyssa are comic-strip writers. They meet at a convention and Holden is instantly smitten. Alyssa appears to be interested, but there is a drawback. Alyssa is apparently a lesbian . . .

For a short while, back in the early 1990s, many independent filmmakers focused on the grunge and slacker generation, and one of the most interesting films to emerge was *Clerks* (1993), directed by Kevin Smith. Smith's strength was his ability to recreate sharp, sparkling conversation and debate between people who may or may not have known what they were talking about. His third film, *Chasing Amy*, demonstrates this talent once more, this time amid the minefield of sexual preference and the eternal triangle.

Being Indie, and clever, and outside the mainstream, Smith has managed to court controversy as much by accident as by design. His propensity for having his lead characters utter endless bad language to emphasize every expression is wearing but presumably accurate. This, and his ability to write explicit sexual dialogue – the sort of conversation you have with your friends every Friday night but is rarely effectively captured on film – rather than the more familiar smutty innuendo, gives him a notorious edge over less brave directors. The controversy surrounding *Chasing Amy* has delighted many (mostly straight men), and upset as many others (mostly lesbians), for the film appears to articulate the old myth that, secretly, all a lesbian needs is the right man.

However, it is clear that although Alyssa spends most of the movie telling everyone she is totally gay, she is in fact *bisexual*, plain and simple. It is only her refusal to establish this certainty that causes anguish all round. So why isn't this rather important fact made clear? One can sympathize with director Smith's dilemma. After all, if Alyssa is revealed as openly bisexual from frame one, there is no dramatic tension. The viewer would simply wait for the two leads to fall in love and that would be that. But, by making Alyssa in theory a hundred per cent lesbian, the familiar dramatic thrust of will-they, won't-they get together is restored. Much to most lesbians' annoyance, who see their sexuality compromised for the sake of a straight male fantasy.

There are compensations to be had throughout the film, however, including an early discussion between Alyssa and Banky which unexpectedly turns into a hilarious account of injuries both have sustained performing cunnilingus. Another revealing, but less satisfactory, conversation has Holden and Alyssa debating what constitutes the loss of virginity. After much banter – most of which dismisses the lesbian sexual experience as not amounting to very much – Holden eventually decides that virginity is lost through physical penetration (though this doesn't appear to apply to *him*).

The way the film aims to win its audience to the romance – sweetly and with much analysis covering all possible points of view – is as unexpected as it is entertaining. By bringing out into the open the sort of questions presumably straight men always wanted to ask about lesbianism, Smith reveals male ignorance and sexual double standards with an enjoyably sardonic wit. But much of the misogyny on view (notably articulated through Banky, Holden's best friend) is forgiven.

Disappointingly, Hooper, Holden's black gay friend (representing as he does the no-axe-to-grind voice of truth) is given the opportunity to tell Holden that Alyssa is not like other lesbians. Most lesbians, he confides, 'look more like you than her'. The age-old message being: the good-looking ones you can get (and you wouldn't want the others anyway). Another disappointment is the way Smith portrays Alyssa's lesbian friends and their reaction when she tells them she's dating a man. Her announcement turns the room stone-silent and one woman remarks 'another one bites the dust', as if lesbianism was an increasingly unpopular sect fearing to lose another member. Very old-fashioned.

Chasing Amy was greeted with considerable excitement by some critics, who commented rapturously on the 'radical' subject matter and the 'daring' involved in dealing with a modern sexual-triangle-with-a-twist. One has to ask whether these critics have seen any of the lesbian (or gay) independent films that have been made in the last ten years. The difference is, of course, that Smith is giving us the heterosexual male point of view, albeit with tenderness, and with warmth. But it isn't *radical*. Perhaps the critics should get out more.

Note: Guin Turner appears briefly as the MC at New York's Miaow Mix lesbian club.

The Children's Hour (The Loudest Whisper)   1961

Director: William Wyler. Country: US. Screenplay: John Michael Hayes (based on the stage play by Lillian Hellman). Production company: Mirisch. Duration: 108 mins, black and white

Cast: Audrey Hepburn (Karen Wright), Shirley MacLaine (Martha Dobie), James Garner (Dr Joe Cardin), Miriam Hopkins (Mrs Lily Mortar), Fay Bainter (Mrs Amelia Tilford), Karen Balkin (Mary Tilford), Veronica Cartwright (Rosalie)

Karen and Martha run a private school for girls. One of the girls – Mary – tells her grandmother a lie: that she saw the women kissing. The grandmother, appalled, removes Mary from the school and encourages other parents to do the same. Denying the accusation, Karen and Martha bring a suit for slander against Mrs Tilford, which is lost when a vital witness fails to appear. Alone in their deserted school, Martha admits to Karen that the implication of the child's words had more than a grain of truth in it. Although Mary's lies are subsequently revealed as such, Martha is unable to face the truth about herself, and takes her own life.

Audrey Hepburn and Shirley MacLaine make an attractive couple. So close are Karen and Martha that by the end of the film even Karen's fiancé must ask whether the accusation is true. He can see the possibility is there. So can we. So, in fact, can everyone. This is interesting, because in 1961 the image of the lesbian was so deeply stereotyped that it was assumed if you didn't look the part you couldn't be the part. These women are hardly obvious candidates. But the townsfolk swallow the rumour instantly, even in the face of extreme denial on the part of both women. Lesbianism, it would seem, is such a strange and awful evil that it can assume the shape of any woman, even two respectable ones like these.

But therein lies the rub, of course, because one woman is not a lesbian at all. The other one is but doesn't know it yet, and when she does realize it – with the surprise and horror usually associated with discovering you have a fatal disease – she is as repelled as any decent woman would be. The only way out, both to free Karen (the woman she has always loved) from the dreadful smear and to affirm her own personal integrity, is to kill herself. The only good lesbian is a dead one.

The film's final scene, at Martha's graveside, suggests tragedy (the waste of a life, the loss of a friend, or perhaps that such a nice woman could turn out to be a lesbian). There is also optimism. The wronged and misjudged Karen Wright asserts her moral superiority, ignores both the townsfolk and her former fiancé and strides with dignity into the distance, alone.

The main thrust of the film's narrative is to show the tragic consequences of a dreadful lie. Initially, as a viewer, one's concern for Martha and Karen is based on a sense of injustice: they are being wronged, and throughout the film there is an overwhelming desire to let the 'truth' come out so that justice is restored. Indeed, if this had been the only drama in the film, it could have emerged as relentlessly homophobic; the notion that lesbianism is a terrible thing is never questioned.

But Lillian Hellman has given us a twist in the story in the hope that the audience will learn something. Instead of allowing the audience simply to reflect on the devastation lies can wreak, we are told that the dreadful lie is in fact a dreadful truth (for one of the women, at least). So now what?

In a highly emotional coming-out scene, during which Martha berates herself far more severely than any of her accusers would have done, this potential problem is solved. The viewer can now feel pity for Martha Dobie (who obviously cannot help herself and despises lesbianism as much as everyone else). Her suicide, unforgivable to a modern lesbian audience but essential for heterosexuals in 1961, is the tragedy required to end the film. What other ending could there possibly be?

Despite the downbeat ending, *The Children's Hour* offers several positive 'firsts' for lesbians in film. Martha and Karen's relationship is exceptionally devoted. Martha is a touching human character endowed with humour and high principles. Karen is portrayed as non-judgemental and steadfastly loyal. Karen appears to agree to marry Joe only when she is sure it will not affect her business with Martha. When Martha tells her the truth about herself, far from running for the door, Karen instead suggests they go away together and make a fresh start. Interestingly, she breaks off her engagement to Joe. Then she also experiences a premonition of disaster; she 'knows' Martha has done something dreadful. After Martha's death, she kneels at the graveside and whispers, 'Goodbye, Martha. I'll love you until I die.'

William Wyler intended *The Children's Hour* to be a more thorough exploration of Hellman's play than his previous film version *These Three* (1936), but he insisted that the film was not about lesbianism. However, to suggest that the film was only about the power of gossip is patently ludicrous. Publicity posters pictured the two women above the caption 'different . . .'. The public knew what was going on.

Whatever Wyler may have intended, *The Children's Hour* was the first Hollywood film to deal with lesbianism as a major theme, and the first film to have a huge star playing a leading role as a lesbian. Shirley MacLaine is terrific as Martha: a witty, straightforward, no-nonsense character with a very human streak of jealousy running through her. Her early scenes with Karen's fiancé Joe (James Garner) strike chords of amused recognition with lesbians everywhere.

Critics at the time treated the film with due respect given the director and original writer, but little else. Most felt rather unmoved by the drama before them, although both actresses were praised for their performances. Almost no one questioned the validity of lesbianism being considered a heinous crime. It was simply accepted that this 'lie' was the worst possible thing you could say about someone.

See also: **JULIA**, based on Lillian Hellman's memoir, *Pentimento*.

Claire of the Moon 1992

Director: Nicole Conn. Country: US. Screenplay: Nicole Conn. Production company: Demi-Monde Productions. Duration: 107 mins, colour

Cast: Trisha Todd (Claire Jabrowski), Karen Trumbo (Dr Noel Benedict), Faith McDevitt (Maggie), Sheila Dickenson (BJ), Caren Graham (Tara O'Hara), Melissa Mitchell (Adrienne)

Straight free spirit Claire goes to a writers' retreat in order to rest and work. She is forced to share accommodation with Dr Benedict, a lesbian academic as

Up close and very personal. Trisha Todd and Karen Trumbo star in *Claire of the Moon*. Courtesy of Strand Releasing USA.

uptight and self-contained as Claire is slack and informal. The two aggravate each other and deny the growing attraction between them.

Claire of the Moon has a cult following in some quarters, for being the nearest thing lesbians have to a Mills and Boon novel realized on screen. For exactly the same reason it leaves some cynical audiences cold, and they find the film's sincerity amusing rather than moving. In simple terms the film tries very hard to be the lesbian movie of the decade, and indeed takes itself very seriously in the process. While it has its heart in the right place, the task of writing, directing and producing a film has proved too much, and the result is not what it might have been.

The plot is fine, the main problem lies in the characterizations. The motley collection of women staying at the retreat seem designed to represent every stereotype that ever existed, from bigoted Southern belle to New Age hippy. In a bizarre and irritating performance, Faith McDevitt as wise crone Maggie speaks her lines as if delivering a Shakespearean monologue. It is her character which launches one of the most mortifying moments of the movie – the illustrated comparison between straight woman and lesbians when it comes to hugging.

A more experienced director might have changed the emphasis of the film and turned it successfully into comedy. However, so sensitive were the producers about the film that a review for the London Lesbian and Gay Film Festival suggesting *Claire of the Moon* was campy melodrama led to a threat to withdraw the film from the festival. Only when an alternative reading of the film was printed and distributed to the audience was the threat withdrawn.

This is a pity, really, because the great aspects of the film – the intense looks between the leads, the eternal wait for them to confront their feelings, scenes of anticipation which seem to linger and drift off into space – all work very well when applied to camp comedy. The two leads are pretty good but, within their 'serious roles', they battle hopelessly against risible dialogue. See it anyway. Take it with a pinch of salt and you'll love it!

See also: **ENTWINED** and **LATE BLOOMERS** for similar romance.

Cleopatra Jones 1973

Director: Jack Starrett. Country: US. Screenplay: Max Julien and Sheldon Keller (based on the story by Max Julien). Production company: Warner Brothers. Duration: 89 mins, colour

Cast: Tamara Dobson (Cleopatra Jones), Bernie Casey (Reubin), Brenda Sykes (Tiffany), Antonio Fargas (Doodlebug), Bill McKinney (Officer Purdy), Shelley Winters (Mommy)

Blaxploitation flick from the 1970s, in which heroine special agent Cleopatra Jones squares up against Mommy and her gang.

Amid a flood of similar pictures that emerged in the 1970s, *Cleopatra Jones* was one of the best, trading as it does on its comic-strip characters and the charisma of lead actress Tamara Dobson (a sequel appeared two years later). Shelly Winters plays Mommy, a soft-butch loudmouth drugs baron who stomps about having histrionics. She presides over an inept and idiotic gang and leads her men a merry dance, although she's a good deal quieter with her girls. CJ is her arch enemy and you know from frame one that Mommy is no match for her.

Mommy has Sapphic tendencies (nothing too overt, a foot massage here, a hair stroke there, just enough to hint at what's going on). Familiar territory then: lesbian as criminal.

Club de Femmes: see under THE WOMEN'S CLUB

The Color Purple   1985

Director: Steven Spielberg. Country: US. Screenplay: Menno Meyjes (based on the book by Alice Walker). Production company: Amblin Entertainment. Duration: 154 mins, colour

Cast: Whoopi Goldberg (Celie), Danny Glover (Albert), Margaret Avery (Shug), Willard E. Pugh (Harpo), Oprah Winfrey (Sofia), Akosua Busia (Nettie), Rae Dawn Chong (Squeak)

Celie and Nettie live with their father in the Deep South. Celie is continually abused by her father, and has two children by him who are taken away at birth. She is literally and figuratively 'given away' to Mister, who treats her more like a servant than a wife. Nettie comes to live with them in order to escape the same abuse Celie suffered, but Mister attempts to force himself upon her. She resists and he throws her out. The sisters are separated for many years, and Celie's life continues to be fraught with difficulty and unhappiness.

Alice Walker's tremendous novel, brought to the screen in the somewhat unlikely hands of Steven Spielberg, is a beautiful and moving experience, dampened only slightly by a certain sentimentality. Celie's life, from downtrodden child and woman to mature and eventually independent adult, is realized in a film which, by focusing on a small group of individuals, tries to reflect a broader situation. The cast are uniformly fantastic, and Whoopi Goldberg, in her first major role, is just perfect as Celie.

In terms of lesbian relationships, the pivotal point in the drama concerns the deeply subjugated Celie and her encounter with Shug, her husband's mistress. The subsequent relationship between the two women proves a liberation for Celie. It is through Shug that she discovers love and a degree of happiness even in the face of Mister's anger. Shug insists that the three continue to live together and Celie, for the first time in her life, is viewed as more than a maid in her own home. Importantly, Shug also enables Celie to find the letters from her sister Nettie, kept from her for years by Mister. These letters give Celie access to a world outside her own, launching her on the road to self-discovery.

Compared to the book, the lesbianism in the film is considerably toned down. Although there are several scenes showing the women together, you might be forgiven for seeing their relationship as girly rather than sexual. Although not as comprehensively written out as in **FRIED GREEN TOMATOES AT THE WHISTLE STOP CAFÉ**, this is nevertheless disappointing. Don't miss it, though.

See also: **BOYS ON THE SIDE** for more Whoopi.

The Company of Strangers (Strangers in Good Company) 1990

Director: Cynthia Scott. Country: Canada. Screenplay: Gloria Demers, David Wilson, Cynthia Scott, Sally Bochner. Production company: National Film Board of Canada. Duration: 101 mins, colour

Cast: Winifred Holden (Winnie), Mary Meigs (Mary), Alice Diabo (Alice), Constance Garneau (Constance), Cissy Meddings (Cissy), Catherine Roche (Catherine), Michelle Sweeney (Michelle), Beth Webber (Beth)

A disparate group of elderly ladies take shelter at a deserted farmhouse when their coach breaks down. Forced to spend time together, the women tell each other about their past lives, and think about what might become of them in the future.

Utterly charming film which somehow strikes a perfect feeling of quiet reflection and solitude. In this atmosphere the women mull over a variety of issues and talk openly of their hopes and fears. Each woman has something to contribute, some aspect of her life which proves fascinating for both the other woman and the viewer. One of the women, Mary Meigs, is a lesbian and tells of her experience. The woman to whom she relates her story is interested and completely nonplussed. Delightful from beginning to end.

The Conformist (Il Conformista) 1970

Director: Bernardo Bertolucci. Country: Italy, France and Germany. Screenplay: Bernardo Bertolucci (based on the novel by Alberto Moravia). Production company: Mars Film Produzione. Duration: 108 mins, colour

Cast: Jean-Louis Trintignant (Marcello Clerici), Stefania Sandrelli (Giulia), Gastone Moschin (Manganiello), Enzo Taroscio (Quadri), Pierre Clémenti (Lino Seminara), Dominique Sanda (Anna Quadri)

Pre-war Italy. As a child Marcello is the subject of sexual attention from the family chauffeur, whom he shoots in retaliation. As an adult he searches for a way to conform with society, even if it means doing whatever the fascist state requires.

Early Bertolucci film is a masterly portrait of the creation of a fascist, and the pointlessness of looking for normality. As a member of the Italian secret service Marcello believes he will find his place in the world as an assassin, if that is what the state wants. He hides his own closet homosexuality by marrying a woman he does not care for, but is finally forced to face himself when he meets Anna Quadri. Dominique Sanda plays Anna, an anti-fascist who is definitely bisexual and might be completely lesbian (it's not clear). She and Marcello's wife bond by talking about sex and going shopping together. In an important and famous scene the two women dance the tango. It's a sexy moment, certainly the other dancers enjoy it, but it's there for the ultimate benefit of Marcello, who must either redeem himself or perish. Lesbianism as indicator of anti-fascist belief and occupying the moral high ground. Very unusual.

See also: **THE LAST EMPEROR** by the same director.

Il Conformista: see under **THE CONFORMIST**

COSTA BRAVA

Costa Brava (Costa Brava – Family Album)   1995

Director: Marta Balletbo-Coll. Country: Spain. Screenplay: Ana Simon Cerezo and Marta Balletbo-Coll. Production company: Marta Balletbo-Coll Production. Duration: 90 mins, colour

Cast: Marta Balletbo-Coll (Montserrat), Desi Del Valle (Anna), Montserrat Malaret (Marta)

Montserrat is a Barcelona tour guide with ambitions to stage her dramatic monologue at any arts festival that will have her. She meets Anna, a seismic engineer new to the city, and the two become friends. To Montserrat's surprise Anna reveals that she once had a lesbian relationship. Later, during a weekend away on the Costa Brava, Montserrat and Anna become lovers.

Anyone who feels that to write, direct and star in a film is to bury yourself in your own grave should go and see *Costa Brava*, a miracle of independent film-making shot in fourteen days and costing just $90,000 to produce. This glorious lightweight comedy romance is a tribute to the formidable talents of Marta Balletbo-Coll, who when she wasn't acting, producing or directing the film was probably making everyone's lunch as well. Bright and breezy and very funny, *Costa Brava* traces the early stages in a relationship from first date to 'moving in together'. Worries over Anna's bisexuality are also explored as well as concerns over career versus commitment. Much of the comedy evolves from Montserrat's self-effacement and her uncertainty about how to proceed in the relationship. Her timing is that of the true comic and some of the interactions between the two women are hilariously well observed. Thoroughly wonderful. And Barcelona never looked more beautiful.

Winner of the Best Feature film award at the 1995 Los Angeles Lesbian and Gay Film Festival, and of the Best Lesbian Feature award at the San Francisco Lesbian and Gay Film Festival.

Costa Brava – Family Album: see under COSTA BRAVA

Coup de Foudre: see under AT FIRST SIGHT

Troubled waters. Marcia Gay Harden and Caitlin Bossley star in *Crush*. Courtesy of Metro Tartan Distribution.

Crush 1992

Director: Alison Maclean. Country: New Zealand. Screenplay: Alison Maclean and Anne Kennedy. Production company: Hibiscus Films. Duration: 96 mins, colour

Cast: Marcia Gay Harden (Lane), Caitlin Bossley (Angela), Donogh Rees (Christina), William Zappa (Colin), Pete Smith (Horse)

Lane and Christina are driving to meet a novelist when Lane causes a crash. Abandoning the scene – and leaving Christina critically injured – Lane goes ahead with the meeting. She insinuates herself into the writer's household and appears to seduce the novelist's daughter, Angela, before dropping her in favour of the father Colin. Angela, upset and angry, discovers a woman called Christina in a nearby hospital . . .

Deeply disturbing story of obsession and revenge, *Crush* is a brutal and remorseless tale. When the exciting American Lane arrives on Angela and Colin's doorstep, neither can quite believe what is happening. Beautiful and sexy, Lane flirts and maybe sleeps her way through both of them, unaware that she is creating, in Angela at least, a jealous and vengeful monster. When Lane casually drops her in favour of her father, Angela's crush turns quickly to hate. She visits the desperately ill Christina in hospital, and begins to care for her. Painfully slowly Christina begins to recover, and starts to remember what happened. The two form a bond based on mutual betrayal and the scene is set for a violent climax.

The lesbian element runs through the film. It is understood that Lane and Christina were probably lovers, although Lane's bisexuality probably caused problems between the two. While it could be asserted that lesbianism is the root of much of the evil in *Crush*, it might be truer to say that treating relationships casually is the real problem (if one can term leaving one's lover for dead *casual*!). The film is too much of a psychological drama with several strands running through it to warrant such a simplistic interpretation. Powerful stuff.

See also: **THE FIRST WIVES CLUB**, in which Marcia Gay Harden plays a straight role.

Dallas Doll 1993

Director: Ann Turner. Country: Australia. Screenplay: Ann Turner. Production company: Dallas Doll Productions. Duration: 104 mins, colour

Cast: Sandra Bernhard (Dallas), Victoria Longley (Rosalind), Frank Gallacher (Stephen), Jake Blundell (Charlie), Rose Byrne (Rastus)

Middle-class Australian family the Sommers are seemingly content with their lot until the charismatic American Dallas Adair turns up and begins to change their lives.

When Dallas is invited to stay with the Sommers, the family quickly realize that life may never be quite the same again. Each individual reacts to her in a different way and all – with one notable exception – are mesmerized by her extraordinary confidence. As if possessed by some magical power, she begins to go through the family one by one, providing them with their dreams. Before long she is assisting Dad with his business (as well as giving him the opportunity to fulfil his masochistic fantasies). She gives the son the sexual experience he needs. For Rosalind, the rather staid wife, she provides an opportunity to change her career and her entire life, but not before a hilarious sequence in which the two play strip-golf in the living room, to the strains of Doris Day singing 'A Woman's Touch'! This lesbian dalliance is viewed positively and can be seen as the route by which Rosalind achieves her liberation.

But dreams usually have a price and the family become disillusioned when Dallas appears to be on the verge of selling out the Australian way of life to overseas interests. She must be stopped! An extremely strange ending puts paid to alien Dallas and life resumes a semblance of normality, with Rosalind the happiest with the outcome.

As a representation of otherness, the fabulous Sandra Bernhard is perfectly cast. Her real-life glamorous weirdness, coupled with her out bisexuality gives the audience a useful persona on which to base Dallas even before the movie starts.

Rumour has it that Sandra Bernhard was a tad 'difficult' on set, and for reasons which are still not completely clear, she appeared to take against the film on release and refused to assist in the publicity campaign. Reports suggest that Bernhard felt director Ann Turner had fallen in love with her and that this somehow warranted her withdrawal of services. Ann Turner denies this, however, and has diplomatically suggested that it was more a result of her star's 'personality'. Whatever the truth is, Sandra Bernhard no longer refers to the movie on her CV, which is a pity, because it is her best film by far.

Daughters of Darkness (Le Rouge aux Lèvres; Blood on Her Lips) 1970

Director: Harry Kümel. Country: Belgium, France, Germany and Italy. Screenplay: Harry Kümel and Pierre Drouot. Production company: Showking Film. Duration: 96 mins, colour

Cast: Delphine Seyrig (Countess Bathory), Danièle Ouimet (Valerie), John Karlen (Stefan), Andréa Rau (Ilona Harczy)

A young honeymoon couple, Stefan and Valerie, arrive at a deserted hotel in Ostend where they are joined by the mysterious Countess Bathory and her 'companion' Ilona. The Countess takes a close interest in the couple and entertains them with lurid tales of her ancestors who bathed in virgins' blood. Stefan's latent sadism is aroused by the stories and a terrified Valerie decides to flee. But the Countess has other plans . . .

Terrific lesbian vampire film based on the apparently real-life vampire Elizabeth Bathory. If, over the years, this immensely stylish and highly entertaining movie has been elevated to classic status it is entirely due to the performance of the exquisite Delphine Seyrig, who imbues every scene with aristocratic sensuality. Sophisticated and effortlessly graceful, she is one of the most elegant vampires ever seen on screen. The lesbianism is subdued and discreet rather than rampant, in contrast to the violence perpetrated by the two women. And, as frequently happens in vampire movies, 'recruitment' of new vamps occurs by means of a heady cocktail of seduction, bloodsucking and magical intoxication. Very tasteful.

Desert Hearts   1985

Director: Donna Deitch. Country: US. Screenplay: Natalie Cooper (based on the book *Desert of the Heart* by Jane Rule). Production company: Desert Heart Productions. Duration: 91 mins, colour

Cast: Helen Shaver (Vivian Bell), Patricia Charbonneau (Cay Rivvers), Audra Lindley (Frances Parker), Andra Akers (Silver Dale), Dean Butler (Darrell)

The year is 1959. Vivian Bell, a professor of English literature from New York, arrives in Reno to obtain a quick divorce. She stays at a local ranch where she meets Cay, a young sculptor who works at the casino by night. The two form a friendship which helps Vivian to break free from her personal inhibitions and detachment from life. When Vivian discovers that Cay is a lesbian she pulls back, fearing that she may have given Cay the wrong impression. But Cay has found someone she wants and will not be deterred, for she senses that underneath it all, Vivian wants her too.

It is no exaggeration to say that in 1985 *Desert Hearts* was the film many lesbians had waited for all their lives. For the first time in cinema history here was a movie which was an unashamedly romantic lesbian love story, aimed primarily at a lesbian audience. This had never happened before, and it is almost impossible to overstate the importance of *Desert Hearts* and the impact it had on a lesbian audience who had been so deprived of positive images. Until then, no American film had been made which addressed lesbianism as its main or only theme which was not also attempting to exploit stereotypes for the benefit of a straight audience. Here was a film made by a highly talented lesbian director who wanted to tell a 'truthful' story.

Director Donna Deitch's documentary-based background suited the method by which this drama is told. The openness and simplicity of the style is one of the most beguiling features of the film. As if saying 'this is the story of two women who fall in love, take it or leave it', the film plays down any potential controversy by aiming for emotional veracity.

The money to finance *Desert Hearts* was obtained laboriously, over a long period of time. Deitch held parties and sold shares for $1000 each. Thus hundreds of 'shareholders' were created who invested for various reasons, perhaps mainly to ensure that for the first time in film history a lesbian love story might eventually make it to the screen. It took two and half years to raise enough money to start filming. The effort was surely worthwhile, for *Desert Hearts* was an instant hit with lesbian audiences, but it also achieved a degree of mainstream success with limited theatrical openings and reviews in both broadsheets and tabloids. It became one of the most successful independent films of the time.

The story, of course, has wide appeal. It helped having two leads that every member of the audience was either attracted to or wanted to be like. The moment Cay Rivvers hit the screen, driving backwards on a desert road, you just knew that lesbians would be attempting the same thing on lonely stretches all over the country. Vivian's gradual coaxing from her position as reserved academic to liberated lesbian academic struck chords everywhere too. Both Patricia Charbonneau and Helen Shaver are excellent in their respective roles. The dynamic coupling of the pair works well throughout, and culminates in a breathtaking love scene, very explicit for the time, but in the context of a relationship of both love and desire it is simply without parallel.

Other aspects of the film also work well, including very strong supporting players and a carefully evoked sense of place (although perhaps less so in terms of the 1950s setting – wouldn't the locals have practically torn them limb from limb rather than letting it all be?)

The reason this film has endured and become essential viewing for every lesbian cinema-goer is simply that the basic ingredients were so good. A director who could direct, actresses who could act, beautiful photography, strong country-music soundtrack and a good story. Very few films get it all right and *Desert Hearts* remains the standard by which all other lesbian films are compared.

Desperate Living   1977

Director: John Waters. Country: US. Screenplay: John Waters. Production company: Charm City Productions. Duration: 91 mins, colour

Cast: Liz Renay (Muffy St Jacques), Mink Stole (Peggy Gravel), Jean Hill (Grizelda Brown), Susan Lowe (Mole McHenry), Edith Massey (Queen Carlotta), Mary Vivian Pearce (Princess Coo-Coo)

'I have never found the antics of deviants to be one bit amusing,' says Peggy Gravel early in the film. John Waters obviously disagrees. Desperate Living starts in everyday suburbia where Peggy, recently released from a sanatorium, finds normality deeply threatening. Before long she and her maid Grizelda have accidentally killed her husband, and feel compelled to go on the run. After a brief encounter with a transvestite cop they find themselves in Mortville, run by the wicked Queen Carlotta and populated by deviants of every shape and size. Things get worse for the duo.

Muffy and Mole are the lesbian couple whom Peggy and Grizelda have the misfortune to encounter upon their arrival in Mortville. Muffy is a vain, temperamental and previously heterosexual Zsa Zsa Gabor lookalike, while Mole is a violent, confrontational, budding transsexual. The two live in tempestuous happiness and regard the intrusion of the runaways as an interesting annoyance.

Peggy finds Mortville's anarchical society much more acceptable than the one she left behind and tries to make the best of things by colluding with the fascist Queen. Lascivious sex takes place everywhere, and the film is distinguished by showing, probably for the first time in cinema history, the female equivalent of a 'cottage', complete with glory hole. Otherwise, the most memorable sequence involves Mole's DIY attempt at a sex change, Muffy's reaction to it and the stomach-turning consequences.

Completely over the top, with performances from the porn-film school of acting, *Desperate Living* is rather like a distant cousin to *Rocky Horror*, but without the restraint.

See also: **PINK FLAMINGOES** by the same director.

Desperate Remedies   1993

Directors: Stewart Main and Peter Wells. Country: New Zealand. Screenplay: Peter Wells and Stewart Main. Production company: James Wallace Productions. Duration: 90 mins, colour

No, let me guess ... Lisa Chappell and Jennifer Ward-Lealand star in *Desperate Remedies*. Courtesy of Electric Pictures.

Cast: Jennifer Ward-Lealand (Dorothea), Kevin Smith (Lawrence), Lisa Chappell (Anne Cooper), Michael Hurst (William Poyser), Cliff Curtis (Fraser), Kiri Mills (Rose)

The year is 1900 in the new town of Hope. Dorothea plans to wrest her opium-addicted sister from the grip of her unscrupulous lover. She contracts Lawrence to ensure the rogue leaves the country, but Lawrence's growing attraction to Dorothea threatens both her forthcoming marriage of convenience and her relationship with her very close friend Anne.

Hilarious bodice-ripper in the style of high camp, parodying everything Barbara Cartland ever stood for. Heavy breathing, quivering lips, sumptuous costumes, dazzling sets and an urgent orchestral soundtrack ensure the story romps along taking everyone with it. Dorothea makes a wonderful object of desire whose morals are constantly compromised for the love of her sister. Her companion Anne is fabulously beautiful and gloriously dashing, prepared to go to great lengths for the sake of her love.

With as much brooding lust and rising passions as actual sex, the film thoroughly enjoys bringing the characters constantly within a hair's breadth of a kiss, only to separate them again. That said, the one explicit love scene between Dorothea and Anne is sensationally sexy even though (or perhaps because) both are fully clothed and exchange no more than intense kisses. Enormous fun throughout and an ending which could not be better. Highly recommended.

Diabolique 1996

Director: Jeremiah Chechik. Country: US. Screenplay: Don Roos. Production company: Morgan Creek. Duration: 107 mins, colour

Cast: Sharon Stone (Nicole Horner), Isabelle Adjani (Mia Baran), Chazz Palminteri (Guy Baran), Kathy Bates (Shirley Vogel)

The wife and mistress of a bullying, arrogant headmaster drown him in a bath. They dispose of the body in the school pool, but when it is drained a few days later the body is no longer there. The suit in which he was drowned is mysteriously returned to the school, freshly cleaned. Later, both women think they see Guy at a classroom window . . .

Remakes of classic films generally fail to live up to the originals, and *Diabolique* is no exception. The US has a penchant for remaking foreign films in American so the good folks back home won't have to read subtitles. Of course the older the original the less likely the audience is to know that there ever was another version in the first place. *Diabolique*, based on the scary and oft-imitated **LES DIABO-LIQUES**, tries to compensate for being an otherwise pointless remake by heavily hinting at Sapphic leanings which never materialize and adding overt violence to the overwrought ending. Terrified that modern audiences will guess the plot twist, the screenplay adds a couple extra and tries to double bluff viewers even at the beginning. The strangest change to the original is the way that the lesbian non-theme is treated. In the book which beget the story many years ago, the two women were portrayed clearly as lovers. In the original 1954 version of **LES DIABOLIQUES**, the lesbian bit was removed (a sign of the times maybe, but it actually improved the film). Now in the 1990s version, the two women are not, never have been and never will be, lovers. Their occasional embraces are little more than sisterly reassurances to each other when the going gets tough. One interesting moment though: when Nicole (Stone) threatens to leave, knowing the police would have no reason to suspect her of the murder, Mia (Adjani) remarks, 'I could tell them we were lovers . . .' 'Well,' replies Nicole in surprise, 'you can take the girl out of the convent . . .'

Never mind. Even if there is less to the film than meets the eye as far as lesbianism goes, there is huge compensation to be found in the two leads (Adjani's infuriating timidity, Stone's granite ruthlessness), the 1950s-style costumes are terrific, but most of all, the totally fabulous Kathy Bates is wonderful as the tenacious private detective. But for an infinitely better film, see **LES DIABOLIQUES**.

See also: **BASIC INSTINCT**, in which Sharon Stone plays a bisexual murder suspect. Kathy Bates plays lesbian in **PRIMARY COLORS** and straight in **FRIED GREEN TOMATOES AT THE WHISTLE STOP CAFÉ**.

Les Diaboliques (The Fiends) 1954

Director: Henri-Georges Clouzot. Country: France. Screenplay: Henri-Georges Clouzot and Jerome Geronimi (based on the novel *The Woman Who Was* by Pierre Boileau and Thomas Narcejac). Production company: Filmsonor. Duration: 117 mins, black and white, subtitled

Cast: Simone Signoret (Nicole), Vera Clouzot (Christina), Paul Meurisse (Michel), Charles Vanel (Inspector Fichet)

The wife and mistress of the brutish headmaster Meurisse conspire together to murder him. But when the deed is done his corpse mysteriously disappears. Then one of the pupils at the school claims to have seen him. Worse, the suit in which he was murdered is returned to his room by the local dry-cleaner ...

Sensational thriller which tagged a plea to the viewer at the end of the film asking people not to give away the ingenious twist to the plot. In the original novel, the two women were lovers, which gave further motivation to the murder of the husband. The film plot is very different and the Sapphic element has been removed, to all intents and purposes. This helps the audience to remain sympathetic with the women throughout the film (after all, murderers are palatable, lesbians are not).

Nevertheless, fragments of their possible relationship remain. Early in the film, when the two women are staying at Nicole's house, Meurisse asks his wife 'Whose is the bed, yours or hers?' 'Ours,' she replies, much to his amusement. The women are seen as strongly bonded by more than just a shared murder. Also, one cannot help but notice how butchly Simone Signoret's Nicole behaves towards Vera Clouzot's passive and sickly femme. However, their allegiance starts to crumble as the evidence mounts up, and they appear to be continually on the verge of discovery. Excellently constructed, with a truly chilling ending.

A Different Story 1978

Director: Paul Aaron. Country: US. Screenplay: Henry Olek. Production company: Peterson Company. Duration: 106 mins, colour

Cast: Meg Foster (Stella), Perry King (Albert), Valerie Curtin (Phyllis), Peter Donat (Sills), Richard Bull (Mr Cooke), Barbara Collentine (Mrs Cooke)

Stella, a real-estate broker and a lesbian too, gives a temporary home to Albert, a Belgian gay hustler. When his ex-lover tells the authorities about his lack of a Green Card, Albert and Stella get married to prevent his deportation. Gradually they find themselves getting closer, until, to their surprise, they find they are in love.

Well-meaning, much maligned comedy which attempted to be gay-positive in both approach and focus. Initially, things begin well. Back in 1978 it was very unusual to see a lesbian represented as good-looking, capable, amusing and interesting. As this is a comedy, the notion that both Stella – independent lesbian – and Albert – camp gay man – conform in some ways to widely believed gay and lesbian stereotypes (e.g. she can't cook or sew, he can do both, etc., etc.) surprisingly serves the comic aspect of the film very well.

In these more confident days (i.e. twenty years later) we are able to shrug off the stereotypes and accept the notion that people fall in love regardless of sexuality or gender – having found their true partners – and good luck to all involved. Back then, however, this was a painful slap in the face. For what do we have here? A lesbian and a gay man who are charming and gorgeous, but who are essentially *not really gay*! Today this would be merely disappointing rather than offensive or upsetting, were it not for the fact that the *other* gay people in the film (and one may as well read 'real' gay people for this) are shown to be quite different. Albert's former boyfriend is a promiscuous, vindictive older man who uses his money to keep himself supplied with young studs until he tires of them. Stella's ex is deeply neurotic, suicidal, very closeted and unable to cope with the rigours of everyday life without help. So, from the viewers' point of view, these are the authentic gays. Stella and Albert are the ones who somehow got caught up in the culture, but who clearly are not like that at all.

DOMESTIC BLISS

The film was widely condemned by gay groups at the time and is still dismissed by many. Seeing it as a period piece certainly helps and it would be a shame to reject it completely. Beautiful Meg Foster is a great screen lesbian (for the hour or so she is one), who does kiss her girlfriend on screen and doesn't end up with a stake through her heart for doing so.

Interesting note: Neither Perry King's nor Meg Foster's career benefited greatly from this film, though both have worked steadily. Meg Foster secured the role of Cagney in the first series of *Cagney and Lacey*, but she was suddenly removed from subsequent series for being 'too butch' (pardon?), and was replaced by the (as we all know) not-butch-at-all Sharon Gless.

Dimenticare Venezia: see under TO FORGET VENICE

The Does: see under LES BICHES

Domestic Bliss   1985

Director: Joy Chamberlain. Country: GB. Screenplay: Gillian Slovo. Production company: Newsreel Collective. Duration: 52 mins, colour

Cast: Mandy More (Emma), Penny Nice (Diana), Yvonne Gidden (Amelia), Martha Parsey (Jenny)

Day in the life of a woman living with her female lover and teenage daughter.

Sponsored by Channel 4, this comedy was scripted from interviews with thirty women about their experiences of relationships and domestic chaos. Amusing script but low production values, small scale, low budget, etc.

However, this little drama was one of the most important moments for lesbians on British television, and for all its shortcomings it represented one of the very first efforts to put a positive spin on a lesbian personality and lifestyle.

See also: **NOCTURNE** by the same director.

Double Obsession 1992

Director: Eduardo Montes. Country: US. Screenplay: Jeffrey Delman, R. J. Marx and Risa Tabacoff. Production company: Reivaj Films. Duration: 84 mins, colour

Cast: Margaux Hemingway (Heather), Maryam D'Abo (Claire), Frederic Forrest (Paul), Scott Valentine (Steve), Beth Fisher (Sherry)

Claire, a married woman with a young daughter, is being stalked by her former university room-mate Heather, a woman of unnatural desires . . .

Many years ago the late Margaux Hemingway, an internationally famous model at the time, starred with her little sister Mariel in the fairly trashy film *Lipstick* (1976), which was all about rape and revenge. Mariel went on to feature or star in some substantial films such as **PERSONAL BEST** and **MANHATTAN**. Margaux, however, never fulfilled her early promise, and before her premature death made some truly awful pieces of rubbish, of which this is an example.

Margaux plays Heather, a very disturbed woman and one of the most profoundly creepy and repulsive lesbians to grace the screen. Heather bonds with new arrival Claire on her first day at Freudville University in 1981 and soon they are best chums as far as Heather is concerned. Heather wants Claire's complete attention and gets mightily upset when she starts dating her soon-to-be husband. Claire's subsequent attempt to console Heather after an argument may have resulted in them going to bed together but it's not completely clear. In any event, time passes and Claire grows up into a normal healthy woman, while Heather matures into a demented psychopath.

The film flashes backwards and forwards and brings us to the present day when Claire is forced to face the mad and bad Heather once more. It transpires that ever since Claire refused to become Heather's friend for life, Heather has been seeking out Claire lookalikes to date and victimize instead. On it all goes until Heather has killed a few people and Claire has to come to the rescue of the latest lookalike – Sherry – who has been roundly abused by the evil dyke. Suddenly it ends. Based on a true story, God help us.

Dracula's Daughter 1936

Director: Lambert Hillyer. Country: US. Screenplay: Garrett Fort. Production company: Universal. Duration: 68 mins, black and white

Cast: Gloria Holden (Countess Marya Zaleska), Otto Kruger (Jeffrey Garth), Marguerite Churchill (Janet Blake), Irving Pichel (Sandor), Edward Van Sloan (Professor Van Helsing), Nan Grey (Lili)

The sequel to Dracula *(1931) involves not the man but his daughter, who comes to London to recover his body so that he may be properly buried. Once in the capital she continues where her father left off and soon a trail of bodies is mystifying police.*

Gloria Holden is wonderful as the timelessly beautiful Countess who struggles to be free of the inclinations she has inherited from her father. She is an extremely interesting character on two levels. First, in her desire for release from the torment she suffers as a result of her 'condition', she manages to inspire the sympathy of the audience. Second, and very importantly, she is the very first cinema vampire who can be clearly viewed as a lesbian, even though she does display a passing interest in men.

Indeed, the most (in fact only) erotic scene in the film is a lesbian one. The Countess sends her manservant Sandor into the London night to find a young girl, ostensibly to pose as a model in her studio. Lili is induced back to the studio with promises of food and warmth. On her arrival the Countess is most attentive, offering the girl every comfort. She tells Lili, 'I'm doing a study of a young girl's head and shoulders. You won't object to removing your blouse, will you?' Lili has no objection at all and even offers to pull down the straps of her camisole. The Countess regards her closely. 'Why are you looking at me that way?' asks Lili, slightly alarmed. The Countess is unable to contain herself any further and moves in. Unfortunately the subsequent gratification is experienced off-camera. As with most vampires, particularly lesbian ones, the Countess does not survive the film. Nevertheless, entertaining fun, and highly recommended.

See also: **THE HUNGER, LUST FOR A VAMPIRE** and **TWINS OF EVIL** for more vamps.

Écoute Voir *(See Here My Love; Look See)* 1978

Director: Hugo Santiago. Country: France. Screenplay: Hugo Santiago and Claude Ollier. Production company: Prospectale. Duration: 120 mins, colour, subtitled

Cast: Catherine Deneuve (Claude Alphand), Sami Frey (Arnaud), Florence Delay (Flora), Anne Parillaud (Chloe)

A young woman is whisked away by a strange sect who may or may not be responsible for some unusual radio waves being picked up in the locality. Claude is soon on the case and revealing more mysteries on the way.

Years before she appeared as a bisexual in **THE HUNGER**, Catherine Deneuve played gay in this curious film, as the utterly suave private detective Claude Alphand. A vision of matchless beauty, even in trilby and trench coat, Claude shows she is made of stern stuff in this interesting, if overlong, glossy French thriller. She is revealed to be a lesbian in the subtle interaction between herself and Flora, with whom we are to assume she had a relationship sometime before. When they meet there are *those* smiles of recognition. Flora asks, 'How's Josiane?' 'We've lost touch,' comes the reply. Flora works in radio. 'It must suit you, being the director,' remarks Claude. Ooh er! Claude encapsulates the Deneuve persona we have come to know and love over the years: cool, capable, detached, intelligent, with impeccable manners and generally immaculate in every respect. In her lesbian role she is all these things, and is in fact even more intriguing.

The plot is fairly impenetrable, though fortunately Claude seems to know what's happening, and watching her at work should be enough for any lesbian viewer. Midway through the film Claude catches up with the missing woman (who is a willing runaway more than anything else), and adopts an unusual approach to get her back: she seduces her (we see only a kiss). This foolproof method guarantees success, and before long Claude has also solved the many mysteries surrounding the cult and discovered who is behind it all, etc.

A film with three lesbians in the leading roles and no particular reason for it? Unique.

See also: **BELLE DE JOUR, THE HUNGER** and **LES VOLEURS** for more Catherine.

Egymásra Nézve: see under **ANOTHER WAY**

11 Harrowhouse   1974

Director: Aram Avakian. Country: GB. Screenplay: Jeffrey Bloom. Production company: Harrowhouse Productions. Duration: 95 mins, colour

Cast: Charles Grodin (Chesser), Candice Bergen (Maren), John Gielgud (Meecham), Trevor Howard (Clyde Massey), James Mason (Watts), Peter Vaughan (Colgin), Helen Cherry (Lady Bolding)

Chesser is an American diamond dealer who wishes to marry his rich widowed girlfriend Maren. Trouble is, if she remarries, she loses her inheritance. Chesser, anxious to hear those wedding bells but unable to provide for Maren in the way she is very accustomed to, feels the solution is to rob a London diamond house.

Highly enjoyable 'caper' movie in which Charles Grodin's droll comic style perfectly complements the stiff British establishment figures with whom he is required to do business. A starry cast and a surprisingly humane subplot involving James Mason as Watts, the unappreciated diamond-house worker, puts *11 Harrowhouse* well above the usual cops and robbers comedy.

The lesbian figure is that of Lady Bolding, an attractive older woman married to an important dealer. When Lady Bolding first meets Maren she remarks, 'Your photographs don't do you justice.' From thereon in, while the men conduct business the women take a swim together and get chummy. Clearly the two women reach some sort of understanding, although this isn't developed. Later in the film Lady B saves the hetero pair from the clutches of her dastardly husband. 'Why is she helping us?' asks a confused Chesser. 'She loves me!' replies Maren. As the happy couple prepare to drive off, Lady Bolding looks at Maren one last time and remarks, with some regret, 'Pity ...'. Indeed.

See also: **THE GROUP**, in which Candice Bergen plays the lesbian.

Emilienne 1975

Director: Guy Casaril. Country: France. Screenplay: Phillippe de Ionas and Eric Lofeld (based on the novel by Claude Des Olbes). Production company: Art House. Duration: 90 mins, colour, dubbed

Cast: Betty Mars (Emilienne), Pierre Ogilvy (Claude), Nathalie Guerin (Nouky)

Married man Claude is having an affair with a young art student Nouky. One evening at a preview Nouky sees Claude's wife, Emilienne, and decides she rather fancies her too. Keeping Claude informed at all times, Nouky seduces the normally chaste but nevertheless interested Emilienne. After a while, Emilienne discovers that her young girlfriend is also seeing her husband and feels understandably hurt and humiliated. However, things soon get very complicated indeed.

Highly entertaining sex film given style and that oh-so-French *Je ne sais quoi* which takes it into a different league entirely from the average cable channel sizzler! With an ambient soft rock soundtrack (beautifully played on an orchestrated Hammond organ), *Emilienne* delivers in a sophisticated, soft-focus manner rarely, if ever, matched by similar British efforts.

The characterizations are surprisingly strong. Emilienne herself is a rather gentle soul with unexplored desires and complicated motivations. Nouky is a selfish, petulant little vixen with a round perm. Upfront without being explicit, this is no nasty little porn film, and it's too amusing to be psychologically challenging. However, it's still a wonder they don't kill each other when the truth comes out. Highlights include a visit to a lesbian club, a highly questionable brothel scene, an encounter with a prostitute and an extraordinary encounter with a coven of blond witches on a remote island (when Emilienne gets going she really doesn't spare herself). Sexy and fun.

See also: **GOLDEN BALLS** and **LENNY**, wherein wives are similarly encouraged to experience Sapphic diversions.

Emmanuelle 1974

Director: Just Jaeckin. Country: France. Screenplay: Jean-Louis Richard (based on the book by Emmanuelle Arsan). Production company: Trinacra Films. Duration: 90 mins, colour, dubbed

Cast: Sylvia Kristel (Emmanuelle), Marika Green (Bee), Daniel Sarky (Jean), Alain Cuny (Mario), Jeanne Colletin (Ariane)

Nineteen-year-old newlywed Emmanuelle arrives in Thailand with her husband. She is soon bored with her bourgeois lifestyle and seeks sexual diversions.

Controversial in its time and successful enough to spawn numerous sequels and countless copies, *Emmanuelle* now resembles a rather quaint period piece. Tracing a youthful girl's evolution from curious innocent to complete slut, this was one of the first soft-porn films to make it into the mainstream simply by taking itself seriously and spending some money on production. As far as the lesbian bits go, there is a simulated sex scene in a club watched by punters, including Emmanuelle's husband. There are also some 'genuine' lesbian scenes as Emmanuelle herself becomes involved with two different women. The second relationship, in particular, is surprisingly tender, although it is insufficient to be regarded as 'the real thing'. Indeed, the question 'does it count with a woman?' is posed early on in the film. Emmanuelle answers this for herself later when she decides that she is definitely 'a woman' because she has fucked a Thai boxer (don't ask). One for the archives.

The Enchantment (Yuwakusha) 1989

Director: Shunichi Nagasaki. Country: Japan. Screenplay: Goro Nakajima. Production company: Fuji Television. Duration: 109 mins, colour

Cast: Kumiko Akiyoshi (Miyako), Kiwako Harada (Harumi), Masao Kusakari (Dr Sotomura)

Miyako, a beautiful young woman, arrives at psychiatrist Dr Sotomura's office claiming she has been beaten by her female flatmate. Although Sotomura is engaged to be married to his assistant Harumi, he finds himself personally interested in Miyako and begins to pursue her case out of hours. The doctor's fiancée also finds herself increasingly involved in Miyako's strange world, and the scene is set for some unusual complications.

Although lesbianism is an implicit theme throughout the film, the real thing doesn't become explicit until an hour into the story. When it does, we are once again in the world of recognizable stereotypes – unhinged lesbian is mad, bad and dangerous to know. However, some interesting plot twists and a male protagonist who is increasingly confused by the mesmerizing Miyako means that this film moves much more into feminist territory than might have been expected. The film also makes some surprising comments about the masculine/feminine dichotomy, and assumptions we make about sexuality generally.

Entre Nous: see under **AT FIRST SIGHT**

Entwined 1997

Director: Raquel Cecilia Harrington. Country: US. Screenplay: Raquel Cecilia Harrington. Production company: Corazon Productions. Duration: 118 mins, colour

Cast: Veronica Sanchez (Elena), Kim Ostrenko (Julia), Marilyn Romero (Daniella), Iris Delgado (Andie), Sarah Lisano (Jodie)

Elena, a film student in Miami, is infatuated with one of her professors, Julia, who appears to be similarly attracted to her. The two meet up and gradually love blooms. They decide they want to be together for ever. Unfortunately, both women have long-term partners to separate themselves from first . . .

Entwined began as a two-woman enterprise and that it exists at all is the result of some tireless work by director/producer Raquel Cecilia Harrington and producer/director of photography Jacqueline B. Frost. Fortunately it does not aspire to be the ultimate lesbian film, and its modesty does it credit.

Impossibly earnest and sweet, *Entwined* shares the stage occupied by romantic melodramas like **CLAIRE OF THE MOON**. Sincerity it has in abundance, but unfortunately its ambition is way beyond its ability to deliver. Acting is enthusiastic but patchy, and the camera focus would have been too soft even for Doris Day. Given the production constraints and the limited crew, *Entwined* is rather like a very elaborate and incredibly accomplished home movie. One or two artistic moments get in the way, however (dream sequences, wherein Elena drifts through a forest in a long white dress, for example), and could have been dropped without compromising the artistic integrity.

The script has passion but lacks depth: despite its intention to raise important issues, such as child custody, the threat of losing promotion at work, etc., moments later the subjects are dropped. However, if what you want from a movie is a romance pure and simple, this is the film for you.

One interesting fact is that it's all set in Miami – possibly a first in lesbian film? – and making more of that fact would have broadened the range. There's also humour here: one or two scenes in the kitchen where Elena and her Mark Bolan lookalike girlfriend Daniella act out their fights have distinct overtones of Almodovar. More shouting and less brooding would have definitely been more fun, but why quibble? You get the picture.

See also: **CLAIRE OF THE MOON** and **LATE BLOOMERS** for more slushy stuff.

Even Cowgirls Get the Blues   1993

Director: Gus Van Sant. Country: US. Screenplay: Gus Van Sant (based on the novel by Tom Robbins). Production company: New Line Cinema/ Fourth Vision. Duration: 96 mins, colour

Cast: Uma Thurman (Sissy Hankshaw), John Hurt (The Countess), Rain Phoenix (Bonanza Jellybean), Keanu Reeves (Julian Gitche), Roseanne Barr (Madame Zoe), Heather Graham (Cowgirl Heather), Lorraine Bracco (Delores Del Ruby)

Possessor of the world's largest thumbs, Sissy Hankshaw's unequalled ability to hitchhike takes her along the high roads and low roads of America, encountering various characters and adventures along the way.

Tom Robbins's cult novel has not translated very well to the big screen. Plagued by numerous problems during production, the result looks like several mismatched scenes cobbled together and given a warm glow with a soundtrack by kd lang. Numerous cameo performances by film and TV luminaries suggest an ambition way beyond its realization, and, although Uma Thurman is always watchable, *Even Cowgirls Get the Blues* seems to be going nowhere. That said, Van Sant is always a thought-provoking director, and the film picks up a degree when the lesbian relationship is introduced. Rain Phoenix is Bonanza Jellybean, cowgirl revolutionary, and the woman with whom Sissy forms a liaison. Amid a strangely dated view of women's liberation, the duo fight the good fight on horseback with the aid of similarly minded cowgirls. Disappointing.

See also: **HENRY & JUNE** for more Uma, and **SWITCH**, in which Lorraine Bracco plays a lesbian businesswoman.

Faster, Pussycat, Kill! Kill! (Mankillers; Leather Girls; Pussycat) 1965

Director: Russ Meyer. Country: US. Screenplay: Jack Moran. Production company: Eve Productions. Duration: 83 mins, black and white

Cast: Tura Satana (Varla), Haji (Rosie), Lori Williams (Billie), Susan Bernard (Linda), Stuart Lancaster (Old Man), Paul Trinka (Kirk), Dennis Busch (Boy)

A trio of go-go dancers speed into the desert – one girl per car – seeking out some fast fun and frolics, led by leather-bound leader Varla. A straight couple competing in a time trial in their motor misjudge Varla's temper and before long there's a body, a hostage and three girls on the run ...

Outstanding cult movie, *Faster, Pussycat, Kill! Kill!* is still one of the most entertaining, ironic and superior 'chick-flicks' ever made. Director Russ Meyer is well known for producing cheap movies filled to the brim with large-breasted women. But he has always been distinguished from the soft-porn and dirty-mac brigade by his genuine ability to direct. Surprisingly, too, his female characters are often strong and frequently dictate the terms.

Faster, Pussycat, Kill! Kill! begins with a hilarious tome-like narration, resembling a public service announcement, advising the (male) audience of the violence simmering just below the surface of any number of women: 'She could be your secretary,' warns the voice, 'or a dancer in a go-go bar.' Cut to our heroines shimmying along to the latest beat before getting into their cars and speeding away. In lesbian terms, karate-chopping Varla is clearly somewhat on the Sapphic side, and her lovelorn sidekick Rosie is her ardent admirer. We don't see any lesbianism going on, although it is mentioned by the straight one of the three – Billie – who suggests that Rosie would be better off if she went 'both ways'. However, this won't stop a lesbian audience enjoying the film, and there's a swinging jazz score and dialogue to memorize and recite. Lesbian camp to the max. Fabulous.

See *also:* **BEYOND THE VALLEY OF THE DOLLS** and **VIXEN** by the same director.

Female Perversions   1996

Director: Susan Streitfeld. Country: US. Screenplay: Julie Hebert and Susan Streitfeld (based on the book *Female Perversions: The Temptations of Emma Bovary* by Louise J. Kaplan). Production company: MAP Films. Duration: 113 mins, colour

Cast: Tilda Swinton (Eve Stephens), Amy Madigan (Madelyn Stephens), Karen Sillas (Renee), Frances Fisher (Annunciata), Laila Robins (Emma), Clancy Brown (John)

Eve Stephens is a successful lawyer, on the verge of promotion to a judgeship. As she prepares for the interview she is called away to help her sister Amy, who has been arrested for stealing. There is no love lost between the two and Amy resents her sister's 'good girl' image. As Eve becomes unwillingly embroiled in her sister's lifestyle, there is a chance she may put some ghosts to rest and recover a glimmer of humanity.

A fascinating, extraordinary film which examines the way in which women are required both literally and figuratively to fit themselves into the most unnatural shapes in order to progress in a man's world.

The 'perversions' of the title refer not to unusual sexual practices (much as the video cover might hint at such a thing) but to the stereotype of 'normal femininity'. Thus a female perversion is the act of trying to meet society's expectations of what a woman should be like. In this way images of walking tightropes and being pulled in several directions by masked beings haunt Eve's dreams, while her waking life is filled with fantasies of failure. Professionally she is ideal for promotion, yet she is plagued by doubts and expects to be 'found out' at any moment. Tilda Swinton, looking every inch a perfect androgynous alien, is so suited to the role that it's hard to imagine any other actress managing to pull it off quite so completely. She gives an amazing, startling performance in which her body appears to be something apart from herself (and in so doing, conveys an astonishing degree of unselfconsciousness). Yet the trappings Eve surrounds herself with — the suits, the lipstick, the car, etc. — are vitally important to her self-esteem. Her world is stylistically dazzling (in strong contrast to her sister's surroundings), but the price appears to have been her very soul.

Eve is characterized as bisexual and has a male, then a female, lover. While professionally Eve is very much in tune with herself, in her private life she is so disconnected with her own feelings that relationships are conducted rather like extravagant business meetings. Thus people are fitted into her schedule as and when, and she has passionate, efficient but uninvolved sex with them. Her girlfriend — if that's the word — is Renee, a doctor, who is initially very interested in Eve but soon wants out, hurt by Eve's disturbing pragmatism. Eve is oblivious to the pain she is causing and takes the news of Renee's departure as if hearing that a contract has been terminated.

As a Freudian study of women's behaviour and sexuality the film is on many levels very successful, though the exposition is sometimes slow. Some of the images will stay with you for a long time and, surprisingly, it may be the witty rather than the symbolic ones you remember.

See also: **ORLANDO** for more Tilda.

The Fiends: see under **LES DIABOLIQUES**

Fire 1996

Director: Deepa Mehta. Country: Canada. Screenplay: Deepa Mehta. Production company: Trial by Fire Films. Duration: 104 mins, colour

Cast: Shabana Azmi (Radha), Nandita Das (Sita), Kulbushan Kharbanda (Ashok), Jaaved Jaaferi (Jatin), Ranjit Chowdhry (Mundu), Kushal Rekhi (Biji)

Present-day New Delhi. Radha is a devoted wife to Ashok and carer to his aged mother Biji. Ashok's younger brother reluctantly marries a young woman he does not love – Sita – and the two of them move into the house. Tensions rise as the proximity of the family members and their separate needs challenge the traditional values holding them all together. Young Sita suddenly realizes that she is in love with Radha and tells her so. The unfolding romance is observed by Biji, mute and disapproving . . .

Truly marvellous film, and ground-breaking, too, as far as the depiction – for the first time – of a lesbian relationship in India is concerned. The initial uncertainty experienced by the two women, the gentleness they express towards each other and the rising passion of the emerging relationship is wonderfully captured. Director Deepa Mehta's greatest achievement is to place the pair's burgeoning relationship against the context of everyday restrictions on women's lives. On top of this the possibility and consequence of discovery seem truly dreadful.

Sita, the younger woman, is more open in her desire to break with tradition. Her efforts initially appear simplistic, amounting to no more than wanting to wear jeans and dance to modern music. By contrast, Radha's needs and desires, buried for so many years, seem achingly profound. Her emotional resurrection is of necessity very slow, but deeply life-affirming.

There are terrific performances from all concerned but particularly the two leads. Nandita Das (Sita) was an unknown at the time and *Fire* was her first film, but Western audiences may not appreciate that Shabana Azmi (Radha) is an extremely well-known and respected actress in India. When interviewed at the 1996 London Film Festival where the film was premiered, she explained how she was attracted to the role because of Radha's dignity. She also playfully remarked that she did not believe that playing a lesbian character would harm her career – in fact, should there be any more films made in India on a lesbian theme she felt it likely that she and Nandita would be offered the roles first! Although *Fire* was critically acclaimed, after the film was shown in India Deepa Mehta found herself at the centre of a horrendous backlash and she received many death threats. In 1998 several cinemas showing the film were attacked and audiences threatened by extremists.

The First Wives Club   1996

Director: Hugh Wilson. Country: US. Screenplay: Robert Harling (based on the novel by Olivia Goldsmith). Production company: Paramount Pictures. Duration: 102 mins, colour

Cast: Bette Midler (Brenda), Goldie Hawn (Elise), Diane Keaton (Annie), Maggie Smith (Gunilla Goldberg), Jennifer Dundas (Chris Paradise), Eileen Heckart (Catherine), Sarah Jessica Parker (Shelly), Dan Hedaya (Morty), Bronson Pinchot (Duarto), Marcia Gay Harden (Dr Rosen)

Tragedy reunites three rich middle-aged women who simultaneously discover that their husbands are trading them in for younger models. Using their combined expertise gained through building up businesses the men are claiming for themselves, the first wives decide to wreak justice where it will hurt the most.

Critics generally didn't rate this film, but ignore them. This is a very funny comedy with some stellar performances all round. True, it is too sentimental at the end, to say nothing of being completely unbelievable (sometimes Americans just can't help themselves). Also, it was a waste to use someone of Stockard Channing's quality as merely the catalyst to kick-start the plot. However, there is a strong lesbian character – Diane Keaton's daughter Chris (Jennifer Dundas) – and her existence in the film leads to the most hilarious scene of all, set in a lesbian nightclub. The episode is far from offensive, and Lea De Laria makes her customary appearance as 'Bull-dyke in a bar'. Get it out on video and you won't regret it.

See also: Marcia Gay Harden as a likely bisexual in **CRUSH**, and Bette Midler having a brief bisexual fling in **THE ROSE**. Lea De Laria also appears in **RESCUING DESIRE**.

Five Easy Pieces 1970

Director: Bob Rafelson. Country: US. Screenplay: Adrien C. Joyce. Production company: Five Easy Pieces Productions. Duration: 98 mins, colour

Cast: Jack Nicholson (Robert Eroica Dupea), Karen Black (Rayette Dipesto), Lois Smith (Partita Dupea), Susan Anspach (Catherine Van Ost), Billy 'Green' Bush (Elton), Fannie Flagg (Stoney), Toni Basil (Terry Grouse)

Robert Eroica Dupea travels the American countryside avoiding his past. Apparently a drifter, Dupea is playing at being an oil rigger to escape his family's musical ambitions for him.

The lesbian scene in the film is just that, one scene, played as an amusing interlude. Dupea encounters two women stranded on the road after their car has broken down. He picks up the hitchhikers – Palm and Terry – who are headed for Alaska. Palm (Helena Kallianiotes) soon alienates her good Samaritan with her neurotic aggressive conversation. Toni Basil plays the other woman, Terry, and the two argue in a familiar way. Just in case you hadn't spotted the lesbian relationship, Palm expresses disgust at 'monkeys ... they do something in the open that I don't go for'. Hmmm.

Note: Actress Fannie Flagg wrote the novel and screenplay on which **FRIED GREEN TOMATOES AT THE WHISTLE STOP CAFÉ** was based.

See also: **BLACK WIDOW** by the same director.

The Fox 1967

Director: Mark Rydell. Country: US. Screenplay: Lewis John Carlino and Howard Koch (based on the book by D. H. Lawrence). Production company: Warner Brothers. Duration: 110 mins, colour

Cast: Sandy Dennis (Jill Banford), Anne Heywood (Ellen March), Kier Dullea (Paul Grenfel)

Jill and Ellen live in unnatural rural togetherness tending a farm. One day a young man, Paul, comes along and imposes his masculine self upon the couple. Very soon the women are torn asunder and normality is restored.

If there is a lesbian film which deserves the title 'most homophobic ever' *The Fox* is probably it. So offensive and upsetting – it fails to amuse on every level – that it is really not the film to see if you're feeling in the slightest bit unsure of your sexuality. And if you're not depressed when you go into the movie, you certainly will be on the way out. In a tale of turgid, sterile lesbianism versus bombastic, virile heterosexuality, the audience is asked to judge whom Ellen March ought to love, and be pleased when she turns inevitably straight.

Ellen March is soft butch, practical – she handles a gun easily – non-communicative (she rarely makes eye contact) but a touch bored with the Sapphic set-up, so isolated is it. We sense that Ellen feels she is missing something. In one scene she looks at her naked body in the mirror, she strokes her body and masturbates. She is missing *passion*, and passion does not exist in her present situation. When the two women get into bed there is no physical affection at all, not even a kiss. Meanwhile, in contrast Jill is the more feminine one of the two, brooding and worrying about things. She cooks, manages the family finances and frets over the finer feelings of animals. She seems non-sexual.

Heavy, overwrought direction brings with it overbearing symbolism, the first sign of which is the intervention of the fox into the women's henhouse. Significantly, Ellen is unable to kill the fox: can it be that she wants his intervention? Similarly, when Paul – prodigal local man – imposes himself on the Sapphic sisters Ellen is deeply disturbed by his presence, yet unable to send him away. Jill, meanwhile, is blissfully ignorant of the tensions mounting in her own home and invites Paul to stay over (it's an icy walk back). He immediately starts performing manly tasks – serving the meat (Ellen's job), offering to mend fences, etc.

Within a couple of days, Paul – taking a break from cleaning guns, shooting and thrusting knives all over the place – suddenly proposes to Ellen. 'It's right,' he pronounces. The next morning he suggests the women should sleep separately, since they must get on each other's nerves. He announces the marriage plans and declares he will build another room to accommodate all three of them. Jill is enraged. Not because his audacity is breathtaking or because she is about to lose her partner but because ... she doesn't want Ellen throwing herself away on a 'drifter'!

As the paper-thin lesbian relationship disintegrates before our eyes, one ever so small exchange might afford lesbian audiences a moment of rejoicing: 'There is no room for a married couple here,' Jill tells the couple firmly. 'There is absolutely no chance of you staying here after you are married.' Later Paul takes an opportunity to challenge Jill and her lifestyle. He defines her problem as never having had a man.

'That's what you want, isn't it? Isn't that what you need?' She slaps him. Cue Ellen to descend the stairs in a red dress and high heels, serving coffee like a good woman should. And before you can say 'Wow, Miss March, you really do look good in women's clothes', she's ripping them off in the barn, all the better to experience real, proper, natural sex the way it was meant to be. She loves it of course, and fulfilment is written all over her face.

At this point in the plot there is a sudden interlude wherein Ellen calls off the marriage for the sake of Jill, but this is merely delaying the inevitable, for we know the fox will come back for his helpless chicken, and so he does. The film looks set to resolve itself into a happy, romantic, heterosexual ending when the director must have noticed the spare woman hanging about in the script, making it look untidy. A little bit of melodrama at the end solves the problem. One day Jill is ineffectually trying to cut down a tree. Paul suddenly arrives, takes over and cuts the tree down easily. He tells her to move out of the way but she won't (stubborn lesbian). The tree falls exactly on her and kills her. Paul manfully prevents Ellen from getting to the body. A moment's doubt is expressed on her lips before she is whisked away.

The strange thing is, you may feel compelled to see this film in order to test your own sensibilities, and it's very possible you will enjoy the feeling of superiority experienced as a result. The acting is very good indeed (though you might dislike all the characters involved). Interestingly, Sandy Dennis was lesbian in real life (although she lived with jazz musician Gerry Mulligan for several years). She died of cancer in 1992.

See also: **THE ROSE** by the same director.

French Twist: see under **GAZON MAUDIT**

Fried Green Tomatoes: see under **FRIED GREEN TOMATOES AT THE WHISTLE STOP CAFÉ**

Fried Green Tomatoes at the Whistle Stop Café (Fried Green Tomatoes) 1991

Director: Jon Avnet. Country: US. Screenplay: Fannie Flagg (based on her own novel) and Carol Sobieski. Production company: Electric Shadow Productions. Duration: 130 mins, colour

FRIED GREEN TOMATOES AT THE WHISTLE STOP CAFÉ

Cast: Kathy Bates (Evelyn), Mary Stuart Masterson (Idgie), Mary Louise Parker (Ruth), Jessica Tandy (Ninny), Cicely Tyson (Sipsey), Chris O'Donnell (Buddy), Stan Shaw (Big George), Gailard Sartain (Ed)

Adaptation of the superb novel Fried Green Tomatoes at the Whistle Stop Café, *following the lives of two sets of women, one in the 1930s, one in the present day.*

Beautifully made, beautifully acted, poignant, hilariously funny and a real tear-jerker, *Fried Green Tomatoes at the Whistle Stop Café* has all the elements of a good old-fashioned 'women's film'. Kathy Bates is wonderful as the present-day housewife Evelyn, struggling to make her life interesting and finding inspiration in the stories told by the elderly Ninny, who recounts the adventures of her childhood companions.

At the time of release, many complained that the film represented another case of the disappearing lesbian. The book from which the screenplay was written clearly indicated a lesbian relationship between Idgie and Ruth, friends and business partners way back in the 1930s.

Certainly, if the quality of the relationship was determined by the physical aspect as viewed on screen, it might be assumed to be no more than a passionate friendship. Lots of platonic arms around the shoulders, and despite quite a few looks of devotion and love, no actual kissing. As frustrating and disappointing as this may be, there can be little doubt about the depth of their mutual emotional involvement. Idgie is transparently in love. She risks life and limb to rescue Ruth from an abusive husband. She has no interest in men or marriage and when she sets up house with Ruth she tells her, 'I'm as settled as I want to be.' Yet the relationship is presented to the viewer as deliberately ambiguous and leaves you to make a personal decision about the degree to which they are physically involved. Thus, as the director intended, the heterosexual majority are not alienated and numbers of straight women are able to cite this film as their favourite without anxiety. Don't be too put off. This is a truly great film and you'll love it.

See also: **BOYS ON THE SIDE**, in which Mary Louise Parker is once more the object of lesbian desire. Kathy Bates plays a lesbian in **PRIMARY COLORS** and a straight detective in **DIABOLIQUE**.

Recruitment. Daniela Bianchi and Lotte Lenya star in *From Russia with Love*. Courtesy of Danjaq, LLC & United Artists.

From Russia with Love 1963

Director: Terence Young. Country: GB. Screenplay: Richard Maibaum and Johanna Harwood (based on the novel by Ian Fleming). Production company: Eon. Duration: 118 mins, colour

Cast: Sean Connery (James Bond), Daniela Bianchi (Tatiana Romanova), Lotte Lenya (Rosa Klebb), Robert Shaw (Red Grant)

International criminal organization Spectre wants the 'Lector' – a Russian decoding machine – and would like to get rid of James Bond at the same time. Spectre sends their best agent – Rosa Klebb – to execute a trap. Bond is dispatched to recover the machine and enlists the help of Tatiana Romanova, a Russian coding clerk working at the Soviet Embassy in Istanbul, who is unwittingly also working for Spectre.

Our lesbian in this film is the gloriously formidable and ruthless Rosa Klebb, played by the highly respected stage actress Lotte Lenya. Crop-haired, severe and inscrutable behind pebble-thick glasses, she is the epitome of fearsome butch, complete with knuckle-dusters and poisoned spikes in her shoes. Klebb is characterized as violent, duplicitous, unattractive, perverted and, of course, communist. She is depicted as irredeemably villainous, and therefore not even worthy of the ultimate Cold War defection weapon: the Bond shag. Instead she provides the perfect contrast to all that is signalled as demure, decent, beautiful and properly female, as revealed in the Romanova persona. Romanova, passive and vulnerable, is shown to be suitably repelled by Klebb (she shudders at her touch), and the audience is invited to experience relief when Bond saves her from an unthinkable fate in Klebb's hands.

From Russia with Love, the second James Bond film, was a huge box-office success. Debate raged in the press as to whether this kind of glossy, glamorous, violent action film could be deemed 'family entertainment', and while most critics enjoyed the film immensely, some wondered whether we were being seduced and corrupted.

Although extreme and designed to frighten the horses, Rosa Klebb was one of the first clearly defined lesbians in any major film. Critics were divided in their approach to her character. Some ignored the obvious lesbian overtones and did not allude to them at all. The *Monthly Film Bulletin* simply remarked that Lenya was 'splendid'. Others found it hard to disguise their distaste. *Variety* felt that 'instead of being sinister, the character may be too grotesque even for this espionage pantomime'. *Films and Filming* felt that '*From Russia with Love* is slick and that, these days, also means sick', citing 'a fashionable excursion into lesbianism' as an example.

See also: **GOLDFINGER**, another great Bond film, featuring the fleetingly lesbian Pussy Galore.

Fun 1994

Director: Rafal Zielinski. Country: Canada and US. Screenplay: James Bosley. Duration: 104 mins, colour and black and white

Cast: Renee Humphrey (Hilary), Alicia Witt (Bonnie), William R. Moses (John), Leslie Hope (Jane), Ania Suli (Mrs Farmer)

FUN

What girls want. Renee Humphrey and Alicia Witt star in *Fun*. Courtesy of Metro Tartan Distribution.

Two girls murder an old woman for 'fun'. The film follows the examination of the two by a counsellor and a journalist, which is intercut by the events of the day that lead to the killing.

Disturbing film which tries to show how it comes about that two relatively ordinary teenagers should want to kill an entirely innocuous old lady simply as another diversion to pass the time. As the female counsellor and the male journalist probe deeper, each elicits information from the girls which illuminates but does not explain the crime.

Interestingly, both interrogators believe that Hilary and Bonnie are strongly bonded by something more than friendship. Hilary describes meeting Bonnie as 'a door opening ... I knew we'd always be together'. If either of them have lesbian inclinations it is likely to be Hilary, although when asked by the counsellor whether she has ever had a lesbian relationship she replies, 'With a woman?!'

Gazon Maudit (French Twist) 1995

Director: Josiane Balasko. Country: France. Screenplay: Josiane Balasko and Telsche Boorman. Production company: Renn Productions. Duration: 103 mins, colour, subtitled

Cast: Josiane Balasko (Marijo), Victoria Abril (Loli), Alain Chabat (Laurent), Ticky Holgado (Antoine), Catherine Hiegel (Dany)

Laurent, a compulsive womanizer, is happily married to his beautiful and unsuspecting wife Loli. One day butch Marijo happens by and seduces Loli. Laurent is predictably furious, but before he can exercise too much self-righteous anger, Loli discovers the truth about his affairs. Herself furious, she demands that Marijo move into the house. There the three of them live in an uneasy truce, until Marijo's ex-girlfriend comes to visit. Laurent welcomes her with open arms ...

First-class comedy, very funny, very French and with enough twists and turns in the plot to ensure that sooner or later everyone in the audience will feel their sensibilities offended. Marijo, a kind of modern-day Sister George, has an appealing confidence in her approach to Loli. Loli, meanwhile, unselfconsciously enters her lesbian affair and makes no apology for it. Nor, however, does she apologize for also wanting her husband. As the power moves from one character to the next, lesbians watching this film may find themselves in the unexpected position of feeling sorry for Laurent. It is to the film's credit that no one occupies the moral high ground for very long, and most of the comedy emerges from this shifting perspective.

Josiane Balasko, who stars as Marijo, also wrote the screenplay and directed. It may be a surprise to some to discover that Ms Balasko is in fact heterosexual (though she clearly has gained her insight into lesbian lifestyles from somewhere). All the cast are excellent, none more so than the consistently excellent Victoria Abril as the wife who decides that she can have her cake and eat it. Highly recommended.

Note: Gazon Maudit is subtitled. You can obtain a dubbed version under the title *French Twist* if you absolutely must ...

See also: **THE GIRL WITH THE GOLDEN PANTIES**, in which Victoria Abril plays a bisexual beatnik.

The Getting of Wisdom 1977

Director: Bruce Beresford. Country: Australia. Screenplay: Eleanor Witcombe. Production company: Southern Cross. Duration: 101 mins, colour

Cast: Susannah Fowle (Laura), Hilary Ryan (Evelyn), Barry Humphries (Reverend Strachey), John Waters (Reverend Shepherd), Alix Longman (Chinky), Kerry Armstrong (Kate)

Victorian Australia. Laura is the daughter of a poor postmistress. Her mother has scrimped and saved to send her to a girls' boarding school. She is mainly self-taught. A brilliant career seems likely.

Lush drama that would evoke warm memories of school and the pursuit of academic success were it not for the irritating leading character on whom the audience is supposed to focus. Unfortunately, Laura is a pompous little pest who is inevitably given a hard time by other, richer girls who find her eccentricity hard to swallow. Her misery is compounded by her unselfconsciousness and naivety, which leave her vulnerable to the petty prejudices and snobbery of all around her. Her lack of social skills relegate her to a separate existence from the others.

Somehow, however, a new girl – Chinky – gets a 'mash' on Laura and steals to buy her a ring. This unwise move leads to Chinky's expulsion from the school and Laura, in a fit of second-hand guilt, gets religion as a result. Christianity obviously has a profound effect, and before long Laura herself manages to have a brief flirtation with an older, rather attractive girl, Evelyn, and the two even make it into bed for a little cuddle. We know this won't last long because Evelyn is rich and gorgeous, and compelled, therefore, to heterosexuality even before a relationship with Laura makes this an appealing option. Annoying overall. Chinky was well out of it.

See also: **BILITIS, MAIDENS IN UNIFORM, OLIVIA, PICNIC AT HANGING ROCK** and **SECRET PLACES** for more schoolgirl crushes.

The Girl with the Golden Panties (La Muchacha de las Bragas de Oro) 1979

Director: Vincente Aranda. Country: Spain and Venezuela. Screenplay: Vincente Aranda, Santiago San Miguel and Maurico Wallerstein (based on the novel by Juan Marse). Production company: Morgan Films. Duration: 101 mins, colour

Cast: Lautaro Murua (Luis Forest), Victoria Abril (Mariana), Isabel Mestres (Soledad), Hilda Vera (Marina's Mother), Perla Vonasek (Elmyr)

Luis, an elderly militant, is writing his memoirs in the coastal resort of Sitges. One day his niece and her girlfriend come to visit him in his empty home, ostensibly to write an article about him. While he is dwelling on his fascist past and sexual indiscretions, the two women inevitably disrupt him in his musings.

Aranda's slow, contemplative film centralizes Luis as its subject, but only when Mariana arrives is the viewer properly woken up. The interest comes as the result of watching turgid, guilty old fascists tormented and teased by beatnik hippies. In other words, it's rather limited. The lesbian bit is revealed in the portrayal of Mariana as an uninhibited type (e.g. she walks around with no clothes on), a free spirit who happens to be with a woman but is equally at home with men. Her girlfriend is a rather strange person who never speaks but also operates the same flexible approach to sex. Just how flexible Mariana is prepared to be is revealed in a plot twist at the end of the film. Lesbianism seen as bohemian, unthreatening and transient. Victoria Abril is great, though, as always.

See also: **GAZON MAUDIT**, in which Victoria Abril plays a straight housewife persuaded into a lesbian affair.

Girlfriends 1978

Director: Claudia Weill. Country: US. Screenplay: Vicki Polon. Production company: Cyclops Film. Duration: 88 mins, colour

Cast: Melanie Mayron (Susan Weinblatt), Eli Wallach (Rabbi Gold), Adam Cohen (Bar Mitzvah Boy), Anita Skinner (Anne Munroe), Jean de Baer (Terry), Christopher Guest (Eric), Nancy Mette (Denise)

Susan, an aspiring photographer living in Manhattan, struggles to make an impact in a man's world.

Claudia Weill's first feature, after much work in documentary, has been occasionally hailed as the first-ever feminist film to reach a wide(ish) audience. The girlfriends of the title are Susan herself and an old room-mate, Anne, but this is firmly heterosexual territory, and the two are not bonded in any particular way. Rather, their characters and lifestyles contrast with each other, and their various up and downs are ostensibly compared, but really it is Susan's tribulations we are watching.

The brief lesbian episode is there to reinforce the straightness of the heroine. One day Susan picks up a young hitchhiker, Ceil (Amy Wright), who stays in her apartment for a while. At one point Ceil makes a pass at Susan, which is rejected and brings to an end her stay in Susan's home.

Brilliantly acted by Melanie Mayron, but dull, dull, dull.

Girls in Prison 1956

Director: Edward L. Cahn. Country: US. Screenplay: Lou Rusoff. Production company: Golden State Productions. Duration: 86 mins, black and white

Cast: Richard Denning (Reverend Fulton), Joan Taylor (Anne Carson), Adele Jergens (Jenny), Helen Gilbert (Melanee), Lance Fuller (Paul Anderson), Jane Darwell (Matron Jamieson)

Anne Carson is involved in a bank robbery and sentenced to five years. She has hidden the money from the robbery and everybody knows it. In prison she is preyed upon by all and sundry determined to get the loot out of her.

Fairly ordinary B-movie in which, very unusually, the criminal is likely to come out of prison a better person than she went in. The lesbian side to things is very low-key indeed, but a couple of lines reveal what is going on for one inmate at least. Melanee tries to befriend Anne. The audience may believe that this is a ploy to trick her out of the money, but there's another agenda at work. Anne rejects her 'advance' and Melanee has a sulk. She exclaims, 'I despise that girl', to which cell-mate Jenny responds, 'I know. Who was it who said something about a woman scorned ...'

And that's about it, folks. Still, these 1950s movies are usually worth watching, and in this case, why not see it and compare it with the very loose remake (below).

Girls in Prison   1994

Director: John McNaughton. Country: US. Screenplay: Sam Fuller and Christa Lang. Production company: Spelling Films International. Duration: 75 mins, colour

Cast: Missy Crider (Aggie), Anne Heche (Jennifer), Nicolette Scorsese (Suzy), Bahni Turpin (Melba), Ione Skye (Carol), Nestor Serrano (Borcelino)

Aggie, an aspiring country singer with a potential hit on her hands, is framed for murder by a bad lot who intend to steal her song. Sentenced to life in a tough city slammer, she meets Carol and Melba, individuals similarly convicted of murder in the first degree (except that they actually did it, but the victims deserved it, etc.). The trio form a close bond, but Aggie's troubles are only just beginning . . .

Not so much a remake of the 1950s classic, more a completely different film with the same name, this is a very amusing romp of a girls-in-the-can movie. The fact that it is completely unbelievable in every respect should not deter you. With a plot as subtle as a prison-yard punch-up, and the line between the good and the bad drawn chasm wide, this is perfect late-night Friday viewing. The strong lesbian relationship between Carol and Melba (consummated in the shower in front of an initially apprehensive Aggie) is presented in every way as positive. The two befriend our heroine and help protect her from the homicidal maniacs lurking in every other cell, while encouraging her to seek justice. Meanwhile, the baddies who framed her in the first place are nervous that Aggie is still alive and decide to recruit a killer within the prison to finish her off.

The villain who has the best time in this movie is the duplicitous Jennifer played by Anne Heche. Long before she came out in front of the entire Western world on the arm of Ellen DeGeneres, the fab Ms Heche vamped it up as the mad, bad girl intent on murder to protect her stolen interests. She doesn't succeed of course, and eventually justice is done (in case you were worried). Seems an awful lot of fuss over one song but that's show business. A hoot from start to finish.

The Glitter Dome 1984

Director: Stuart Margolin. Country: US. Screenplay: Stanley Kallis (based on the novel by Joseph Wambaugh). Production company: Telepictures. Duration: 90 mins, colour

Cast: James Garner (Al), Margot Kidder (Willie), John Lithgow (Marty), John Marley (Captain Woofer), Stuart Margolin (Herman)

Police drama set in LA and styled on the hard-boiled cop stories of the 1940s. Al investigates the murder of a movie mogul, which leads him into the seedier side of life in the big city, including child pornography and murder.

One of the murder suspects is a middle-aged lesbian played by Coleen Dewhurst. She's a cool customer, unintimidated by the police, clever and responsible. She takes care of a pretty fifteen-year-old girl (with whom she might be sleeping) and is trying to keep her off the streets. She is shown to be smart and honourable. Lesbianism as surprise factor and to underline the LAPD's eternal struggle in dealing with all human life, etc., etc.

Go Fish 1994

Director: Rose Troche. Country: US. Screenplay: Rose Troche and Guinevere Turner. Production company: Can I Watch Pictures. Duration: 85 mins, black and white

Cast: Guinevere Turner (Max), T. Wendy McMillan (Kia), Migdalia Melendez (Evy), V. S. Brodie (Ely), Anastasia Sharp (Daria)

Max is looking for a girlfriend. Ever so cute Max, rather incredibly, has not had a date in ten months and speculates with her friends as to where she should look for Ms Right. A chorus of like-minded twentysomethings decide on matchmaking our heroine with an unlikely prospect, the hippy, trippy, long-haired Ely. Initially unimpressed, Max is eventually convinced they might be right.

Brilliant independent feature from first-time director Rose Troche, *Go Fish* is a feel-good movie aimed directly at lesbians but which has achieved an astonishing crossover appeal to straight audiences. That said, much of the comedy for lesbians comes from those moments of recognition and detailed observations of everyday life. Some truly hilarious scenes, mainly involving the Sapphic sisters under the skin who literally put their heads together to contemplate life, love and everything. Subjects for discussion include Lesbian Bed Death, the preferred terminology for *that* part of the body, and the vexing taboo surrounding lesbians who sleep with men. Some quirkiness too (including nail-clipping as a prelude to seduction ...), and a touch of politics thrown in here and there with a deft lightness of touch.

Go Fish was conceived in August 1991, the project of Rose Troche and Guinevere Turner. Initially intended as an avant-garde documentary, *Go Fish* expanded into a more straightforward narrative film as Guinevere's script took shape and the production progressed. Various set-backs, delays and lack of money beleaguered the production (at no point could Troche and Turner even view the previous day's filming, as they couldn't afford to have the rushes processed). Recruiting the cast from clubs and bars kept costs low, but when no one suitable was found to play the leading role of Max, Guinevere Turner herself stepped in. Rose Troche has rather disarmingly admitted that 'everyone was chosen for their looks!' Filming schedules were tailored to fit around outside work (everyone had a full-time job), and the cast were frequently pleaded with not to change their appearance during the course of filming. This had particular relevance for V. S. Brodie – who plays Max's girlfriend-to-be Ely – whose real long hair is shorn during a 'transformation' sequence.

One year later, when the project was floundering, producer Christine Vachon (*Swoon* [1991], **I SHOT ANDY WARHOL**, *Velvet Goldmine* [1998]) came on board and things gradually picked up again. The film eventually took two and a half years to make.

An insight into the bars and cafés making up the Chicago scene, a soft jazz score coupled with a free-flowing camera and a witty script make this one of the most important lesbian films so far and essential viewing for that reason alone. Comparisons with early Spike Lee and even 1970s Woody Allen are tempting, but stylistically *Go Fish* is its own movie. Filled to the brim with wit and wisdom and a very funny, knowing humour. Cool, clever and sexy!

See also: (if you must) **PREACHING TO THE PERVERTED** for more Guin. Guin fans should also see **THE WATERMELON WOMAN**

The Goddess 1958

Director: John Cromwell. Country: US. Screenplay: Paddy Chayefsky. Production company: Columbia Pictures. Duration: 105 mins, black and white

Cast: Kim Stanley (Emily Ann Faulkner), Lloyd Bridges (Dutch Seymour), Steve Hill (John Tower), Betty Lou Holland (The Mother), Elizabeth Wilson (The Secretary), Joan Copeland (The Aunt), Gerald Hiken (The Uncle)

Tracing the rise to fame of a small-town girl in the Depression to the big time in Hollywood.

Kim Stanley is Emily, the small-town girl who manages to achieve childhood dreams of success through a mixture of judicious marriages and unbridled ambition. Her start in life is unpromising. However, Emily marries a film star's son, has a child (whom she refuses to bring up), suddenly somehow becomes a star, divorces and marries a boxer.

Ten years later she is very rich and lives in a huge house. Recovering from a nervous breakdown, she is profoundly lonely and calls people she barely knows her 'best friends'. By the end of the film Emily is being cared for by a Miss Heywood (Elizabeth Wilson), the lesbian character. 'She likes me to be in the room when she wakes up,' says Miss Heywood to John, Emily's first husband. John remarks, 'So, she finally found a mother.' The expression on Miss Heywood's face suggests that this is not how she sees herself at all. She refers to Emily as 'My girl', and declares, 'I kind of love her ... I'll take good care of her.'

Thus the film closes with Emily neurotic, on medication, friendless and facing a life in the dubious care of a creepy lesbian. Lesbianism as an indication of how low a person can sink. A lesson for all ambitious women.

See also: CAGED by the same director.

Golden Balls (Huevos de Oro) 1993

Director: Bigas Luna. Country: Spain. Screenplay: Cuca Canals and Bigas Luna. Production company: Lolafilms. Duration: 95 mins, colour, subtitled

Cast: Javier Bardem (Benito Gonzalez), Maria De Medeiros (Marta), Maribel Verdu (Claudia), Elisa Touati (Rita), Raquel Bianca (Ana), Alessandro Gassmann (Melilla's Friend), Albert Vidal (Father-in-law)

Construction worker Benito Gonzalez aspires to create mighty erections for all the world to admire. A ruthless personality and an ability to seize the main chance sees him achieve his ambitions. But lust and greed can be their own punishments, and soon both his wife and mistress are making demands . . .

Very amusing Spanish comedy, in which the excesses of machismo – coupled with a 1990s desire to make money and be damned – are gradually built up, in order to be completely demolished. The rise and fall of ambitious Benito is something to see, but it is the relationship between his wife and his mistress which is even more interesting.

Initially, Benito marries Marta, the banker's daughter, in order to obtain backing for his business. He keeps his mistress, Claudia, on the side. As time passes Benito unexpectedly finds that he rather likes his wife and wants to bring together the two women into the one bed. At first Marta is both horrified and upset. But soon the women begin to talk and find that they share much in common, mostly involving their frustration with Benito himself. So the women comply with his sexual wishes and sleep together, and at certain times they seem more interested in each other than their shared man. An idyllic threesome develops, for a while.

Much later in the film, when Claudia is out of the picture, Benito brings home another woman as a substitute. Marta is beside herself with rage. 'Do you think we women are all alike?' she cries. Lesbianism given a certain respect, though always in relation to the heterosexual principle.

See also: **HENRY & JUNE**, in which Maria De Medeiros plays bisexual again. Other notable films wherein wives are encouraged to experience Sapphic diversions include **EMILIENNE** and **LENNY**.

Goldfinger 1964

Director: Guy Hamilton. Country: GB. Screenplay: Richard Maibaum and Paul Dehn (based on the novel by Ian Fleming). Production company: Eon Productions. Duration: 109 mins, colour

Cast: Sean Connery (James Bond), Honor Blackman (Pussy Galore), Gert Frobe (Goldfinger), Shirley Eaton (Jill Masterson), Tania Mallett (Tilly Masterson), Harold Sakata (Odd-Job)

Goldfinger plans to attack Fort Knox, the centre of the USA's gold reserves. James Bond is sent in to sort it out.

GOLDFINGER

The lady *is* for turning. Honor Blackman and Sean Connery star in *Goldfinger*. Courtesy of Danjaq, LLC & United Artists.

One of the best Bond movies, with all the usual ingredients: mad megalomaniac villain, clever gadgets, exciting music and great locations. This one also has Pussy Galore.

In Ian Fleming's book she was a Sapphic working for the enemy who became a man's woman after a roll in the hay with Bond, James Bond. In the film the concept of lesbian is altered to mean 'hard to get and dresses a bit on the butch side'. As Pussy Galore is the leading Bond girl in the film, there is no way that she will not comply with the standard requirements of putting out for the hero. In this case the vague hint of lesbianism provides evidence of classic mythology, in which 'a real man can make a real woman out of her'. All is not lost for the lesbian viewer, however. Honor Blackman (fresh from *The Avengers* at the time) is first class as the weak link in Goldfinger's plan, and is at least given some important screen time. She still has her team of lovelies, of course, female pilots willing to do whatever she says (including switch allegiances at the eleventh hour). Her name – presumably a reference to a reckless past – is a source of continual heterosexual amusement both for Bond and the straight audience, but there is no reason why lesbians should not smile too.

See also: **FROM RUSSIA WITH LOVE**, another great Bond film.

The Good Father 1986

Director: Mike Newell. Country: GB. Screenplay: Christopher Hampton (based on the novel by Peter Prince). Production company: Greenpoint Films. Duration: 90 mins, colour

Cast: Anthony Hopkins (Bill Hooper), Jim Broadbent (Roger Miles), Harriet Walter (Emmy Hooper), Frances Viner (Cheryl Langford), Simon Callow (Mark Varda), Miriam Margolyes (Jane Powell), Joanne Whalley (Mary Hall)

Bill Hooper is a former feminist now living in a miserable state of separation from his wife and with only limited access to his young son. When friend Roger hears that his own former wife plans to leave the country with their child – and her female lover – Bill encourages him to fight her in the courts.

Family breakdowns and custody battles are the themes behind this often unpleasant drama, filled to the brim with conflicting agendas and bitter rivalries. Bill Hooper is a complex character, and the war he fights with his own and Roger's wife Cheryl is an explosive battle of the sexes. We learn that Bill previously bought into feminism in a big way, but now feels betrayed and angry with a judicial system that favours his wife. He seems worthy of our sympathy, until he hires an unscrupulous lawyer to help fight Roger's corner using the weapon of lesbianism to secure a victory. He takes a vicious pleasure in Cheryl's distress even though Roger himself is too devastated – and still in love with his wife – to want revenge.

We later learn that Bill rejected his wife, not because of her short-term infidelity but because he felt jealous of the attention she gave their son. On an unconscious level he even feels murderous towards the boy. Thus the film attempts to restore a little balance to the rather misogynistic tone that colours most of the movie. The performances are solid enough – from a sterling bunch of British thesps – and the writing is sharp, but the overall effect is depressing.

Grace of My Heart   1996

Director: Allison Anders. Country: US. Screenplay: Allison Anders. Production company: Cappa Productions. Duration: 115 mins, colour

Cast: Illeana Douglas (Denise Waverly), Matt Dillon (Jay), Eric Stolz (Howard), John Turturro (Joel), Patsy Kensit (Cheryl), Bridget Fonda (Kelly)

Denise Waverly, an aspiring singer/songwriter, has left behind her wealthy Philadelphia family in order to pursue a musical career. On her way to eventual recognition she endures many tribulations and problems in her personal life.

Wonderful comedy/drama, some say based on the life of Carole King, or perhaps an amalgam of 1960s singer/songwriters who struggled for fame and fortune way back when. Some great tunes written by the likes of Dave Stewart, Elvis Costello, Carole Bayer Sager and the legendary Burt Bacharach add to the veracity of the piece, and the solid talent of Illeana Douglas makes the film a first-rate drive down the middle of the road.

The lesbian scene is brief but memorable. Denise is given the job of writing a song for a popular singer of the moment, Kelly Porter (Bridget Fonda in a terrific cameo). Musing over the sort of theme she might base her song upon, Denise overhears Kelly talking to her female lover. As a result, Denise pens a tune she calls 'My Secret Love', which Kelly sings her little heart out over. Just great.

Great Moments in Aviation (Shades of Fear)   1994

Director: Beeban Kidron. Country: GB. Screenplay: Jeanette Winterson. Production company: BBC Films. Duration: 89 mins, colour

Cast: Rakie Ayola (Gabriel Angel), Vanessa Redgrave (Angela), John Hurt (Professor Rex Goodyear), Jonathan Pryce (Duncan), Dorothy Tutin (Gwendoline)

GREAT MOMENTS IN AVIATION

Keeping company. Vanessa Redgrave and Dorothy Tutin star in *Great Moments in Aviation*. Courtesy of British Film Institute: Still, Posters and Designs.

In 1957 a cruise ship takes a number of motley characters from the Caribbean to England. Each has a mission, vendetta or ambition to fulfil. Among them is Gabriel Angel, a young black woman on her way to meet her husband. Her optimistic innocence causes the others to examine their lives and see things as they really are.

Written by the supremely talented Jeanette Winterson, and produced by the same team that brought the highly acclaimed *Oranges Are Not the Only Fruit* to television, *Great Moments in Aviation* is a little gem of a British film. Inexplicably overlooked and never given proper distribution, the film has occasional outings on BBC TV but has never made it to the big screen. Be sure to catch it if you can, although this is not, one must hastily add, a lesbian film as such. However, among the group of principal characters are an archetypal tweedy couple of women, Gwen and Angela, middle-aged, eccentric and sweet. Other passengers assume they have some sort of Boston marriage. 'Lesbians,' pronounces Professor Rex Goodyear, observing them by the ship's bathing pool. 'Is that a kind of missionary?' asks Gabriel. In fact, until the fateful cruise journey, Gwen and Angela are engaged in a profound friendship that only develops further once Gwen has decided to seize the day. In a golden scene, beautifully photographed and exceptionally well paced, the two women gradually realize they have been in love for years. For women of a certain age this may be the most heart-rending (not to say, inspirational) depiction of a coming-out moment ever seen on screen. Whimsical, comic, dramatic and gentle.

See also: **THE BOSTONIANS, JULIA** and **MRS DALLOWAY** for more Vanessa.

The Greengage Summer (Loss of Innocence) 1961

Director: Lewis Gilbert. Country: GB. Screenplay: Howard Koch (based on the novel by Rumer Godden). Production company: PKL. Duration: 99 mins, colour

Cast: Kenneth More (Eliot), Danielle Darrieux (Mme Zizi), Susannah York (Joss), Claude Nollier (Mme Corbet), Jane Asher (Hester), Elizabeth Dear (Vicky), Richard Williams (Willmouse)

Coming-of-age drama in which sixteen-year-old Joss forms a relationship with a middle-aged man during a family holiday in France.

Enjoyable romantic drama set in the green and golden champagne country of France. Four English children are en route to a summer holiday in France when their mother is suddenly taken ill. The children thus arrive at the hotel unescorted, which does not go down well with the two Frenchwomen – Mme Zizi and Mme Corbet – in charge. Eliot, a charming man with whom Mme Zizi is having an affair, intervenes and insists the children are allowed to stay.

As the summer progresses a number of interesting relationships develop, particularly between the eldest child Joss (Susannah York in her first major role) and the suave Eliot, who notices the girl's burgeoning charms. An unexpectedly melodramatic plot twist has Eliot revealed as a jewel thief, but not before Joss has experienced love and disillusionment in equal measures.

The lesbian aspect is a subtle reference to the relationship between the two managers of the hotel. Mme Corbet is in love with Zizi and laments, 'We were so happy before he came, so happy.' Zizi clearly returns the compliment, though she is mightily keen on the affable Brit, played with friendly appeal by Kenneth More. Interestingly, although the lesbian suffers seeing her girlfriend having an affair with a man, the bisexual Zizi suffers too, for she must witness Eliot's growing affection for the younger, fresh as a daisy, Joss.

See also: **THE KILLING OF SISTER GEORGE, THE MAIDS** and **ZEE & CO** for Susannah in lesbian or bisexual mode.

The Group   1966

Director: Sidney Lumet. Country: US. Screenplay: Sidney Buchman (based on the novel by Mary McCarthy). Production company: Famous Artists Productions. Duration: 150 mins (GB 147 mins), colour

Cast: Candice Bergen (Lakey), Joan Hackett (Dottie), Elizabeth Hartman (Priss), Shirley Knight (Polly), Joanna Pettet (Kay)

It's 1933 and eight Vassar girls graduate with all the excitement and aspirations of privileged youth. The film follows their fortunes over the ten years into World War II.

Tremendous adaptation of Mary McCarthy's novel. *The Group* makes for compelling viewing as we watch, with sympathy and occasional horror, youthful enthusiasm gradually turn into resignation and disappointment. With a careful and clever delineation of revealing scenes, together with constant cross-referencing, we care about the characters from beginning to end.

Candice Bergen plays Lakey, integral member of the group, the most assured (which is saying something) and probably the richest. Lakey is an art history major and soon departs to Europe to study. This trip proves so successful that she does not return for years. Unfortunately, this means that she is also missing from the film for quite some time. When she returns she has found herself a lover, the stylish but rather stern-looking Baroness Maria d'Etienne, who comes back to America with her. The group respond to this surprise with varying degrees of discomfort, but all politely accept it as a personal idiosyncrasy.

Lakey is characterized as glacially cool, superior, elegant and independent. She is completely uninterested in men sexually: in one scene she casually removes a male friend's hand from her waist and in another ignores the advances of a keen painter. The only time we see the softer side to Lakey is at the wedding of Kay and Harold. Lakey has tears in her eyes as she watches Kay leave with her husband. As Dottie observes to Lakey: 'Kay adores you and you used to like her best in your heart of hearts ...'

At the end of the film, when the group have been reunited through tragedy, Lakey has an opportunity to be alone with Kay's estranged husband Harold. His attitude to her is, at first, amused: 'I never had you down for a Sapphic.' When she fails to rise to his remarks he becomes angry and demands to know if there had ever been 'anything between' herself and Kay. The audience knows there was nothing physical between them but Lakey chooses to answer ambiguously, thus inflaming him even further. As Harold was persistently cruel to his wife while he was with her, the audience is given the satisfaction of seeing him receive a come-uppance at the hands of someone who cared for his wife. It is very unusual to position a lesbian in this role, but any notion that Lakey is a solid force for good must be tempered by the fact that Harold is *misled* into believing something about Kay which isn't true. If there *had* been something going on, the chances are that the lesbian viewers would have been the only ones enjoying the last laugh.

See also: **11 HARROWHOUSE** for Candice as the object of desire.

The Handmaid's Tale   1989

Director: Volker Schlöndorff. Country: US and Germany. Screenplay: Harold Pinter (based on the novel by Margaret Atwood). Production company: Cinecom Pictures. Duration: 109 mins, colour

Cast: Natasha Richardson (Kate), Faye Dunaway (Serena Joy), Aidan Quinn (Nick), Elizabeth McGovern (Moira), Victoria Tennant (Aunt Lydia), Robert Duvall (Commander)

Atwood's frightening vision of a post-feminist future has women either married to rich men or interned and bar-coded to produce children as surrogate mothers. Kate resists her fate.

In the puritanical, fascistic police state of Gilead, women's bodies and the uses to which they will be put are decided by the authorities. Heterosexual women are bound by their status in relation to men and their ability to conceive. Love or tenderness of any sort are not part of the game and women are encouraged to view (and judge) each other with the same contempt. All actions are examined with puritanical Calvinism. Women are punished for masturbation – 'Men can't help it, but we're different,' Kate is advised.

A separate fate awaits lesbians, or at least those attractive enough to warrant the attentions of men. Categorized as 'gender traitors', they are dispatched to glamorous brothel/bar/clubs where they service men in need. This is what happens to Moira, played by the likable Elizabeth McGovern. This role is, unfortunately, much smaller than it should have been – she appears only briefly at the beginning and, again, in a short scene at the end of the film. A pity, because she is characterized as brave, heroic and wise. 'Gilead,' she cannily observes, 'is a fucking loony bin.'

The Haunting   1963

Director: Robert Wise. Country: GB. Screenplay: Nelson Gidding (based on the novel by Shirley Jackson, *The Haunting of Hill House*). Production company: Argyle Enterprises. Duration: 112 mins, black and white

Cast: Julie Harris (Eleanor), Claire Bloom (Theo), Richard Johnson (Dr Markway), Russ Tamblyn (Luke Sannerson), Fay Compton (Mrs Sannerson), Rosalie Crutchley (Mrs Dudley), Lois Maxwell (Grace Markway)

Four people arrive at a reputedly haunted house in order to conduct experiments. Within hours things are going bump in the night and Eleanor, particularly, seems susceptible to the strange atmosphere. The very house itself seems equally interested in Eleanor . . .

Claire Bloom performs a highly entertaining turn as Theo, the sophisticated butch lesbian – well dressed, intelligent, practical, emotionally tough, as well as somewhat predatory and manipulative. From the moment she meets Eleanor she turns on the charm and waits to see what will happen next. As it happens, Theo is far too sophisticated for the sheltered Eleanor, and one has the strongest feeling that she is merely passing the time flirting with her. Theo would probably prefer someone more like herself, and indeed she hints that there is someone waiting for her at home. Nevertheless, any port in a storm. Theo operates on the 'all girls together' strategy and ensures compliance by demonstrating a keen interest in Nell's life. She also has the somewhat unnerving ability to read minds, which allows her to make accurate observations about Eleanor's real motives. In any case, given the year the film was made, Theo is not too offensive a portrayal of a lesbian, just a highly predictable one. As required, she is seen largely alone, unable to capture Eleanor and in fact insulted by her once Nell has finally realized what is actually going on. Do not be deterred. *The Haunting* is enormous, good-quality fun. It's genuinely scary, too.

Heavenly Creatures 1994

Director: Peter Jackson. Country: New Zealand. Screenplay: Peter Jackson and Frances Walsh. Production company: Wingnut Films. Duration: 98 mins, colour

Cast: Melanie Lynskey (Pauline), Kate Winslet (Juliet), Sarah Peirse (Honora), Diana Kent (Hilda), Clive Merrison (Henry), Simon O'Connor (Herbert)

New Zealand 1953. Pauline Parker and Juliet Hulme strike up an intense friendship at school. They invent an imaginary fantasy world into which no one else is admitted. As time passes, separation is threatened and the girls contrive a terrible plan in order to stay together. Based on a true story.

Strikingly effective drama/horror, telling the tale of a massive scandal that occurred in Christchurch in 1954, when two young schoolgirls were found guilty of the murder of Honora Parker, Pauline's mother. As a story of mounting obsession, and with a shockingly violent ending, *Heavenly Creatures* might be notable merely as an accomplished horror film. But the film is most memorable not just as a study of escalating madness but as a brilliant insight into being fourteen and in love with your best friend. In doing so the film achieves something remarkable: it lets you understand why the terrible deed is committed.

Melanie Lynskey is superb as the scowling, sulky Pauline who finds fault with almost everything except her cherished friend. Kate Winslet is equally accomplished as Juliet, the beautiful, superior English girl, materially rich but with pragmatic rather than loving parents. The two are initially drawn together through a passion for the 'world's greatest tenor' Mario Lanza, but also find themselves bonded through the various illnesses they have experienced. The sheer exuberance the two girls feel in simply being together, the feeling of being above and beyond everyone else, and of being understood at last, becomes the tie that binds them. The invention of their private 'Fourth World' allows them to exclude everyone but themselves from their friendship. The fantasy also allows them to sleep together in the guise of impersonating a hero or two.

When Juliet's father begins to suspect that the relationship is 'unhealthy' he persuades Pauline's parents to send their daughter to a psychiatrist. He diagnoses the condition known as 'homosexuality' and the parents' thunderstruck reaction leads the girls to fear they may be separated. Somehow Pauline's mother becomes the focus of the fear and hatred, and the two conceive of a murder plan, something they describe as a 'happy event'.

Heavenly Creatures is much more than just schoolgirl crush time, and equally this is no tiresome 'killer dykes' movie either. The film suggests that if the girls had been left to experience their blissful romance to its conclusion, then the murder would probably not have happened. The director, who has beautifully described his own film as 'a murder story about love', portrays both girls as locked in a maelstrom of obsession that dictates the only action they feel they can take. The death of their love or the death of an 'obstacle'? No choice.

Henry & June 1990

Director: Philip Kaufman. Country: US. Screenplay: Philip Kaufman and Rose Kaufman. Production company: Universal. Duration: 136 mins, colour

Cast: Fred Ward (Henry Miller), Uma Thurman (June Miller), Maria De Medeiros (Anaïs Nin), Richard E. Grant (Hugo), Kevin Spacey (Osborn), Jean-Philippe Ecoffey (Eduardo)

Story based on the diaries of Anaïs Nin and chronicling her affair with the then unknown Henry Miller and her involvement with June Miller, his wife.

A frank and fairly erotic drama, *Henry & June* is a lengthy but interesting film, sustained and nurtured by some excellent acting. Uma Thurman smoulders as June Miller, the woman who abandons her husband in Paris so that she can pursue both her acting career and her female lover in New York. This is very much the story of Henry and Anaïs though, he all rough male virility and she the somewhat cosseted and receptive female. However, the relationship between Anaïs and June has its moments, and certainly they both seem desperately keen to get into bed with each other, although this is only able to occur to anyone's satisfaction during a brief dream sequence.

What is made explicit, though, is that once aroused, Anaïs's interest in women extends through June to other women. In one of the film's most interesting scenes Anaïs and her husband visit a brothel and pay to watch an 'exhibition'. This involves two women making love to each other, one of them pretending to be a man. Having selected two women who resemble herself and June, Anaïs and her husband then watch as one of the prostitutes 'forces' herself upon the other (à la mode one assumes). 'You like something else?'

asks one of the women. Anaïs replies, 'Yes, stop pretending to be a man.' The sex suddenly becomes more co-operative.

Lesbianism in this film is expressed in both passionate and gentle terms, and on both sexual and emotional levels, but it is always seen as secondary to the 'real' sex which goes on between Henry and Anaïs.

See also: **EVEN COWGIRLS GET THE BLUES** for more Uma, and **GOLDEN BALLS** for more Maria. **THE UNBEARABLE LIGHTNESS OF BEING** is by the same director.

Higher Learning 1994

Director: John Singleton. Country: US. Screenplay: John Singleton. Production company: Columbia Pictures. Duration: 128 mins, colour

Cast: Omar Epps (Malik Williams), Kristy Swanson (Kristen Connor), Michael Rapaport (Remy), Ice Cube (Fudge), Tyra Banks (Deja), Laurence Fishburne (Professor Maurice Phipps), Jennifer Connelly (Taryn)

Columbus University at the present day, and the young freshmen are starting their academic lives with a mixture of excitement and trepidation. The experience of half a dozen young men and women – black and white – is detailed, as over a few months they become part of campus life.

Singleton's excellent film, much more than a superficial skim over student parties, nervous sex and macho grandstanding, takes a long cool view at its main protagonists and watches their personalities evolve in front of us. Painful issues of race and sexism are at the forefront, and, cleverly, Singleton moves our sympathies all over the place, proving, as we all know in our hearts, that nothing is simple and there are no easy answers.

The leading female is Kristen, a nice, well-meaning, naive woman. A drinking game with a group of students turns into date-rape, which leads to a fear of sex with men. Along comes a young feminist, Taryn, who offers an alternative in the form of a lesbian relationship. This rather unsubtle explanation for a conversion is tempered by the way the relationship is depicted. Taryn is no seductress, and it is the straight Kristen who has to make the running, not the other way around. At one point Taryn resists a pass, explaining that she doesn't want Kristen unless she is sure, 'not just because you're fascinated'. Singleton risks lesbian disappointment (not to say anger) when he counterpoints the lesbian liaison with Kristen's tentative involvement with another man (a sensitive one this time). Thus the long-awaited love scene between the two women is interwoven with a similar scene with the male beau. Slightly unnerving to watch unless you are bisexual, in which case it is probably the most satisfying (very brief) love scene ever filmed!

This will all be too pat for some, and of course there is no guarantee Kristen will not simply straighten out when graduation comes (or sooner, given that after the love scene/s she is pictured with the boyfriend first). But Taryn is lovely, intelligent and gentle, and sends out the message that not every lesbian is going through a passing phase.

Homemade Melodrama   1982

Director: Jacqui Duckworth. Country: GB. Screenplay: Jacqui Duckworth. Production company: Jacqui Duckworth. Duration: 51 mins, colour

Cast: Lyndey Stanley (Katie), Joy Chamberlain (Francis), Cass Bream (Jude), Madelaine McNamara (Liza)

A group of women discuss, and act out, the merits of non-monogamy.

As the title suggests, this is a domestic drama played out in melodramatic little scenes. The theme of sexual politics is the main thrust of this grainy, low-budget, dated, but important little film. These days home video is of better quality and at times the film can be difficult to watch (although it looks as if it was fun to make!), but this shouldn't detract from the achievement of putting lesbian images on the TV screen when Beth Jordache was still in her cradle. Archive gold.

The Hotel New Hampshire   1984

Director: Tony Richardson. Country: Germany/Denmark/Portugal/US. Screenplay: Tony Richardson (based on the novel by John Irving). Production company: Woodfall. Duration: 108 mins, colour

Cast: Rob Lowe (John), Jodie Foster (Franny), Paul McCrane (Frank), Beau Bridges (Win), Lisa Banes (Mary), Jennie Dundas (Lilly), Nastassia Kinski (Susie the Bear)

Odd, amusing story following the fortunes of the idiosyncratic Berry family and chronicling their various adventures and mishaps.

Though the film starring Jodie Foster as a fully-fledged lesbian character has yet to be made, *The Hotel New Hampshire* is a promising start. This beguiling, underrated comedy about a dysfunctional family provides us with individual family members who are rather sweet and display a sometimes extraordinary degree of open-mindedness towards sexual mores. Jodie plays Franny, who is at one stage paired off with Susie the Bear (Nastassia Kinski), the friend who adores her. As much out of a sense of friendly duty as curiosity, Franny agrees to give of herself and the two sleep together. The scene is very brief and filmed at a polite distance. It does not result in Franny becoming a lesbian; indeed, she passes on a little later to none other than her own brother (Rob Lowe). Still, baby steps, baby steps ...

The House of the Spirits 1993

Director: Bille August. Country: Germany/Denmark/Portugal/US. Screenplay: Bille August (based on the novel by Isabel Allende). Production company: Constantin Film Productions. Duration: 138 mins, colour

Cast: Jeremy Irons (Trueba), Meryl Streep (Clara), Glenn Close (Ferula), Winona Ryder (Blanca), Antonio Banderas (Pedro)

Epic tale, with an epic Hollywood cast, which follows the fortunes of the Trueba family from early personal struggles in the 1920s to the consequences of the country's political unrest in the 1970s.

Dismissed by many critics as an unwieldy melodrama, *The House of the Spirits* contains an interesting and touching lesbian romance. Ferula, Trueba's lonely and neglected sister, develops a passionate love for Clara in one of the many plotlines of this wide-ranging story. Ferula, as played by Glenn Close, is a deeply sympathetic and ultimately tragic character. She is a woman who has spent her life caring for her mother, while her brother has left home and made his fortune. When the mother dies Ferula is forced to throw herself on her brother's charity. Trueba, recently married, feels well disposed towards his sister and allows her to live in his house. She meets Clara, Trueba's wife, who is gentle and kind towards her. This inspires complete devotion from Ferula, who has been deprived of tenderness and love all her life. A strong bond develops between them, of which Trueba is occasionally jealous. Ferula's feelings for Clara find further expression in her private thoughts, and she goes to a priest to confess her 'sins'. 'I want to climb into her bed and feel the warmth of her skin, her gentle breathing,' she tells him.

The relationship is ruined when Trueba returns home early one day and finds Clara and Ferula asleep on a bed. In an act of extraordinary cruelty Trueba banishes Ferula from his house for ever, despite her protestations that 'nothing happened'.

This is one of the few instances in the cinema where separating two women suspected of lesbianism to reinforce a heterosexual relationship is presented as utterly heartless and morally wrong. Strong playing by Glenn Close ensures that only the most homophobic viewer will feel otherwise. This is also one of the fews films where the lesbian relationship in the film has been fleshed out in comparison to the book.

See also: **SERVING IN SILENCE**, in which Glenn Close plays another lesbian role, and **MANHATTAN** and **SILKWOOD** for more Meryl.

Huevos de Oro: see under GOLDEN BALLS

The Hunger 1983

Director: Tony Scott. Country: US. Screenplay: Ivan Davis and Michael Thomas (based on the novel by Whitley Strieber). Production company: Richard Shepherd Company. Duration: 96 mins, colour

Cast: Catherine Deneuve (Miriam), Susan Sarandon (Sarah Roberts), David Bowie (John), Cliff de Young (Tom Havel), Beth Ehlers (Alice Cavender), Dan Hedaya (Lieutenant Allegrezza)

Miriam Blaylock is a vampire who possesses the secret of eternal life. She is able to convert humans to her own state of being, but after a few hundred years they suddenly age and die. Her current lover, John, begins to age overnight. Miriam contacts Sarah Roberts, a researcher in the ageing process, with a view to finding either a cure or a replacement for John . . .

Glamorous, glossy vampire film, with a bold and extremely exciting seduction scene, especially given that in 1983 it was still a very rare sight to see two attractive women kissing each other as if they meant it. Catherine Deneuve plays the irresistible, supernaturally beautiful vampire as if to the manner born. Susan Sarandon is wonderful as the newly converted Sarah, and she found herself with legions of new fans overnight as a result of this movie.

Critics saw the film as lacking substance, and as usual failed to see the film's significance to lesbians. Even lesbian reviewers of the time took a dim view of the film and many saw the exploitation aspect before anything else. However, there is a great deal here for lesbians to savour. Susan Sarandon herself was responsible for the seduction build-up – it was originally written as a cut to the chase – and this adds much to the enjoyment of the film. Ms Sarandon has also commented on the script's absurd requirement that her character be drunk or intoxicated in order to 'explain' the fact that she is seduced by a woman, and has astutely remarked that 'You don't have to be drunk to go to bed with Catherine Deneuve.' Quite so. Recommended.

See also: **BELLE DE JOUR, ÉCOUTE VOIR** and **LES VOLEURS**, for more Catherine.

I Shot Andy Warhol   1996

Director: Mary Harron. Country: US and GB. Screenplay: Mary Harron and Daniel Minahan. Production company: Playhouse International Pictures. Duration: 106 mins, colour

Cast: Lili Taylor (Valerie Solanas), Jared Harris (Andy Warhol), Stephen Dorff (Candy Darling), Martha Plimpton (Stevie), Lothaire Bluteau (Maurice Girodias), Donovan Leitch (Gerard Malanga)

Literary terrorist Valerie Solanas, founder and sole member of the Society for Cutting Up Men, attempts to sell her manifesto while making a lean living hustling on the street She meets Andy Warhol and becomes a marginal member of the fashionable coterie inside 'The Factory'. Desperate to be recognized, but increasingly convinced that Warhol plans to steal her work, Valerie takes matters into her own hands.

Opening with an urgent, dramatic musical score over the title sequence, this tremendous, stylish drama traces the life of the enigmatic Valerie Solanas. A woman of exceptional intellectual abilities, the brilliant, energetic and paranoid Valerie argues the natural superiority of women over men to whoever will listen. Few are interested, however, and the increasingly edgy Valerie pours her efforts into persuading Andy Warhol to take her seriously.

We are told that Valerie sleeps with men for money and women for enjoyment. We don't actually see her in a relationship with a woman, however, or indeed making love with anyone unless it is for payment. In one scene she fakes wild sex with a female friend for the

Streetwise. Lili Taylor stars in *I Shot Andy Warhol*. Courtesy of Electric Pictures.

benefit of a paying customer. However, this is not a film about sexuality. Instead, the important element is the extraordinary intensity of Valerie's genius and madness, her strength and her fragility. An absolutely stunning performance by Lili Taylor underpins the film, supported by Stephen Dorff, extraordinary as Candy Darling. The recreation of the 1960s is excellently evoked, particularly the Warhol Factory and the louche, casual arrogance of its members: celebrities, artists and hangers-on. Fabulous.

Note: The film was co-produced by Christine Vachon, who also produced **GO FISH**.

I, the Worst of All (Yo, la Peor de Todas) 1990

Director: Maria Luisa Bemberg. Country: Argentina. Screenplay: Maria Luisa Bemberg and Antonio Larreta (based on 'The Traps of Faith', from the book *Sor Juana: Her Life and World* by Octavio Paz). Production company: GEA Cinematografica. Duration: 105 mins, colour, subtitled

Cast: Assumpta Serna (Sister Juana Ines de la Cruz), Dominique Sanda (Vicereine Maria Luisa), Hector Alterio (Viceroy), Lautaro Murua (Archbishop of Mexico), Alberto Segado (Father Miranda), Franklin Caicedo (Santa Cruz, Bishop of Puebla), Graciela Araujo (Sister Ursula)

Seventeenth-century Mexico. Sister Juana is a highly intelligent young nun who writes plays and poetry. She is patronized and befriended by the country's cultural Viceroy and his wife. Their protection allows Juana to fulfil her intellectual ambitions, to a degree, but she has many enemies who seek her destruction.

Mexico at the time of the Spanish Inquisition is portrayed as a dangerous place for intelligent women. Juana's unselfconscious approach to her own education (she is passionate about art and learning) is seen as deeply threatening to the established Church. Her lack of interest in politics and her close friendship with the Vicereine, whom she loves, and who returns something similar, is also condemned by those who observe it. Her poetry is viewed by the misogynistic Archbishop's committee as 'lascivious' and containing references to her unnatural love. (There is nothing very outrageous between the two women: at one point the Vicereine kisses Juana on the lips, but this is the sum total of their physical relationship.) We learn that Juana's motive for becoming a nun in the first place may have been to avoid marriage. In a flashback sequence we see the nine-year-old Juana dressed as a boy. She reveals that 'I couldn't dress as a man, so I dressed as a nun.'

I, the Worst of All is a theatrically staged film, based on the true story of Sister Juana. The title of the film comes from the Sister's final confession of her sins. A little slow at times, the film is nevertheless an interesting account of a persecuted woman now regarded as one of Spain's greatest poets. Assumpta Serna is excellent as the doomed Juana and Dominique Sanda (who appeared as an alluring bisexual in **THE CONFORMIST**) assumes a regal stillness and wisdom as the gentle Vicereine.

See also: **THE CONFORMIST**, in which Dominique Sanda plays a bisexual.

I, You, He, She: see under **JE, TU, IL, ELLE**

In a Lonely Place (Behind This Mask) 1950

Director: Nicholas Ray. Country: US. Screenplay: Andrew Solt (based on the novel by Dorothy B. Hughes). Production company: Columbia Pictures. Duration: 93 mins, black and white

Cast: Humphrey Bogart (Dixon Steel), Gloria Grahame (Laurel Gray), Frank Lovejoy (Brub Nicolai), Carl Benton Reid (Captain Lochner), Art

Smith (Mel Lippman), Jeff Donnell (Sylvia Nicolai), Martha Stewart (Mildred Atkinson)

Fifties Hollywood. Lonely scriptwriter Dixon Steel is suspected of murdering a young woman. Unexpectedly, girl-next-door Laurel Gray lies to the police and provides Dixon with an alibi. The two form a relationship, but as Dixon's violent temper begins to reveal itself Laurel begins to wonder if he really is the killer.

First-rate noir thriller in which all the characters are brilliantly realized and have a resonance well beyond the scope of the plot. Bogart and Grahame are particularly good as the insecure lovers – it's probably Bogart's finest role – but the layers of complexity extend further than just these two. The lesbian character, so subtle as to be almost invisible (well this *is* 1950), is Martha, Laurel's personal masseuse (played by Ruth Gillette). The two have a close, comfortable relationship, so much so that Martha calls her young client 'Angel'. Martha is the one who voices her mistrust of Dixon – but of course as Martha is a lesbian in thin disguise we must assume that this concern is motivated solely by male-fearing jealousy. In any case, Martha is rewarded with the sack for her suspicions and Laurel rushes off to be with her man. There is a brief reconciliation later on but nothing to disturb the heterosexual principle.

See also: **JOHNNY GUITAR** by the same director.

The Incredibly True Adventure of Two Girls in Love 1995

Director: Maria Maggenti. Country: US. Screenplay: Maria Maggenti. Production company: Fine Line Features/Smash Pictures. Duration: 90 mins, colour

Cast: Laurel Holloman (Randy Dean), Nicole Parker (Evie Roy), Dale Dickey (Regina), Stephanie Berry (Evelyn Roy), Maggie Moore (Wendy), Kate Stafford (Rebecca Dean), Sabrina Artel (Vicky)

Randy is a rebellious working-class teenager who lives with her lesbian aunt and her aunt's lover. She struggles at school, against academia and unpopularity in equal proportions. One day while at her after-school job at a gas station she meets Evie Roy. Evie is a pretty, smart black teen with money and popularity to spare. The two find that opposites attract.

Likeable, lightweight coming-of-age comedy/drama centring around two young things who, against all the odds, find 'true love forever' with each other.

Seventeen-year-old Randy is characterized as an extremely untogether teen. She's always late for everything, and is about to fail at school. Her chaotic non-nuclear home life doesn't help much, and together with the daily social exclusion she faces at school, she's a mess. Surprisingly, though, she's also having an on-off affair with a married woman, Wendy (engagingly played by Maggie Moore in a scene-stealing performance).

In polar opposite to Randy, mature Evie Roy is charming, bright, capable and successful in all she does. Her 'problem' is that she intellectualizes her life and does not emotionally engage. She is the quintessential 'mama's perfect little girl', and something inside her is struggling to break free.

Chasm-like differences established, the film then brings the two girls together in gentle steps, until the two finally giggle their way into bed via a bacchanalian feast courtesy of Evie's absent mother. They are discovered of course, and must face the consequences. What will everyone think?

With tenderness and good humour the film reminds us of the spirit of youthful true love. There is a natural, convincing performance from Nicole Parker as Evie Roy and quite a good turn from Laurel Holloman, if a touch mannered and self-conscious. *The Incredibly True Adventure of Two Girls in Love* is both fun and funny. Best seen at seventeen probably, but even if your innocent years are long gone, give it a try anyway and enjoy reliving the embarrassing intensity of your first teenage crush (and be grateful that it's all behind you).

Internal Affairs 1990

Director: Mike Figgis. Country: US. Screenplay: Henry Bean. Production company: Paramount. Duration: 115 mins, colour

Cast: Richard Gere (Dennis Peck), Andy Garcia (Raymond Avila), Nancy Travis (Kathleen Avila), Laurie Metcalf (Amy Wallace), Richard Bradford (Grieb), William Baldwin (Van Stretch)

Excellent, clever thriller in which two Internal Affairs officers (Metcalf and Garcia) investigate the possibly corrupt LA police officer Peck.

The lesbian in this movie is a minor but significant character played by

Laurie Metcalf (best known as Jackie in *Roseanne*). Amy Wallace is one half of the Internal Affairs team, efficient and dedicated, dryly humorous and laconic. While we don't know too much about her private life, we can assume she is probably single – or at least that she is prepared to place her relationship second to her job (she tells Garcia to go home to his wife while she continues working well into the night).

Her lesbianism is underlined – with subtlety – on several occasions in the film. The first time is a wonderful little moment when both she and Garcia check out a woman who walks past their car. Amy's interest in the woman lasts longer than her partner's and he catches her looking. She sinks back into her seat looking amused rather than embarrassed. Later in the film her sexuality becomes ironic when Garcia's wife accuses him of having an affair with her. Director Mike Figgis has said that when the Amy Wallace character was first invented, the script represented her largely as a figure of fun, but he decided he was going to 'de-joke' her. He saw her as being very strong, and felt that the lesbian 'characteristic' added something positive to her as a person. The result is a brave, heroic lesbian who is unquestionably one of the good guys.

Intimate Confessions of a Chinese Courtesan   1973

Director: Chu Yuan. **Country:** Hong Kong. **Screenplay:** Kang-chien Ch'iu. **Production company:** Shaw Brothers. **Duration:** 91 mins, colour, dubbed

Cast: Lily Ho (Ai Nu), Yueh Hua (Chi Te), Betty (Chun I), Tung Lin (Pao Fu), Wan Chung-shan (Yeh Shun-tzu)

Teacher Ai Nu is kidnapped and brought to a brothel, where she is forced into a life of prostitution.

She's fantastically glamorous, ridiculously violent (she kills a man for deflowering a new recruit) and terrific at martial arts. Yes, she's the brothel-keeper, Chun I, a lesbian naturally. She rather fancies the new girl and makes no secret of it. The unfortunate Ai Nu meanwhile is suffering all sorts of horrors, including beatings, whippings and rape. Chun I offers special treatment to Ai Nu in return for 'co-operation', but being a nice straight girl Ai Nu would rather suffer all the above than defile herself Sapphically.

Compliance seems like the best idea later in the film, however, when an escape attempt goes wrong. A little kiss follows. Ai Nu, finding new resources within herself, kills a man deliberately. She tells

Chun I that she did it because she is becoming more like her (a homicidal maniac? No, silly! a lesbian who hates men, of course).

Complete hokum, but very entertaining if you like violent trash. In many ways Chun I precedes *Basic Instinct*'s Catherine Tramell in her *modus operandi*. Even the dubbing is enjoyable: all the women sound like Lady Penelope.

Isle of Lesbos 1996

Director: Jeff B. Harmon. Country: US. Screenplay: Jeff B. Harmon. Music and lyrics: Jeff B. Harmon. Production company: Duce. Producer: Jeff B. Harmon. Co-producer: Daniel Stoeker. Duration: 98 mins, colour

Cast: Kirsten Holly Smith (April Pfferpot), Danica Sheridan (Blatz Balinski), Jeff B. Harmon (Pa Pfferpot/Dr Colon), Sonya Hensley (Emphysema), Janet Krajeski (Ma Pfferpot), Alex Boling (Lance), Michael Dotson (Dick Dickson)

In Bumfuck, Arkansas, it is April Pfferpot's wedding day and she is about to become Mrs Dick Dickson. Instead, she flees from the church and attempts to blow her brains out with a gun. Magically she is whisked through her bedroom mirror into the isle of Lesbos, where she falls in love with the ultimate diesel dyke, Ruler Blatz Balinski.

Chorus line. Danica Sheridan and Dionysius Burbano set the pace on the *Isle of Lesbos*. © Courtesy of Duce Films.

A unique experience as far as cinema-going is concerned, this all-singing, all-dancing musical comedy is like nothing else you will have ever seen. Filmed entirely on a single sound set, with unknowns cast throughout, this is a very clever, *very* vulgar 'tribute' to the musical comedies of the 1940s (with more than a nod to *The Wizard of Oz* [1939]). April's journey into the Isle of Lesbos and her experiences on the way are revealed in a series of show-stopping songs sung by the worshipful lesbian chorus and the angry rednecks back in Bumfuck.

Written, composed, directed by and starring (as both Pa and Dr Colon) Jeff B. Harmon, *Isle of Lesbos* is a remarkable achievement. Nothing in Mr Harmon's past as a war correspondent could possibly prepare his future audiences for this foray into the world of lesbian film, but he is more than up to the task. If it seems audacious that a male would attempt such a vision, rest assured that there is something here to upset everyone. A low budget has limited Jeff Harmon only slightly! This is one to catch if you can, if only to find out whether you are still shockable ...

It's in the Water   1996

Director: Kelli Hurd. Country: US. Screenplay: Kelli Hurd. Production company: Water Island Films. Duration: 100 mins, colour

Cast: Keri Jo Chapman (Alex Stratton), Teresa Garrett (Grace Miller), Derrick Sanders (Mark), Timothy Vahle (Thomas), Nancy Charter (Sloan), John Hallum (Spencer), Barbara Lasater (Lily), Matthew Tompkins (Robert Stratton)

In the quiet Texan town of Azalea Springs things are pretty normal. The men are butch and sweaty, the women beautiful and backcombed. The Women's League runs the social side of things and most people are content with their lives until one day an AIDS facility opens in the town. Suddenly, townsfolk are worrying that an influx of 'those people' will be a bad influence. Worse, when Spencer drunkenly confides to his grandma that the reason he is gay is because 'it's in the water ...' all hell breaks loose.

Kelli Hurd's debut feature, made for a quite unbelievable $300,000 dollars (but looking as if it cost twenty times as much), is the best lesbian/gay independent feature film in years. It's as camp, glossy and glamorous as an episode of *Dynasty* and it's also one of the few films ever to include both a strong lesbian and a gay romance. Keri Jo Chapman makes a wonderful, gorgeous Alex, married to Robert but

Is it in her kiss? No, *It's in the Water*! Keri Jo Chapman and Teresa Garrett star. Courtesy of It's in the Water Productions.

delighted when her old school friend Grace returns to Azalea Springs to work at Hope House. Their renewed friendship is thrown into sharp relief when Alex opts to work at the House herself, against the wishes of both her husband and – worse – her Mother! Meanwhile Mark, desperately trying not to be gay and assiduously attending the 'Turn or Burn' meetings at the local church, suddenly meets the man of his dreams! What will he do?

As a satire on American values, especially Southern extremism, the film works brilliantly, but much more than that *It's in the Water* is a fresh, knowing and very sexy film. Apparently, while on location and presumably inspired by the film, two of the cast came out (which two, which two?!) Made in Texas with local actors and crew, the film is a remarkable achievement. As a debut feature it is nothing short of extraordinary. A deliriously funny comedy, and containing the best pre-kiss line you'll ever hear! Unmissable.

I've Heard the Mermaids Singing   1987

Director: Patricia Rozema. Country: Canada. Screenplay: Patricia Rozema. Production company: Vos Productions. Duration: 84 mins, colour

Cast: Sheila McCarthy (Polly Vandersma), Paule Baillargeon (Gabrielle St Peres), Ann-Marie MacDonald (Mary Joseph), John Evans (Warren), Brenda Kamino (Japanese Waitress), Richard Monette (Clive)

Polly comes to work for beautiful, capable Gabrielle in her art gallery. Socially awkward and self-deprecating, Polly finds herself infatuated with the curator and dazzled by her worldliness.

Wonderful film, a sad and uplifting comedy in which the insecure and insignificant Polly eventually proves herself better than her superiors.

In a confidential manner, Polly addresses the audience via a video camera she has set up in her 'furnished bachelorette'. In her own utterly endearing manner, she tells us of her adventures in the gallery each day. She is heartbreakingly honest in her accounts of her social inadequacy and the various humiliations she endures as a result. Her love for the curator is unnoticed and unreturned. Gabrielle has her

Happy daze. Sheila McCarthy stars in *I've Heard the Mermaids Singing*. Courtesy of Contemporary Films.

own girlfriend, and besides, Polly is simply not a contender, she would never be taken seriously. There is a plot here, in which Polly struggles to establish her photography as something of worth and accidentally stumbles upon an art fraud in which the curator is involved. But really this film is about personal relationships, innocent love and motiveless devotion. And about the excruciating embarrassment which results when you choose the wrong dish at a Japanese restaurant.

See also: **WHEN NIGHT IS FALLING** by the same director.

Jane Street 1996

Director: Charles Merzbacher. Country: US. Screenplay: Charles Merzbacher. Production company: Beads and Trinkets Productions. Duration: 90 mins, colour

Cast: Mark Berlin (Brian), Jane Jenson (Corinne), Christa Kirby (Suzanne), Kevin Carroll (Ry)

Brian comes to New York with no prospects and no job. He finds dwellings in an empty apartment and, in order to get some cash, sublets to a couple of lesbians, one of whom he is attracted to. His hopes of seducing Corinne come to nothing, and he feels worse when the two declare they are planning to have a baby. Confused and resentful, Brian decides to interfere with the plans in the only way his provincial brain can think of.

Described as a 'provocative comedy', *Jane Street* is more a sad slice of life based on a small-town character completely at sea in modern Manhattan. Quite why the two women – who seem sensible enough – agree to move into the one-room apartment with dorky Brian is a bit of a mystery. At night young Brian is just a few feet away when Corinne and Suzanne make love (although he turns to face the wall in a decent fashion when they do so). To be fair, the story is based on Brian, not on the issue of two lesbians having a baby, but we really do not get to know the women very much at all.

The attitude Brian expresses towards the two lesbians is apparently based on the views expressed by the director's male film students at New York University. This admission would be depressing enough were it not for the complete forgiveness the film expresses towards nerdy Brian as he – too late – develops some intelligence and respect for his flatmates. The film suggests that if you fancy a woman (and she has the audacity to be a lesbian), then to 'have' her in some other way is misguided but comic. Very unfortunate. The film's happy ending has all the hallmarks of a good-natured telling-off for Brian along the lines of 'Well, you got away with it once, my boy, now don't be so silly again'. Disheartening.

Je, Tu, Il, Elle (I, You, He, She) 1974

Director: Chantal Akerman. Country: Belgium. Screenplay: Chantal Akerman. Duration: 85 mins, black and white

Cast: Chantal Akerman (Young Woman), Niels Arestrup (Truck-Driver), Claire Wauthion (Woman's Lover)

Act 1: A naked young woman writes a letter and eats sugar in a white room. Act 2: She hitches a ride with a truck-driver, and has a brief sexual liaison with him. Act 3: She goes to Paris and visits a female lover. The two eat jam and have sex (eventually). They fall asleep.

Akerman's first feature, a critically acclaimed avant-garde independent in three acts, intends to reveal something about the nature of separation and loss. This film is a precursor to her later, more accomplished, work, and displays some of the influence of avant-garde luminary Jean-Luc Godard. Like him she prefers to explore the medium of film, continually reminding the audience that they are watching film, rather than allowing them to drift towards enjoying a story. The lack of close-ups makes identification with any character difficult, not that this would concern the director particularly. An important film, but tough going for the average movie-watcher. It is difficult enough in real life observing someone write a letter (and do nothing else). At the cinema it is a challenge like none other.

Jest of God: see under RACHEL, RACHEL

Johnny Guitar 1954

Director: Nicholas Ray. Country: US. Screenplay: Philip Yordan (based on the novel by Roy Chanslor). Production company: Republic Pictures Corporation. Duration: 110 mins, colour

Cast: Joan Crawford (Vienna), Sterling Hayden (Johnny Guitar), Scott Brady (Dancing Kid), Mercedes McCambridge (Emma Small), Ward Bond (McIvers), Ben Cooper (Turkey)

Vienna runs a saloon in some deserted God-forsaken bit of the Wild West. She is waiting for the railroad to be built nearby. She has an enemy in the guise of Emma Small who wants her out of the town. Along comes Johnny Guitar.

The girls slog it out in the strangest western you may ever see. Although there are significant male characters everywhere, it is the relationship between the two women that matters. It seems to be the only thing that matters. Locals have spotted the antipathy between the two, and the gender reversal of both women: 'I've never seen a woman who was more like a man. She acts like one, thinks like one, and sometimes makes me think that I'm not,' complains a local of Vienna.

When the stage is held up, Emma's brother is killed and she perversely blames the Dancing Kid, whom she secretly loves. Vienna comments that 'He makes her feel like a woman and that frightens her.' Sometime later the two women have a verbal fight. 'Get out!' demands Vienna. 'That's big talk for a little gun,' replies Emma. Later still, when Johnny Guitar addresses the townsfolk he declares, 'There are those who have a weakness for whiskey and for women,' looking pointedly at Vienna.

Real-life bisexual Joan Crawford plays Vienna, resplendent in male attire, complete with six-shooters on both hips. What is going on?! Heaven knows. This is a very bright, perceptive and witty script. So full of hidden depths there's more undertone than surface. There's definitely a western in there somewhere, but what it's really about is the women, the women ...

See also: **WALK ON THE WILD SIDE** for more Joan, and look out for Mercedes playing a butch misogynist in **TOUCH OF EVIL**. **IN A LONELY PLACE** is by the same director.

Julia 1977

Director: Fred Zinnemann. Country: US. Screenplay: Alvin Sargent (based on a chapter of Lillian Hellman's memoir, *Pentimento*). Production company: Twentieth Century Fox. Duration: 117 mins, colour

Cast: Jane Fonda (Lillian Hellman), Vanessa Redgrave (Julia), Jason Robards (Dashiell Hammett), Maximilian Schell (Johann), Hal Holbrook (Alan Campbell), Rosemary Murphy (Dorothy Parker), Meryl Streep (Anne Marie)

Account of Lillian Hellman's long friendship with Julia, an exceptional, talented woman, who asks for her old schoolfriend's help in a highly dangerous mission smuggling money into pre-war Germany.

Generally a great film, excellently acted and directed, and lovely to look at. Beautifully realizes memories of childhood and teenage infatuations with older, more competent, girls. However, the film goes to extraordinary pains to dispel any uncomfortable notions that Lillian's friendship with Julia was any more than platonic. Incredibly, no mention is made of the fact that the play Lillian is writing at the beginning of the film (and which brings her national success) is *The Children's Hour*, a drama concerned with lesbianism and the power of rumour.

Later, when the obnoxious Sammy (John Glover) suggests to Lillian that she and Julia have something Sapphic going, she slugs him with a right hook. Thus, the issue of lesbianism is raised in order to be powerfully dismissed. While there is no evidence that there was anything sexual between the two women, raising the subject via such a character suggests that even the thought of it is perverse (Sammy himself has just announced that he has been sleeping with his sister). But why fell him to the ground? Where is the insult? Would Lillian Hellman herself have reacted in this way? Very disappointing.

But see it anyway. Both leads are utterly tremendous, the story is powerful and dramatic and overall the film is one of Zinnemann's best.

See also: **THE CHILDREN'S HOUR**, written by Lillian Hellman, and for more Vanessa see **THE BOSTONIANS, GREAT MOMENTS IN AVIATION** and **MRS DALLOWAY**.

Just One of the Guys   1985

Director: Lisa Gottlieb. Country: US. Screenplay: Dennis Feldman and Jeff Franklin. Production company: Columbia. Duration: 96 mins, colour

Cast: Joyce Hyser (Terry), Clayton Rohner (Rick), Billy Jacoby (Buddy), Toni Hudson (Denise), William Zabka (Greg), Sherilyn Fenn (Sandy)

Terry, an aspiring journalist, believes that her cuteness is preventing her being taken seriously. So she drags up to prove it.

Amusing cross-dressing comedy with one or two inevitable (but entertaining) pseudo-lesbian moments to spice things up. First we have the opening shots of the movie, revealing Terry as one hell of a real gal. She has the body, the boyfriend and the popularity to go with it. Once she drags up, the 'situations', unrelated to her career intentions, begin.

At college, she has a run-in with a couple of bonehead jocks for being a smart-alec (but not, interestingly, for the fact that now in drag she strongly resembles a soft gay boy or a baby-dyke). Later, a becoming young woman by the name of Sandy (Sherilyn Fenn in a very early role) takes a fancy to Terry, and our nervous heroine, unable to resist or think of a good excuse, arranges a double date. She is resentfully assisted by her brother, a youthful reactionary who has been exasperated by Terry from the start. 'Who do you think you are, Tootsie?' he says.

In an unexpectedly rude moment during the date, Sandy kisses our Terry on the cheek and then discovers the socks she has stuffed down her trousers to increase her manliness. Things go from bad to worse as Terry flirts with Rick (the boy she secretly fancies), and Rick immediately assumes 'he' must be gay, etc., etc.

Eventually, at the prom, everything comes out and everyone learns something about gender and sexuality. In a happy ending, Rick will now consent to go out with Terry, once the sex roles have been firmly re-established. Thank goodness for that.

See also: **MOROCCO, ORLANDO, QUEEN CHRISTINA, SWITCH** and **YENTL** for more cross-dressing, gender-bending capers. See also: **THREE OF HEARTS** and **TWO MOON JUNCTION** for more Sherilyn Fenn.

Kamikaze Hearts 1986

Director: Juliet Bashore. Country: US. Screenplay: Juliet Bashore, Tigr Mennett and John Knoop. Production company: Legler/Bashore. Duration: 77 mins, black and white

Cast: Sharon Mitchell (Mitch), Tigr Mennett (Tigr), Jon Martin (Jon), Sparky Vasque (Sparky), Jerry Abrahms (Gerald Greystone), Robert McKenna (Bobby Mac)

Mitch is making a film called Carmen *in which she plays an opera singer who can't sing. She is doing this as a favour to her director girlfriend Tigr, who is*

obsessed with her. At the same time, she is being filmed by a documentary crew who are trying to encapsulate her life.

An interesting foray into a shady backstage world, Kamikaze Hearts takes us – in grainy semi-documentary style – into the porn industry, laying it bare in all its seediness, revealing the petty jealousies, the pressures and the strains of being either the star or the producer of such a commodity.

Mitch describes the film she is making to the audience thus: 'Surrealistic look at myself and my girlfriend and the way we look at the X-rated film business and our relationship with each other.' So it goes. Tigr complains of Mitch, 'She fucks on-camera the same way she does off-camera. You don't ever know what's real.' As Tigr's love for her idol overcomes her she is drawn further inside Mitch's world of sex for sale and drugs to get through it. No doubt about it, this is strong stuff even if the politics are a bit confused. In any case, the filming of the sex itself is fascinating and if you've ever wondered whether porn stars stop what they're doing the moment the director shouts 'Cut!', this film will tell you. Diverting, but startlingly unerotic.

Kazetachi No Gogo: see under AFTERNOON BREEZES

Kika   1993

Director: Pedro Almodóvar. Country: Spain. Screenplay: Pedro Almodóvar. Production company: CiBy 2000. Duration: 114 mins, colour, subtitled

Cast: Veronica Forqué (Kika), Victoria Abril (Andrea), Peter Coyote (Nicholas), Alex Casanovas (Ramón), Rossy de Palma (Juana)

Kika, a make-up artist, encounters various domestic crises including suffering an endless rape, murders happening all around her and enough media attention to drive her from her home. But while madness ensues, Kika maintains an optimistic view of the world.

Almodóvar feature containing some of his best virtues: an unparalleled disdain for normality and a glorification of his wonderful leading women, this time the unflappable Kika (the fantastic Veronica Forqué). Shrugging off the most outrageous crimes against the person, Kika's sense of humour and affable nature never desert her. Our lesbian in the movie is the ever-marvellous Rossy de Palma, who plays Kika's maid Juana. Juana is hopelessly in love with her mistress, but oblivious to her mistress's professional beauty tips. 'Men don't have the monopoly on moustaches,' says Juana, when Kika suggests she remove hers. Too witty to be offensive, too funny to be upsetting. A riot of colour and energy.

See also: **PEPI, LUCY, BOM** by the same director.

The Killing of Sister George   1968

Director: Robert Aldrich. Country: US. Screenplay: Lukas Heller (based on the stage play by Frank Marcus). Production company: Palomar Pictures International. Duration: 138 mins, colour

Cast: Beryl Reid (June Buckridge), Susannah York (Alice 'Childie' McNaught), Coral Browne (Mercy Croft), Ronald Fraser (Leo Lockhart), Patricia Medina (Betty Thaxter)

June Buckridge is a popular soap star in a long-running TV series where she plays Sister George, the village nurse. Sister George's homely advice and cheerful nature have made her a favourite with the nation. In real life June is so identified with her TV character that everyone calls her 'George'. Her true character is far removed from the provincial Florence Nightingale she plays, however, and far more interesting. George is an aggressively butch tweedy dyke who demands constant attention. She is worried, with some justification, that Sister George is about to be killed off. It gradually becomes clear that this may well be the case. Sister George is perceived as a dated character and the fickle public are turning their affections towards the vile Leo Lockhart, among others. Meanwhile, George's relationship with her girlfriend Childie is becoming strained. Mercy Croft, a BBC executive with the task of breaking the bad news to George, takes a shine to Childie, and the scene is set for George's total ruin.

One of the all-time greats as far as lesbian films go, although this tends to be a retrospective view and certainly did not reflect the prevailing feeling at the time of its release. As with all mainstream films of the period that dealt with lesbianism as its main theme ('all' being about three), when *The Killing of Sister George* appeared in the late 1960s, it was expected to present the eager public with the last word on lesbianism. The media colluded with this process completely. Critics commented on how true to life the film was(!), while adding that they thought it was perverted and nasty. Meanwhile, many lesbians felt profoundly embarrassed by the film – even more so than the heterosexuals who went to see it – and could not identify with any of the three stereotypes on view (butch tweedy dyke, glamorous older woman and baby-doll femme).

These days, though, now that the pressure is off to see George and her friends as definitive lesbian images, it is time to reclaim her. George really is one of the great screen lesbians whom straight society defeats but doesn't quite destroy. Her bolshiness, temperamental stroppiness, contrasted with her devilish wit and deeply felt vulnerability, make her unexpectedly frail and sympathetic.

The film begins by showing us her rather more 'manly' qualities. From the opening credit sequence she is portrayed as butch, hard-drinking and no respecter of authority. Instead, she is a real lover of life who refuses to toe the line. Eccentric and occasionally outrageous, one hilarious scene sees her drunk and attempting to hail a taxi. She leaps into a cab when it stops at traffic lights, only to find it full of nuns. 'Well! Hello, girls!' she says, with a lecherous grin, and closes the door behind her. Traffic jams and car accidents ensue, all the while George continues in her own blissfully carefree stupor. Lesbianism causing chaos on the high street!

Director Aldrich recognized the sensationalist potential of his material and chose to brutalize an often tender comic stage play for the sake of controversial shock value. Three scenes stand out in this respect. The first is the implicitly sado-masochistic cigar-chewing ritual, in which Childie must show her 'contrition' to George for displeasing her. Second is the club scene in which George and Childie attend a fancy-dress party at Gateways, the real-life lesbian club of the time. (Newspapers luridly reported how there were 'real lesbians' in this scene, and that Aldrich had adopted practically a documentary style of filming. Heterosexuals could have the benefit of seeing real lesbians as well as pretend ones.) The third sequence was, of course, The Sex Scene, saved up as the climax to the film.

Beryl Reid had told Aldrich before filming began that she would not be involved in any overt sex scenes, although both Susannah York and Coral Browne initially agreed. When the time came, however, both actresses had changed their minds. Reid subsequently revealed in an interview that the two women locked themselves in their dressing rooms and refused to come out. As a consequence, Beryl had four days off while the argument raged. Eventually, Aldrich threatened the two women with everything he could think of and they both relented. On seeing the film, one can understand their reticence. The resulting scene is extraordinarily perverse. The lighting is very low and it's difficult to see what is going on. Strangely (and cleverly) it appears to be explicit while for the most part there is very little to see (albeit that whatever it is Mercy Croft is doing, it's remarkably effective). It is unlikely that any heterosexuals were better informed about lesbian sex after that scene, except to assume that it must be performed in some kind of twilight zone.

Exceptionally well acted and sharply funny, *The Killing of Sister George* has an important place in lesbian film history. Aldrich's achievement, paradoxically, is to show us how things were back in the 1960s by directing a film that itself demonstrates the degree of fascinated homophobia with which lesbians were treated. In other words it tells us as much – maybe more – about the film-maker's own prejudices as it does about its controversial subject matter. Nevertheless, George's essential humanity shines through, and it would be a granite heart who did not want to welcome George into the fold, with honours. Essential viewing.

Note: Amazingly, Doris Day was offered the role of George initially (with Rock Hudson as Childie presumably). Fortunately she turned it down and the role went to Beryl Reid, who had already spent a year playing George on the London stage.

See also: **THE MAIDS** and **ZEE & CO**, in which Susannah York takes another turn, and **THE LEGEND OF LYLAH CLARE** by the same director.

The L-Shaped Room 1962

Director: Bryan Forbes. Country: GB. Screenplay: Bryan Forbes (based on the novel by Lynne Reid Banks). Production company: Romulus Films. Duration: 142 mins, black and white

Cast: Leslie Caron (Jane), Tom Bell (Toby), Brock Peters (Johnny), Cicely Courtneidge (Mavis), Bernard Lee (Charlie), Avis Bunnage (Doris), Pat Phoenix (Sonia)

London in the 1960s, and young, pregnant Frenchwoman Jane finds the going tough in her clapped-out rented bedsit. Various characters come and go in the house, each assisting or hindering Jane in her situation.

Mavis is the busybody of the house, a sweet and gentle old lady who takes great interest in all around her. Although she now lives with only her cat for company we discover that she did have one great love in her life. It is never spoken of, but when Jane is invited to look at a photo of the former love, we gather from the expression on her face that she is seeing something unexpected. (We don't see the photo at that point, but it is on view ever so briefly near the beginning of the film.) 'It takes all sorts,' says Emily, by way of explanation. Subtle, unapologetic and very tender.

Note: The book did not contain a lesbian character; director Bryan Forbes invented her.

The Lair of the White Worm   1988

Director: Ken Russell. Country: GB. Screenplay: Ken Russell. Production company: White Lair. Duration: 93 mins, colour

Cast: Amanda Donohoe (Lady Sylvia Marsh), Hugh Grant (Lord James D'Ampton), Peter Capaldi (Angus Flint), Catherine Oxenberg (Eve Trent), Sammi Davis (Mary Trent)

Based on the novel by Bram Stoker. Lord James D'Ampton and Angus Flint begin an investigation into the identity of a mysterious, bizarrely shaped skull. Their search leaves them to past pagan religions, a secret vampire and virginal sacrifices.

Irresistibly camp and silly nonsense in which four young things, led by Hugh Grant, go looking around the nearby manor house in search of ancient reptiles, missing parents and so on. Amanda Donohoe is perfect as the strange aristocratic Lady of the Manor with a fine line in seduction but a fatal bedside manner. Entirely heterosexual except that Amanda sports a lethal dildo which she plans to use on Catherine Oxenberg during the hilarious climax to the film. Also, during an earlier dream sequence a little earlier Amanda and Catherine have a wrestle dressed as air-hostesses (well, this *is* Ken Russell). Hugh Grant's pencil gets an erection as a result.

See also: **THE RAINBOW** for Amanda in a bisexual mood (also directed by Ken Russell).

Lake Consequence 1992

Director: Rafael Eisenman. Country: US. Screenplay: Zalman King, Melanie Finn and Henry Cobbold. Production company: 10dB Inc. Duration: 86 mins, colour

Cast: Billy Zane (Billy), Joan Severance (Irene), May Karasun (Grace)

Irene is a suburban housewife with a nice husband and a cute little boy. But when she spots Billy trimming the trees outside her house she comes over all of a heap and hardly knows where to look. Billy, meanwhile, a hunky, pretty thing with brooding good looks and a fabulous body, thinks Irene is a bit of all right, too.

A quirk of fate and some unbelievable plotting allows the two lust birds to end up together at Lake Consequence with Billy's part-time girlfriend. The scene is set for some sexual awakening, which for some reason occurs in a nearby Chinese bathhouse. Irene gets to do it first with the handsome hunk in a jacuzzi and then with the gorgeous girl when Grace decides to join them. The lesbianism is depicted as an interesting build-up to real sex. Billy watches the women first before intervening, selecting a woman and completing the act properly. Everyone is deliriously satisfied. But, hey! Nothing lasts for ever and soon Billy is driving the reluctant Irene back to hearth and home, a big sacrifice as he has now fallen totally in love with her ...

Make no mistake, *Lake Consequence* is an awful film. The only reason it exists at all is to realize a few sessions of glossy hetero hanky-panky in the style of **TWO MOON JUNCTION**. Unlike that film, however, at least the 'other female' gets a proper (though by no means comprehensive) look in. Lesbianism for straight couples.

The Last Emperor 1987

Director: Bernardo Bertolucci. Country: Italy and GB. Screenplay: Mark Peploe with Bernardo Bertolucci. Production company: Yanco Films Ltd. Duration: 163 mins, colour

Cast: John Lone (Pu Yi), Joan Chen (Wan Jung), Peter O'Toole (RJ), Ying Ruocheng (The Governor)

Epic saga relating the story of one Pu Yi, a man who began his life as Emperor of China and ended it as a simple gardener. Ambitious and gorgeously photographed, Bertolucci's magnificent drama traces a man's journey from ignorant puppet to self-realization.

Eastern Jewel (Maggie Han) provides the (limited) lesbian interest. We know she is a baddie from the moment she comes on screen dressed top to toe in a tight leather flying outfit. She is an aviator and happily states that her ambition is to bomb Shanghai. Although ostensibly attached to the Emperor and his wife to protect them both, in fact she is an ambassador for the Japanese, and her mission is to ensure Pu Yi's compliance. Unfortunately, the Emperor's wife Wan Jung is none too keen on the Japanese, so Jewel acts and hooks her into an addiction to opium. We shortly learn that Pu Yi will not sleep with her because of her drug habit.

In a later scene Jewel comes on to Wan Jung and a seduction is implied (although all we see is some enthusiastic toe-sucking). Jewel, clearly bisexual, is viewed as unscrupulous and opportunistic. Wan Jung's dalliance with her is another step on the slippery slope towards total degradation.

See also: **THE CONFORMIST** by the same director.

Late Bloomers 1996

Director: Julia Dyer. Country: US. Screenplay: Gretchen Dyer. Production company: One Mind Productions. Duration: 104 mins, colour

Cast: Connie Nelson (Dinah Groshardt), Dee Hennigan (Carly Lumpkin), Gary Carter (Rom Lumpkin), Lisa Peterson (Val Lumpkin), Esteben Powell (Jamie Hooper)

Much to their own amazement, and to the astonishment of all around them, middle-aged maths teacher Dinah Groshardt falls in love with married school secretary Carly Lumpkin. Such an unexpected liaison causes consternation for all concerned, not least Carly's husband. As the word spreads, the two lovers find themselves the subject of endless speculation, and a great deal of condemnation from the community. Will they find it in themselves to fight for what they want?

Sister film-makers Julia and Gretchen Dyer have written, produced and directed a bittersweet comedy which they describe as 'not really a lesbian story as much as a love story'. While many lesbians may feel they have already seen much of this film in the form of **LIANNA** some years ago, in thematic terms *Late Bloomers* probably owes more to triumphant feel-good movies like *Shirley Valentine* (1989). Dinah and Carly, both lonely in different ways, both believing that the best of life has passed them by, cannot quite understand what is

Ball girls. Dee Hennigan and Connie Nelson star in *Late Bloomers*. Courtesy of Strand Releasing USA.

happening as love grows between them. Indeed, most of the comedy in the early part of the film stems from this disbelief. Dee Hennigan is particularly good as the frumpy housewife who suddenly discovers a reason to take herself seriously, even in the face of open hostility from her daughter. We are spared any earth-moving moments in the form of explicit sex scenes, but the film's determination to be a little quirky allows for a superfluous naked one-on-one basketball scene to enter the proceedings. No matter. Romantics will love this movie and find much to identify with. And for those of you who think that there are simply not enough lesbian weddings in films these days, here's one to cheer you up.

See also: **CLAIRE OF THE MOON** and **ENTWINED** for more slushy romantic stuff.

Leather Girls: see under FASTER, PUSSYCAT, KILL! KILL!

The Legend of Lylah Clare   1968

Director: Robert Aldrich. Country: US. Screenplay: Hugo Butler and Jean Rouverol. Production company: Associates and Aldrich. Duration: 127 mins, colour

Cast: Kim Novak (Lylah Clare/Elsa Brinkmann), Peter Finch (Lewis Zarkan), Ernest Borgnine (Barney Sheean), Milton Selzer (Bart Langner), Rossella Falk (Rossella), Gabriele Tinti (Paolo), Valentina Cortese (Countess Bozo Bedoni)

Elsa Brinkmann is plucked from obscurity to play the lead in a film about the life and mysterious death of film star Lylah Clare. Her resemblance to the late Lylah is uncanny, and soon people around her cannot help but treat her in the same way they treated the former film star. Soon Elsa is confusing her own personality with that of the dead woman.

In the same year that Robert Aldrich produced **THE KILLING OF SISTER GEORGE** he also directed this hilarious offering, an overblown examination of some of the more extreme examples of Hollywood's movers and shakers, 1960s fashion.

Among the cast of egoists, neurotics and losers is the required lesbian character. Describing herself, somewhat unbelievably, as Lylah's dialogue coach (she has a strong Italian accent), Rossella is a drug taker who is just about keeping it together day by day. Lylah was her one true love, and amazingly, it appears that this may have been requited, at least in part. They shared rooms for a while, until Lylah's wedding night, which was also the night of her death.

The long-deceased Lylah is described as having been first 'discovered' in a brothel. She was apparently promiscuous and took a delight in humiliating those around her. Aldrich effortlessly couples lesbianism with dubious antisocial behaviour. That said, Rossella is shown to have had a very real love for Lylah – which she transfers to Elsa – and more than anyone else she truly appears to care for her (hopelessly, of course – bisexuality is the one aspect of Lylah's personality that Elsa has not assumed).

See also: **THE KILLING OF SISTER GEORGE** by the same director.

Lenny 1974

Director: Bob Fosse. Country: US. Screenplay: Julian Barry. Production company: United Artists. Duration: 111 mins, black and white

Cast: Dustin Hoffman (Lenny Bruce), Valerie Perrine (Honey Bruce), Jan Miner (Sally Marr), Stanley Beck (Artie Silver), Gary Morton (Sherman Hart), Rashel Novikoff (Aunt Mema)

Biopic account of the 1960s Jewish American comedian Lenny Bruce.

Rather more pot-boiler than careful dissection, *Lenny* is an interesting cruise through second-rate comedy clubs, detailing the reactions of the Establishment to the man's particular brand of obscene humour. Dustin Hoffman is great and Valerie Perrine won an Oscar for her role as Lenny's stripper wife Honey.

The lesbian part is brief but very revealing. Lenny decides to 'force' his wife to sleep with a woman so that he can watch. She reluctantly acquiesces. Unfortunately for him, she likes it. She continues to want lesbian sex whether he is watching or not. He is not pleased and incorporates his anger into his nightclub routine: 'You know why we don't make jokes about lesbians? Because sometimes we're married to them ...'

See also: **EMILIENNE** and **GOLDEN BALLS**, wherein wives are similarly encouraged to seek Sapphic diversions.

Lianna   1982

Director: John Sayles. Country: US. Screenplay: John Sayles. Production company: Winwood Company. Duration: 112 mins, colour

Cast: Linda Griffiths (Lianna), Jane Hallaren (Ruth), Jon DeVries (Dick), Jo Henderson (Sandy), Jessica Wight McDonald (Theda), Jesse Solomon (Spencer), John Sayles (Jerry)

Lianna, married with two children, finds herself falling into an affair with her female night-class teacher. When she tells her serially adulterous husband what has happened he throws her out and threatens worse. Abandoned by her straight friends Lianna realizes she is to pay a high price for her new life. Also, it soon becomes clear that her new lover does not intend to stay around to weather the storms with her.

Very well-meaning drama skilfully directed by independent specialist John Sayles. Lesbian cinema-going opinion is divided over *Lianna*. Some have always championed it as their favourite film even over such winners as **DESERT HEARTS**. Others have found it vaguely embarrassing and too cheaply shot to be revered in this way (and a lesbian film directed by a man is still a moot point to many). But *Lianna* is a strong piece of work, which tries hard to open up some rarely explored issues such as the reactions of children and friends to the revelation. Also, the fact that while Dick's adultery has no impact on the family's life at all, Lianna's affair has enormous consequences for everyone is interestingly explored. Significant, too, is the fact that Lianna's choice immediately plunges her into poverty. Lianna grows as a person and becomes stronger, but there are no easy answers or happy endings. Her lover Ruth's reluctance to become involved is partly due to fear of losing her job. She is slightly older than Lianna and has maintained her position in the world by exhibiting a cool reserve and a strict control of her private life. Lianna, new to the game, is much more vulnerable because she has not spent twenty years learning coping strategies. This is a two-way street – Lianna wants to express affection in public and does so; she's not oppressed enough to know she shouldn't do it.

Two scenes from *Lianna* live for ever in the memory: one is the sex scene, in which barely audible whisperings of sweet nothings (possibly in French) form a backdrop for some 1970s romantic lesbian sex: closed-mouth kissing, a bit of stroking, but not much else. There is a suggestion that oral sex is taking place but the position of the various limbs indicate that Lianna is going down onto the mattress.

The other scene is the visit to a lesbian bar, not much bigger than your average lounge, the My Way tavern. Populated by about a dozen women (at most), it's very cruisy with everyone looking sideways at everyone else. You may never again see so many eyes in close-up. Recommended.

See also: **LOSING CHASE** and **A QUESTION OF LOVE** for more lesbian mothers.

Lilith   1964

Director: Robert Rossen. Country: US. Screenplay: Robert Rossen and Robert Alan Aurthur. Production company: Centaur Enterprises. Duration: 116 mins, black and white

Cast: Warren Beatty (Vincent), Jean Seberg (Lilith), Peter Fonda (Steven), Kim Hunter (Bea Brice), Anne Meacham (Yvonne Meaghan)

Vincent starts work as a trainee therapist at the local asylum. Gradually, he becomes involved with Lilith, a young schizophrenic woman who engages him emotionally but wants his body as well as his mind. Her desire to put her mark on every living creature unnerves Vincent, and he becomes increasingly drawn into a world in which he cannot cope.

Rossen's last film, complex and interesting, delicately but relentlessly depicts the rise and fall of a doomed relationship. The very disturbed Lilith, at first indistinguishable from a typical girl next door, is gradually revealed to be what she is, and the cost of realizing it seems to be Vincent's own sanity. Lilith's personal need to touch other people's lives by providing them with what she thinks they want leads her to the fairly brief lesbian aspect of the film. Shortly after she has 'given herself' to Vincent, Lilith is seen walking hand in hand with Yvonne, another inmate. The two walk towards a barn, and once Vincent has caught up with them he sees Yvonne apparently doing up her trousers! What has occurred? Vincent thinks he knows and accuses Lilith of being a bitch. She suggests to him that just because she loves others doesn't mean she loves him less. Nice try but he doesn't quite buy it. She *is* disturbed after all.

Liquid Sky   1982

Director: Slava Tsukerman. Country: US. Screenplay: Slava Tsukerman, Anne Carlisle and Nina V. Kerova. Production company: Z Films Inc. Duration: 112 mins, colour

Cast: Anne Carlisle (Margaret and Jimmy), Paula E. Sheppard (Adrian), Susan Doukas (Sylvia), Otto von Wernherr (Johann)

Miniature aliens arrive in New York and site themselves on Margaret's roof. The aliens want the chemicals secreted in human brains during orgasm. Thereafter, whomsoever Margaret sleeps with ends up having their brains drained at the crucial moment and experiencing the little death in a big way. Once Margaret realizes what's going on she decides to use her new power to sort out her enemies.

New Wave sci-fi used to explore post-punk urban trash drug culture, or, to put it another way, Russian emigré director looks at the West and does not like what he sees.

Anne Carlisle plays Margaret, a lesbian model, the woman who finds she can 'kill with her cunt'. She also plays Jimmy, an attractive androgynous junkie who bullies and steals his way to the next fix. Carlisle is by far the best and most interesting aspect of the film, her own androgynous qualities contributing both to the look and feel of the film. However, *Liquid Sky* generally fails to engage. No one in the film is very likable, and even the relatively sympathetic Margaret is not exactly Ms Charm School. Another problem is the insistent, computer-generated musical soundtrack. It's the sort of music that is put into films to suggest 'futuristic', but which inevitably sounds monotone, repetitive and dirge-like. Possibly the only way to get into the mood of the film and enjoy it is to be as completely stoned as most of the characters. A case of jack up, tune in and pass out.

Locked In: *see under* CAGED

Look See: *see under* ÉCOUTE VOIR

Losing Chase   1996

Director: Kevin Bacon. Country: US. Screenplay: Anne Meredith. Production company: Showtime Networks Inc. Duration: 88 mins, colour

Cast: Helen Mirren (Chase), Kyra Sedgwick (Elizabeth), Beau Bridges (Richard), Michael Yarmush (Little Richard), Lucas Denton (Jason)

At the family cottage in Martha's Vineyard, Chase Phillips is recovering from a nervous breakdown, or, as she prefers to call it, a 'collapse'. Her weary husband hires a childminder/companion in order that Chase can rest and recover. When Elizabeth arrives, Chase's initial hostility develops into something more positive. She finds herself feeling better.

Sensitive drama outlining a complex relationship between two women, each struggling with unresolved family problems. Helen Mirren is excellent as the troubled Chase, loved by one son, harangued by the other and dictated to by her husband. Her unpredictable behaviour has taken a toll on them all and Elizabeth's arrival is a source of relief.

When the two women first meet it's a case of the baiting game and Chase tests the young Elizabeth with a variety of mental challenges, mainly in the form of barbed insults. Encouraged by the husband, Elizabeth persists and very gradually Chase is won over. In an interesting turn, Elizabeth is revealed to have almost as many problems as Chase. When the carer and patient roles are reversed, both women begin to experience 'recovery'.

Over the summer, Chase's feelings for Elizabeth become more intense and she gradually falls in love with the young woman. One day on the beach she kisses her in front of her eldest boy. Although Elizabeth feels strongly for Chase, this demonstration of love is not returned. Elizabeth sees Chase quite differently: she has placed her in the role of her mother. Much confusion ensues, and the brattish son jumps to the correct conclusion and tells Dad what he thinks is happening. The resulting family row means that Elizabeth has to leave the household, much against Chase's will, and the two are separated.

Handled with surprising tenderness, *Losing Chase* is one of the few films ever made to suggest lesbianism might be a sign of *recovery* from mental illness rather than an indicator of it.

See also: **LIANNA** and **A QUESTION OF LOVE** for more lesbian mothers.

Loss of Innocence: see under **THE GREENGAGE SUMMER**

The Loudest Whisper: see under **THE CHILDREN'S HOUR**

Love and Human Remains   1993

Director: Denys Arcand. Country: Canada. Screenplay: Brad Fraser. Production company: Max Films. Duration: 100 mins, colour

Cast: Thomas Gibson (David), Ruth Marshall (Candy), Cameron Bancroft (Bernie), Mia Kirshner (Benita), Joanne Vannicola (Jerri)

A few weeks in the life and loves of a group of friends. Gay resting actor David lives with straight Candy, who used to be in love with him. She is lonely and needs a relationship. David's straight friend Bernie is a businessman who is growing increasingly disillusioned and misanthropic. Meanwhile, the city is in the grip of fear as a serial killer is picking off young women. Benita, a dominatrix with telepathic powers, senses danger nearby . . .

One of the many plot strands in this cold urban drama/comedy is a lesbian one. Down at the local gym, attractive Jerri hits on slightly unnerved Candy. Jerri is nice, nicer than all the other characters, in fact. She's a primary school teacher, steady and kind. Quite why she goes for Candy is a mystery: for Candy is neither charismatic or cute and only consents to a date when she feels used by a man. Candy is essentially heterosexual but, as she has already said to David earlier, she might date a woman to see what it's like. Interestingly, the film is careful to show that Candy's attitude helps no one: Jerri falls hard for her and is inevitably rejected, and Candy is no closer to the relationship she wanted. Jerri's characterization is very positive in the main. She is thoughtful, sweet and sexy. She is also slightly obsessive, but this seems to be an (unsuccessful) attempt to turn her into a potential serial killer suspect.

The film itself is a strange mixture: engaging one minute and disconnecting the next. The straight press simply could not find a character to identify with and generally found the whole experience alienating. But there is a lot for gays and lesbians to enjoy, especially the domestic arrangements between David and Candy and the inside knowledge of gay culture.

Love and Other Catastrophes   1996

Director: Emma-Kate Croghan. Country: Australia. Screenplay: Yael Bergman, Emma-Kate Croghan and Helen Bandis. Production company: Screwball Five Pty Ltd and Australian Film Commission. Duration: 78 mins, colour

Cast: Matt Day (Michael), Frances O'Connor (Mia), Matthew Dyktynski (Ari), Alice Garner (Alice), Radha Mitchell (Danni), Suzi Dougherty (Savita), Kim Gyngell (Professor Leach)

It's winter on a Melbourne college campus and Mia has problems. It's her last chance to swap courses and her current lecturer is being obstructive. Her girlfriend needs more commitment and wants an answer. Her flatmate hasn't had a date in three years but fancies the campus gigolo, oblivious to the attentions of shy medic Michael, who is desperately searching for a new place to live . . .

Life, Love, Sex, Death and the Movies are the themes of this wonderful low-budget Australian independent comedy. Energetic, original and clever, *Love and Other Catastrophes* is like a breath of fresh air blowing through traditional 'youth' movies and finding an exciting and thoroughly entertaining way to tell familiar tales. For the story is basic enough. A group of students face relatively mundane problems in the course of one day, most of which are unravelled or solved come night-time.

The lesbian relationship concerns Mia and her unappreciated girlfriend Danni, who on this day decides that enough is enough. Trouble is, Mia hasn't the time for this personal crisis, as she must face the bureaucracy of the college system to save her education. Gentle and rather put-upon Danni is not pleased and consoles herself with a new friend.

Bright, cheerful, intelligent and aware, *Love and Other Catastrophes* was directed with terrifying precociousness by its young director (Emma-Kate Croghan was twenty-three when she made the film). It was made in a tremendous rush: seventeen days to put together the script and two weeks to shoot it, which goes some way to explaining its joyful enthusiasm. Frances O'Connor is a delight as Mia, the principal character around whom most of the drama unfolds. Supporting characters are equally assured and the standard of acting is astonishingly accomplished and relaxed.

If you love films, you'll love the in-jokes, and, like the central characters themselves in one pivotal scene, you may find yourself striving to name your favourite three films (and the reasons why).

Unless you have a particular aversion to students, you will love this movie!

Lune de Novembre: see under **NOVEMBERMOON**

Lunes de Fiel: see under **BITTER MOON**

Lust for a Vampire   1970

Director: Jimmy Sangster. Country: GB. Screenplay: Tudor Gates. Production company: Hammer. Duration: 95 mins, colour

Cast: Ralph Bates (Giles), Barbara Jefford (Countess Herritzen), Suzannah Leigh (Janet Playfair), Michael Johnson (Richard), Yutte Stensgaard (Mircalla), Helen Christie (Miss Simpson)

Richard Lestrange arrives at a European village dominated by the castle of the Karnstein family. The locals tell him that the family are the undead — vampires

Irresistible! Yutte Stensgaard and Suzannah Leigh star in *Lust for a Vampire*. Courtesy of Canal + Image UK Ltd.

– *who, on this very day (the fortieth anniversary of their last appearance), are due to begin a killing spree again. Before long local girls begin to disappear.*

Fairly tame but hilariously enjoyable Hammer horror, loosely based on the Dracula myths but this time centred around a girls' finishing school (at which, incidently, no pupil looks younger than twenty-five and none is seen in anything less than full make-up at all times). The 'girls' are in perpetual danger from (wouldn't you know it) one of their own – a new girl who is in fact an undead relative of the vampire family. As all the girls spend much of their time 'innocently' canoodling with each other, it's not a problem for the vamp Mircalla to trap a few wayward femmes. We don't see too much of the action until near the end of the film when we get a – very short – bed scene indicating rather more full-blooded lesbianism, as it were. One of a trail of vampire films to use lesbianism as titillation for a straight audience.

See also: **DRACULA'S DAUGHTER, THE HUNGER** and **TWINS OF EVIL** for more girls with fangs.

Mädchen in Uniform: see under **MAIDENS IN UNIFORM**

Maidens in Uniform (Mädchen in Uniform)   1931

Director: Leontine Sagan. Country: Germany. Screenplay: Christa Winsloe and F. D. Andam (based on the play by Christa Winsloe, *Gestern und Heute*). Production company: Deutsche Film-Gemeinschaft. Duration: 91 mins, black and white

Cast: Dorothea Wieck (Fraulein von Bernburg), Hertha Thiele (Manuela von Meinhardis), Ellen Schwannecke (Ilse von Westhagen), Emilia Unde (Headmistress), Hedwig Schlichter (Fraulein von Kesten)

At a Prussian boarding-school for the daughters of the rich, young Manuela develops a passionate crush on her teacher Fraulein von Bernburg. Although supported by many of her classmates, the condemnation of the headmistress, among other things, drives Manuela to attempt suicide.

Until the early 1960s, *Maidens in Uniform* was probably the best-known lesbian film in the Western world. Critics, then and now, generally love this film. It is seen either as a moving statement on pure love, or else a revolutionary indictment against fascism. Written by lesbian poet Christa Winsloe as an expression against totalitarianism, the film features a warm and tender (reciprocated) friendship between a teacher and pupil, which is prevented from developing by the harsh pro-Nazi headmistress. The school is depicted as fearsome and oppressive. The girls are housed in harsh conditions and fed an inadequate diet in a regime that believes Prussia will be great again but only through austerity and self-deprivation.

Certain scenes stand out, such as the goodnight kiss imparted by the beloved teacher upon the forehead of all the schoolgirls each evening before lights out. Manuela is the only one to receive a kiss on the lips. The girls' miserable existence in the militaristic school is briefly alleviated by this gentle affection. In another scene Manuela ardently declares her love for Fraulein von Bernburg in the middle of school assembly. Such is the depth and purity of the love speaking its name that the only negative reaction is from the vindictive headmistress.

Lesbian director Leontine Sagan ensured that the ending of the film was a positive one – Manuela's suicide attempt ends in failure when her school friends step in and save her. But shortly after the film's release the Nazi censors stepped in and ensured that the unfortunate Manuela fell to her death, her punishment a warning to others. The film was widely praised by critics all over Europe and the USA (although interestingly it was censored almost everywhere it was shown – the lesbianism was toned down). Despite the changed ending, Goebbels banned the film in Germany, describing the subject matter as 'unhealthy'. In the wake of such suppression, several copies of the film disappeared or were buried in archives.

There have been two remakes, a Mexican version, *Muchachas en Uniforme* (1950), and another German version which emerged in 1958, featuring Lilli Palmer and Romy Schneider.

See also: **BILITIS, THE GETTING OF WISDOM, OLIVIA, PICNIC AT HANGING ROCK** and **SECRET PLACES** for more schoolgirl crushes.

The Maids 1974

Director: Christopher Miles. Country: GB and Canada. Screenplay: Robert Enders and Christopher Miles. Production company: Cinevision. Duration: 95 mins, colour

Cast: Glenda Jackson (Solange), Susannah York (Claire), Vivien Merchant (Madame), Mark Burns (Monsieur)

A version of Genet's play based around the true story of two French sisters who killed the mistress for whom they worked.

Awful histrionic version of Genet's slightly more subtle play. It must have seemed like a good idea at the time but the other versions (**LES ABYSSES** and **SISTER MY SISTER**) are more successful – and interesting – than this one, for several reasons. Here the action is very contained – betraying the theatrical origins – with barely a nod to the fact that this is a film not a play. Although both York and Jackson act all over the place, the action appears muted and static. In this respect it rather resembles **THE BITTER TEARS OF PETRA VON KANT**, another chamber piece wherein nothing very much happens (although in that film style alone was enough to keep the viewer fascinated). The two women engage in strange games of domination, passions rise and fall, power moves from one sister to the other. Is this an incestuous relationship? It's hard to tell. At one point Solange says to her sister, 'I have the perfect way to end all suffering,' and they both go into a room, off camera. Does this imply sex? No idea. For thespians rather than lesbians.

See also: **LES ABYSSES** and **SISTER MY SISTER** for other versions of the same story. Also, Susannah York plays lesbian and bisexual respectively in **THE KILLING OF SISTER GEORGE** and **ZEE & CO**.

Man of Flowers   1983

Director: Paul Cox. Country: Australia. Screenplay: Paul Cox and Bob Ellis. Production company: Flowers International. Duration: 91 mins, colour

Cast: Norman Kaye (Charles Bremer), Alyson Best (Lisa), Chris Haywood (David), Sarah Walker (Jane), Julia Blake (Art Teacher)

Lonely male art collector pays a young female model to ritually strip for him every week. He becomes involved in her private life. Meanwhile, he undergoes psychotherapy, which gradually unravels his personal obsessions.

Low-key drama in which a short lesbian moment enters the proceedings. Lisa lives in an atmosphere of artistic turbulence with her coarse painter boyfriend. After an argument she goes to stay with her friend Jane, a lesbian, who has offered her bed to Lisa in the past. In this scene Lisa has decided to 'give it a go' and the two discuss what it might be like. Lisa, with matter-of-fact curiosity, asks 'Am I going to like this?' Jane flatly replies, 'I don't know.' Hardly a ride on a passionate tidal wave then, and made even worse by Lisa's subsequent announcement: 'I reserve the right to be disgusted.' As a prelude to a gentle seduction this must be one of the most deflating comments ever, but Jane is undeterred and the two begin to kiss. Fade-out. Lesbianism as very secondary to heterosexuality but something a nice girl might do – without conviction – if she has a boorish male partner.

Manhattan 1979

Director: Woody Allen. Country: US. Screenplay: Woody Allen and Marshall Brickman. Production company: United Artists. Duration: 96 mins, black and white

Cast: Woody Allen (Isaac Davis), Diane Keaton (Mary Wilke), Michael Murphy (Yale), Mariel Hemingway (Tracy), Meryl Streep (Jill), Anne Byrne (Emily), Karen Ludwig (Connie)

A slice of life in which Woody Allen examines sex, drugs, TV, relationships and urban cultural living in twentieth-century New York.

A comic masterpiece, *Manhattan* is a wonderful mixture of the grown-up and the immature, the gravely important and the sweetly silly. Isaac and his friends work and play in the city negotiating the rough terrain between depressive neurosis and 'normal' anxiety. One minor sub-plot involves the trials and tribulations Isaac experiences as a result of being left by his wife, who has set up home with another woman. Jill, played by Meryl Streep, is one half of the lesbian couple, and Karen Ludwig plays her lover Connie. They are both attractive, smart and seen as a stable couple.

Jill is also quite severe and deals briskly with Isaac. She is going to humiliate him in her biography and seems to care little for his feelings on the matter. Nevertheless, one is left with the impression of a strong, intelligent, sorted-out woman who is in fact less neurotic and fucked up than most of Isaac's friends. She is bringing up their son well, despite Isaac's anxiety over the boy's masculinity, and she views their broken marriage with clear eyes. Isaac admits to having tried to kill Connie with a car, but typically this reference is quickly turned into a comedy opportunity. The scene may be brief, but Woody Allen uses it for some of his very best lines. When he complains that he cannot understand how she can prefer her female lover to him, Jill replies, 'You knew my sexual history before you married me.' To which he responds, 'I know, my psychiatrist warned me ... but you were so beautiful I got another psychiatrist.'

See also: **THE HOUSE OF THE SPIRITS** and **SILKWOOD**, in which Meryl Streep plays the object of lesbian desire in both cases.

Mankillers: see under **FASTER, PUSSYCAT, KILL! KILL!**

Masks: see under **PERSONA**

May Fools (Milou en Mai)   1990

Director: Louis Malle. Country: France and Italy. Screenplay: Louis Malle and Jean-Claude Carrière. Production company: NEF/TFI Films. Duration: 108 mins, colour

Cast: Michel Piccoli (Milou), Miou-Miou (Camille), Michel Duchaussoy (Georges), Marcel Bories (Léonce), Dominique Blanc (Claire), Rozenn Le Tallec (Marie-Laure), Harriet Walter (Lily)

When the matriarchal head of the family dies, various relatives assemble at their country home to discuss, and dispute, the will. Meanwhile, the Paris riots of 1968 convince the family that they are in danger of attack by communist students.

Pastoral comedy which unfortunately delivers a rather disappointing lesbian figure in the form of Claire, niece to the central character Milou. Pragmatic and serious both in attitude and appearance, she is presented in stark contrast to her ballerina girlfriend, Marie-Laure, who accompanies Claire to the reunion. Claire seems reserved, although there are hints of something more interesting when the youngest member of the family, Françoise, goes to wake the two women up in the morning and finds Marie-Laure tied to the bed.

This said, Claire is a taciturn creature, with a barely concealed streak of violently jealous anger inside her, the product of her insecure possessiveness in relation to Marie-Laure. This insecurity turns out to be justified when the fun-loving girlfriend discovers the joys of heterosexuality – a development which cannot surprise the audience. It's a conversion waiting to happen. Claire watches, powerlessly, as in front of her eyes Marie-Laure falls for a young man.

Meantime: see under **BOUND AND GAGGED: A LOVE STORY**

Milou en Mai: see under **MAY FOOLS**

Mirror Images   1991

Director: Alexander Gregory Hippolyte. Country: US. Screenplay: Georges Des Esseintes. Production company: Axis Films. Duration: 88 mins, colour

Cast: Delia Sheppard (Kaitlin/Shauna), Jeff Conaway (Jeffrey), Richard Arbolino (Carter Sayles)

Ludicrous 'erotic drama', in which a bored twin sister takes the place of the other in order to experience a bit more life. In so doing she uncovers an international drug-smuggling operation involving political candidates (the way you do).

En route to solving the crime our heroine beds several passionate types, including a Sapphic secretary, all lip gloss and long fingernails. The secretary doesn't survive till morning, but this is due to a drug rather than sex overdose (indeed, they barely touch, and it is the tips of their tongues rather than mouths which actually meet). It is this incident which sparks our heroine into action. Lesbianism as minor titillation and vague plot hook. Delia Sheppard, who starred in another Hippolyte masterpiece, **NIGHT RHYTHMS**, must be so *tired* of these roles.

See also: **NIGHT RHYTHMS**, and indeed **MIRROR IMAGES II** for more of the same from Mr Hippolyte.

Mirror Images II   1993

Director: Alexander Gregory Hippolyte. Country: US. Production company: Axis Films. Duration: 92 mins, colour

Cast: Shannon Whirry (Carrie and Terrie), Kristine Kelly (Dr Rubin)

Identical twins, one good, one bad, fight it out in this sex film with a thriller plot tagged on to it somewhere. The bad sister – Terrie – is thought to be dead, and can therefore seduce the good sister's boyfriend and no one is any the wiser. But inevitably it gets worse, and eventually the sisters meet. The scene is set for murder, at least.

Two is obviously better than one as far as Gregory Hippolyte is concerned and indeed it's a case of here we go again in terms of plot premise. Hippolyte puts lesbian sex scenes in his films for pure diversionary titillation and nothing else. This one involves good sister Carrie visiting her psychiatrist in order to sort out a childhood trauma. In no time at all Dr Rubin has put aside doctor/patient ethics for the sake of a roll on the couch. The sex is fascinating. Apart from breast-stroking and finger-sucking nothing actually seems to happen, but watch out for those fingernails.

See also: **MIRROR IMAGES** and **NIGHT RHYTHMS** by the same director.

Mona Lisa   1986

Director: Neil Jordan. Country: GB. Screenplay: Neil Jordan and David Leland. Production company: Handmade Films. Duration: 104 mins, colour

Cast: Bob Hoskins (George), Cathy Tyson (Simone), Michael Caine (Mortwell), Robbie Coltrane (Thomas), Clarke Peters (Anderson), Kate Hardie (Cathy)

Interesting and stylish thriller in which a small-time con man, George, freshly released from prison, is enticed by a high-class prostitute to help find her friend who has disappeared into the seedy and dangerous world of London vice.

Very successful British thriller (and the first screen role for Cathy Tyson), which revealed a grim and frightening view of the London underworld. George is a working-class hero, lost and misled from beginning to end by various protagonists including Simone, with whom he falls hopelessly in love. It is the relationship between these two, he racist bigot but diamond in the rough, she tart with pragmatic heart, which forms the emotional core of the film. Lesbianism is the unknown factor which drives the plot along. Director Neil Jordan likes to surprise (some years later he would present us with *The Crying Game* [1992]), and in *Mona Lisa* the shock, if you like, is that Simone has enlisted George's help to find her female *lover*, not friend. The fact that George has placed himself in real danger for the love of Simone and now discovers his mission was futile (from his point of view) is likely to have had many viewers thinking 'What a shame'. This 'twist' to the plot has dramatic force because we care for George; as a result, it is not the most positive screen image of lesbianism. However, the characterization of Simone is so compelling, and excellently acted by Cathy Tyson, that reservations may be suspended. After all, no one emerges from this film in a haze of golden light.

Monique 1969

Director: John Bown. Country: GB. Screenplay: John Bown. Production company: Tigon. Duration: 84 mins, colour

Cast: Joan Alcorn (Jean), David Sumner (Bill), Sibylla Kay (Monique), Jacob Fitz-Jones (Edward), Nicola Bown (Susan)

Bill and Jean are a modern 1960s couple with an Ideal Home and no worries, except that Jean has no interest in sex. Jean is also bored with housework and irritated with the children. She persuades her husband that they should take on an au pair. Monique, all French and flirtatious, arrives and soon their lives are transformed. Seducing first one, then the other, Monique brings charm and happiness into the couple's lives before she, inevitably, must return to her boyfriend in France.

This wonderful low-budget 1960s sex film has some unusual elements. First, the director has bothered to write a plot, which has moments of both comedy and drama. Second, the characters are quite well drawn, and in many ways the whole endeavour is endearingly innocent. The one thing it doesn't really have is very much sex, but the build-up of tension between all three, especially the two women, is remarkably well paced. In one sequence the husband goes to bed and leaves the women together decorating the Christmas tree. We see nothing more until Jean comes to bed looking slightly shell-shocked, and undresses in front of her sleeping husband. As she takes off her sweater we see her bra is already undone ... that's subtlety for you.

Also interesting is the way that a genuine friendship is created between Jean and Monique, and that their sexual affair is presented as only positive, to both her and her husband.

In fact, the film makes an astonishingly convincing case that adultery, including lesbianism, can save and improve a marriage. No talk of divorce or custody rights here; instead, the new non-nuclear family are better off than they were before, with Monique rather like a latter-day Mary Poppins descending on a family and making everything work properly. Quaintly charming and great fun.

Morocco   1930

Director: Josef von Sternberg. Country: US. Screenplay: Joseph von Sternberg and Jules Furthman (based on the book *Amy Jolly* by Benno Vigny). Production company: Paramount Publix Corporation. Duration: 92 mins, black and white

Cast: Gary Cooper (Tom Brown), Marlene Dietrich (Amy Jolly), Adolphe Menjou (La Bessiere), Ulrich Haupt (Adjutant Caesar), Juliette Compton (Anna Delores), Francis McDonald (Corporal Tatoche)

Amy Jolly sacrifices everything for her man, legionnaire Tom Brown, in von Sternberg's Hollywood drama.

Marlene Dietrich's first American film had the fabulous real-life bisexual playing it relatively straight (and getting an Oscar nomination for it). Fairly standard heterosexual couplings in this film are spiced up with Marlene's turn in the local club, wherein cross-dressing tease Dietrich kisses a woman ever so briefly, while dragged up and performing a cabaret song. Designed to inflame her man, not the woman, the woman is nevertheless enthralled by such attention, and later becomes jealous when Marlene's attention is diverted. It goes no further than that, but it is enough to throw the film nicely off balance. Dietrich's thrilling screen persona, a blend of sexual ambiguity and sultry androgyny, means that even when she is straight, a question mark follows her everywhere.

See also: **JUST ONE OF THE GUYS, ORLANDO, QUEEN CHRISTINA, SWITCH** and **YENTL** for other cross-dressing, gender-bending capers.

Mrs Dalloway   1997

Director: Marleen Gorris. Country: Netherlands, US and GB. Screenplay: Eileen Atkins (based on the novel by Virginia Woolf). Production company: Overseas Filmgroup. Duration: 97 mins, colour

Cast: Vanessa Redgrave (Mrs Clarissa Dalloway), Natascha McElhone (young Clarissa Dalloway), Michael Kitchen (Peter Walsh), Alan Cox (young Peter Walsh), Sarah Badel (Lady Sally Rosseter), Lena Headey (young Sally Seton)

London 1923. Mrs Dalloway prepares to throw the perfect party. As the day progresses she muses on her early life, and wonders how things would have been had she not married her bourgeois politician husband.

One very small, but memorable, lesbian moment stands out in Marleen Gorris's excellent period drama. The privileged young Clarissa Dalloway (Natascha McElhone, looking exquisitely handsome) and her friend Sally spend an evening flirting with interested young men and speculating about their futures. Under a moonlit sky, Sally takes Clarissa aside and kisses her on the lips. The moment is sublime for Clarissa, whose eyes remain closed well after the kiss is complete, until the girls are disturbed by the reappearance of the boys. Clarissa is furious to have her exhilaration halted so abruptly and her eyes betray her anger. Very exciting. Leads to nothing else, however.

See also: **ANTONIA'S LINE** by the same director, and for more Vanessa see **THE BOSTONIANS, GREAT MOMENTS IN AVIATION** and **JULIA**.

La Muchacha de las Bragas de Oro: see under **THE GIRL WITH THE GOLDEN PANTIES**

Muriel Fait le Désespoir de Ses Parents: see under **MURIEL'S PARENTS HAVE HAD IT UP TO HERE**

Muriel's Parents Have Had It Up to Here (Muriel Fait le Désespoir de Ses Parents) 1995

Director: Philippe Faucon. Country: France. Screenplay: Philippe Faucon and Catherine Klein. Production company: Ognon Pictures. Duration: 79 mins, colour, subtitled

Cast: Catherine Klein (Muriel), Dominique Perrier (Nora), Serge Germany (Fred), David Bigiaoui (Antoine), Marie Riviere (Muriel's Mother), Jean-Louis Caillat (Muriel's Father)

At seventeen Muriel is beginning to sort out her sexuality. She is in love with Nora, her flirtatious best friend, who attracts the attention of men wherever she goes. Nora is straight, but that doesn't stop her giving Muriel surprisingly sexy kisses now and then. Muriel begins to know what she wants and unselfconsciously tells her mother that she prefers girls to boys. Her mother is not pleased.

Absolutely marvellous drama, beautifully observed and acted, and handled by director Faucon with a light touch. The timbre of the film is set by the title, although the parents themselves are largely absent. Uplifting in its own way, due largely to the wonderfully knowing performance by Catherine Klein (who also co-wrote the screenplay) as the young Muriel. She is able to generate vulnerability one moment and juxtapose it with a very satisfying directness. This makes her much sexier than her appearance suggests. Once she realizes what she wants she does not hesitate or look back. 'I won't change,' she tells her mother. Her mother is very annoyed and says, 'I expected better.' Muriel and Nora take a couple of boys down to the beach. The boys don't know where they stand from one moment to the next. Muriel tells Nora that she wants to make love to her, but on that occasion heterosexuality prevails.

But it's just a matter of time before Muriel finds what she's looking for. How refreshing to have a lesbian heroine whose main coming-out problem is not shame or angst, but the ordinary everyday search for a partner.

My Father Is Coming 1991

Director: Monika Treut. **Country:** US and Germany. **Screenplay:** Monika Treut and Bruce Benderson. **Production company:** Hyäne Filmproduktion. **Duration:** 82 mins, colour

Cast: Shelley Kästner (Vicky), Alfred Edel (Hans), Annie Sprinkle (Annie), Michael Massee (Joe), Flora Gaspar (Lisa)

A young woman living in New York anxiously awaits the arrival of her father, who has decided to pay her an impromptu visit. Unfortunately, she has told her father that she is married, and now he can't wait to meet her husband . . .

Treut's low-budget New York-based comedy traverses a wide range of issues and sexualities with a broad brush and a humorous outlook. Vicky, a very un-innocent abroad, is an aspiring actress whose sexuality is up for grabs if she can only decide what it is she really wants. With Pa on his way, much confusion ensues as Vicky is forced to paper over the cracks of her non-existent career, to say nothing of desperately summoning up a pretend husband. The story takes an unexpected turn, however, once Pa arrives in the Big Apple. Far from being in a position to criticize his daughter for her various 'failures', it is he who takes up with sex goddess Annie Sprinkle on a riotous sexual journey through the East Village's alternative – and polymorphous – erotic underworld. Much worse, from Vicky's point of view, when Pa tags along to one of her auditions, it is *he* who lands a part in a major TV commercial rather than her.

Some fine acting, particularly from Alfred Edel as the transformed father, as well as some wonderful observations surrounding culture clashes and gender confusion.

See also: **SEDUCTION, THE CRUEL WOMAN** by the same director.

The Night of the Iguana   1964

Director: John Huston. Country: US. Screenplay: Anthony Veiller and John Huston (based on the play by Tennessee Williams). Production company: Seven Arts Productions. Duration: 118 mins, black and white

Cast: Richard Burton (Reverend Laurence Shannon), Ava Gardner (Maxine Faulk), Deborah Kerr (Hannah Jelkes), Sue Lyon (Charlotte Goodall), Skip Ward (Hank Prosner), Grayson Hall (Judith Fellows), Cyril Delevanti (Nonno)

Defrocked clergyman turned tour guide Reverend Shannon is escorting a group of female teachers in a bus through Mexico.

Our lesbian in this film is the very proper Miss Fellows, played by Grayson Hall (who won an Oscar for her performance). She is looking after the young nymphet Charlotte, whose burgeoning (hetero)sexuality is causing Miss Fellows some distress. As time passes, Judith spots a relationship developing between the girl and the much older Reverend Shannon, and determines to stop it. She warns Shannon to keep away from the infatuated Charlotte ostensibly because she is under age. She threatens that she will have to 'take steps' if he attempts anything.

Shannon is a man of the world and naturally sees Judith for what she really is. He comments to Maxine that 'Charlotte is travelling under the wing – the military escort – of a butch vocal teacher.' Judith is characterized as possessive, domineering and vindictive. She is also desperate, pathetic and, to underline it all, ungainly. Her fight with Shannon over Charlotte is doomed to failure, but it is implied that she can be forgiven for her perversity because she is unaware of it. This is indicated later in the film (once heterosexuality has prevailed and Miss Fellows has left, defeated) when Shannon remarks, 'Miss Fellows is a highly moral person. If she ever recognized the truth about herself it would destroy her.' Thus, in her absence, Miss Fellows becomes a figure of pity (just about).

See also: **SEVEN WOMEN**, in which Sue Lyon is the object of desire for another repressed lesbian.

Night Rhythms   1992

Director: Alexander Gregory Hippolyte. Country: US. Screenplay: Alan Gries and Robert Sullivant. Production company: Axis/Davis Joint Venture. Duration: 99 mins, colour

Cast: Delia Sheppard (Bridget), Martin Hewitt (Nick), Tracey Tweed (Honey)

Soft-core porn drama from the man who brought you **MIRROR IMAGES**, *if that's any recommendation.* Night Rhythms *revolves around a late-night DJ – Nick – who talks sweet and dirty to his adoring female listeners. One of his more forthcoming fans – Honey – arrives at the studio and offers him sex there and then. Unfortunately for Nick, his liaison not only goes out live to the listening public but his passionate encounter is also interrupted mid-coitus by a killer who knocks out Nick and disposes of Honey. Thus Nick is framed for the murder and must find the killer before the police find him . . .*

But all this is irrelevant. The point of the film is soft-core, soft-focus sex involving Nick and one woman, Nick and two women, or two women being watched by Nick. All the women look and behave in the same way, all have that Californian big hair and all have silicone to thank for their extraordinary shapes. It's as if the Stepford Wives had been designed by *Playboy* magazine.

Oh, and who is the mystery killer? Suffice to say that **BASIC INSTINCT** has a lot to answer for.

See also: **MIRROR IMAGES** and **MIRROR IMAGES II** by the same director.

Nineteen Nineteen (1919)   1984

Director: Hugh Brody. Country: GB. Screenplay: Hugh Brody and Michael Ignatieff. Production company: British Film Institute Production Board. Duration: 99 mins, colour

Cast: Paul Scofield (Alexander Scherbatov), Maria Schell (Sophie Rubin), Frank Finlay (Voice of Sigmund Freud), Diana Quick (Anna), Clare Higgins (Young Sophie), Colin Firth (Young Alexander), Sandra Berkin (Nina)

Two elderly people meet up and recall the experiences of their youth, when they were both patients of Sigmund Freud. Massive historical changes have come about since they last saw each other, and they talk over their lives, speculating whether Freud helped or hindered them.

Pregnant pause. Clare Higgins and Diana Quick star in *Nineteen Nineteen*. Courtesy of British Film Institute.

The first twenty minutes of *Nineteen Nineteen* are painfully slow, and the tone suggests the film will be as stifled as the consulting room in question. However, things warm up a little and become more interesting with the use of flashbacks taking us back to 1919, when the early scenes are set. Clare Higgins plays the young Sophie, who reveals that she tried to kill herself after the end of a relationship with a woman. She is swift to tell Freud that she is seeing him because of her suicide attempt, lest he should think she wants a cure for her homosexuality. Nevertheless, Freud concludes that Sophie secretly desires her father, not Anna (Diana Quick), the woman she adored. Sophie describes her love for the beautiful middle-class woman, and there is an amazing scene in which the two women are in bed, kissing, and we suddenly see that Anna is six months pregnant. Sophie sadly remarks that the moment was 'the happiest night of my life'.

The acting is faultless, and the script is sharp and sensitive, if a touch airless.

See also: **THIN ICE** for Clare Higgins playing it straight.

No Exit 1962

Director: Tad Z. Danielewski. Country: US and Argentina. Screenplay: George Tabori (based on the play by Jean-Paul Sartre). Production company: Aries Cinematografica Argentina. Duration: 87 mins, black and white

Cast: Viveca Lindfors (Inez), Morgan Sterne (Garcin), Rita Gam (Estelle)

Three people meet in a room in Hell, condemned to spend eternity together as punishment for their sins. Garcin is a journalist who betrayed his colleagues in the Resistance. Estelle is an avaricious woman who killed a child for money. Inez is a lesbian who seduced the wife of a friend and destroyed them both.

Excellent psychological drama in which three people of different class, gender and sexual proclivity realize that they have been selected to be together for ever because none of them can or will provide anything that the others need. 'Hell is other people,' as Jean-Paul Sartre observed. So Estelle tries in vain to seduce Garcin, who cannot comply due to impotence and guilt, and Garcin must wait in vain for the approval of Inez, who sees him as a coward. Inez, expertly played by Viveca Lindfors, is a typical screen lesbian of the time: inherently evil and deceptively attractive! She admits that she was in love with her girlfriend but that she likes to watch others suffer. Describing herself as a torch in Florence's heart, she declares, 'I burned everything out.' She is by far the most adept at the power games they must all play, but she cannot get the girl – Estelle is relentlessly heterosexual – and that is her eternal torment. *No Exit* offers a surprisingly overt depiction of a lesbian for its time.

Note: There is another version of *No Exit* entitled *Huis Clos* (1954), directed by Jacqueline Audry, who also directed **OLIVIA**.

Nocturne 1990

Director: Joy Chamberlain. Country: GB. Screenplay: Trish Fairbanks. Production company: Maya Vision. Duration: 65 mins, colour

Cast: Lisa Eichhorn (Marguerite), Caroline Patterson (Sal), Karen Jones (Ria), Helena McCarthy (Mrs Ruddock), Maureen O'Brien (Mother), Jackie Ekers (Tutor), Jenny Long (Young Marguerite)

A woman approaching middle age tries to take possession of her life after the death of her mother. She is visited one afternoon by two young lesbians

NOCTURNE

One for the road. Lisa Eichhorn and Caroline Patterson star in *Nocturne*. Courtesy of Maya Vision.

sheltering from the rain. Inviting them to dinner, Marguerite finds her guests challenging and liberating.

Strange and interesting psychological drama starring the excellent Lisa Eichhorn (*Yanks* [1979], *Cutter's Way* [1981], etc.), and also Caroline Patterson (*EastEnders*). Marguerite is a deeply repressed woman who, arriving back at her childhood home for her mother's funeral, decides to change her life. Taking the opportunity to invite into the house two young women of whom her mother would certainly have disapproved, Marguerite begins a night of self-discovery. Her two wild-child guests, with their lack of manners and flirtatious, careless abandon, offer the older woman a chance for free expression, possibly for the first time in her life. (We see, via the use of flashbacks, a glimpse of Marguerite's inhibited and subdued childhood, liberated briefly by the arrival of a loving tutor.) In a night of drunken reverie, and with the help of her daring visitors, Marguerite is able to come to terms with her past. Very fine performance from the underrated Lisa Eichhorn.

See also: **DOMESTIC BLISS** by the same director.

Novembermond: see under **NOVEMBERMOON**

Novembermoon (Lune de Novembre; Novembermond) 1984

Director: Alexandra von Grote. Country: Germany and France. Production company: Ottokar Runze Productions. Duration: 107 mins, colour

Cast: Gabriele Osburg (Novembermoon), Christiane Millet (Ferial), Danièle Delorme (Ferial's mother), Stéphane Garcin (Laurent), Bruno Pradal (Marcel)

World War II. Novembermoon is a German Jew who manages to escape to Paris. By chance she meets a beautiful woman, Ferial, and the two fall in love. As the war progresses the danger for November increases and she goes to the countryside to hide with farming people until the situation is safer. Ferial persuades her mother to allow November back into their shared flat. In order to avert suspicion, and to try to avoid having her flat searched, Ferial compromises her beliefs and her moral integrity by working on a collaborationist newspaper. At the end of the war the women are free, but Ferial discovers that local people were taken in by her pro-Nazi stance more than she realized.

War zone. Christiane Millet and Gabriele Osburg star in *Novembermoon*. Courtesy of Cinenova.

Absolutely marvellous film that works on many levels and has the story of two lesbians in love at its core. *Novembermoon* gives a lesbian viewer something we hardly ever see – a proper story with drama, a plot and real depth of character. By using the lesbian thread as a central theme, the value of the story as a whole is much enhanced.

The two women meet completely by chance in a queue for food. November discovers that she is standing beside Ferial, the sister of the young man who flirts with her at the restaurant each day. Their amusement at this discovery leads to a chat over coffee and the two begin realize they are attracted to each other. Later, Ferial tells her brother what has happened. When he realizes that November has chosen Ferial over himself, he graciously withdraws. The two women consummate their relationship shortly afterwards – we see just a couple of intense kisses (more would have been wonderful, it's the only disappointment of the film).

With a delicacy that should be envied by more experienced directors, Alexandra von Grote generates an intense and enthralling relationship between the two women. The war forms the backdrop against which the love story is set, with November's position as a Jew adding a sharp tension. Riveting, and one of the best lesbian dramas ever.

Now I Lay Me Down: see under RACHEL, RACHEL

Olivia (Pit of Darkness)   1951

Director: Jacqueline Audry. Country: France. Screenplay: Colette Audry (based on a chapter of the novel by Dorothy Bussey). Production company: Memnon Films. Duration: 94 mins, black and white

Cast: Edwige Feuillère (Mlle Julie), Simone Simon (Mlle Cara), Claire Olivia (Olivia), Yvonne de Bray (Victoire), Suzanne Dehelly (Mlle Dubois), Marina de Berg (Mimi)

Olivia arrives at a girls' boarding-school run by two sisters, Julia and Cara. Each woman has a group of admiring pupils whom she indulges with special attention and occasional favours. Olivia falls for the charismatic Mlle Julie, who appears to want to return her love.

Turn-of-the-century drama, directed by, written by and starring almost exclusively women, sees the familiar adolescent crush developed into a passionate and intense yearning on the part of both the girl and the headmistress.

Schoolmistress ... Edwige Feuillère and Claire Olivia star in *Olivia*. Courtesy of Cinenova.

Olivia forms an urgent desire for Mlle Julie, which she one day openly expresses in pronouncements of love. Mlle Julie responds in a cool fashion, while looking into the distance. She is tempted by this jailbait ... Her ability to suppress her own desire gets the better of her, however, and although she promises the girl a great deal (including at one stage that she will visit her in her room at night), restraint is the order of the day and Olivia is rejected. Later Mlle Julie talks about her inner turmoil and remarks, 'It's been a struggle all my life, but I've always been victorious and proud of it.' She wonders, though, 'Would failure have been kinder to us all?' Very controversial on release, and heavily censored in Britain and the USA, these days the content will appear mild rather than shocking. Beautifully acted by both Edwige Feuillère and Simone Simon, and containing both humour and tragedy, *Olivia* is the consummate schoolgirl crush film.

See also: **BILITIS, THE GETTING OF WISDOM, MAIDENS IN UNIFORM, PICNIC AT HANGING ROCK** and **SECRET PLACES** for more schoolgirl crushes.

Only the Brave 1994

Director: Ana Kokkinos. Country: Australia. Screenplay: Ana Kokkinos and Mira Robertson. Production company: Pickpocket Productions. Duration: 61 mins, colour

Cast: Elena Mandalis (Alex), Dora Kaskanis (Vicki), Maude Davey (Kate Groves), Bob Bright (Reg)

Alex and Vicki are close friends. Disillusioned with school and life, they pass the time setting fire to fields and empty buildings. While Vicki is sexually available to her boyfriend, Alex will not sleep with hers. Instead, she develops a crush on a female teacher.

Raw and desperately grim examination of youth in the dead-end Australian suburbs, centring on two close female friends (Mandalis and Kaskanis, both excellent). Alex dreams of finding the mother who abandoned her as a child, while Vicki has more problems at home than even Alex knows about. The two are intense friends until differences in sexuality divide them for a while. Uncompromising and brutal, in one vicious scene Alex is forced into a fight with another girl in the school toilets, having been taunted for being 'a lesbo'. Alex has indeed been drawn to her female literature teacher, who seems to offer a glimmer of hope on an intellectual, but not a sexual, level. As the film moves towards an inevitable tragedy, it is – unusually – the lesbian Alex who seems to get a grip and moves on to a possibly better future.

See also: **ALL OVER ME** for more teenage angst.

Open City (Roma, Città Aperta; Rome, Open City) 1945

Director: Roberto Rossellini. Country: Italy. Screenplay: Sergio Amidei, Federico Fellini and Roberto Rossellini. Production company: Excelsa/Minerva. Duration: 101 mins, black and white

Cast: Aldo Fabrizi (Don Pietro Pellegnini), Anna Magnani (Pina), Marcello Pagliero (Manfredi), Harry Feist (Major Bergmann), Maria Michi (Marina), Nando Bruno (Sexton), Giovanna Galletti (Ingrid)

Rome during the last days of the German occupation. Ordinary people are caught up in acts of persecution and betrayal in this, one of the greatest Italian neo-realist films ever made.

Shot in the style of a documentary, this extraordinary film gives a strong impression of being absolute *vérité* – right there at the end of World War II. Many of the cast were not actors; Rossellini had very few of the luxuries a normal film director would expect. The result, though, is quite amazing, the central characters emerging as heroic (against an admittedly one-dimensional enemy).

From a lesbian point of view, however, the film contains one of the most evil and startlingly unpleasant characters ever seen in film history. She is a woman working for the Nazis, who seduces youthful girls into becoming whores for the local army officers. Ingrid is a sophisticated and utterly ruthless woman who uses whatever it takes to ensure compliance. In the case of Marina it is drugs which are used as the bait. In one scene Ingrid gives Marina narcotics and a fur coat in exchange for information which leads to several arrests. Once she is drug dependent, Ingrid hands over the hapless Marina to the Gestapo for rape and prostitution. As she is taken away, Ingrid retrieves her coat: 'For the next time.'

Orlando 1992

Director: Sally Potter. Country: GB/Russia/France/Italy/Netherlands. Screenplay: Sally Potter. Production company: Adventure Pictures. Duration: 93 mins, colour

Cast: Tilda Swinton (Orlando), Billy Zane (Shelmerdine), Quentin Crisp (Queen Elizabeth I), Heathcote Williams (Nick Greene/Publisher), Dudley Sutton (King James I), Lothaire Bluteau (The Khan), Charlotte Valandrey (Sasha)

It is the year 1600. Orlando catches the eye of Queen Elizabeth I, who promises the young man a huge inheritance, provided that he does not lose his beauty and age. This casts a spell on the youth, who proceeds to live a remarkable life through the centuries, changing sex along the way.

Sally Potter's wonderful film, a magnificent parade through English history, sees the androgynous Tilda Swinton perfectly cast as the immortal, soft-hearted nobleman who experiences history first-hand. With a shrewd sense of humour, an eye for the spectacular in terms of theatrical staging and a magnificent score (she wrote the soundtrack, too), Potter's film is a clever, funny and finely filmed *tour de force*.

Orlando's adventures through history lead him to love and romance. He falls for the beautiful Sasha, who fortunately returns his affection. In one exceedingly romantic scene Orlando declares his love against an icy background of snow and bleak desolation. They kiss. Of course, this is not a lesbian moment as such because at this point Orlando is, after all, a male. This may be a little too second-hand for some, but it is enthralling nevertheless. It is worth remembering that Virginia Woolf's extraordinary novel, on which the film is based, was apparently inspired by, and a tribute to, the great female love of her life, Vita Sackville-West.

See also: **FEMALE PERVERSIONS** for more Tilda, and **JUST ONE OF THE GUYS, MOROCCO, QUEEN CHRISTINA, SWITCH** and **YENTL** for more cross-dressing, gender-bending capers.

Out of Season 1998

Director: Jeannette Buck. Country: US. Screenplay: Kim McNabb. Production company: IMJ Productions. Duration: 98 mins, colour

Cast: Carol Monda (Micki Silva), Joy Kelly (Roberta), Dennis Fecteau (Charlie), Nancy Daly (Shelley), Rusty Clauss (Jane), Gregory A. Reid, Jr (Dexter)

City-dweller Micki Silva is forced to return to her small home town to care for her sick Uncle Charlie. At the local diner she meets Roberta, who is singularly unimpressed with Micki's casual flippancy. The two women are compelled to spend time together, however, after it transpires that Roberta is Charlie's best friend . . .

Interesting drama, the strength of which centres around the acting, which is superb, and the ensemble playing, which is exceptionally entertaining. Most especially, the antipathy expressed between various characters gives the film an unexpected zing! of authenticity. The character of Shelley – manager of Zoe's diner – is a real treat. Abrupt and dismissive, she gives no one respect until they have earned it and treats the newcomer with curiosity and disdain in equal measures. The film is at its most effective when the three female leads are in the diner, verbalizing over food or whatever. And from a dramatic point of view this is very convincing, because you really don't see how Roberta and Micki are ever going to get together.

Unexpectedly, this is where the film's only weakness occurs. The fact is, these two women are having such an interesting 'non-relationship' that it would have been more satisfactory if they *didn't* find romance together. Once they do, the film fades into predicability. Themes of commitment and finding one's roots are there of course, but they are just a backdrop to the central connection between Micki and Roberta. When the friction between the two disappears, our interest diminishes too. See it for the raillery and the banter, though, and you won't be disappointed.

Pandora's Box 1928

Director: G. W. Pabst. Country: Germany. Screenplay: Ladislao Vajda (adapted from plays by Frank Wedekind). Production company: Nero Film. Duration: 104 mins, black and white, silent

Cast: Louise Brooks (Lulu), Fritz Kortner (Dr Peter Schon), Franz Lederer (Alwa Schon), Carl Götz (Schigolch), Alice Roberts (Countess Anna Geschwitz)

Pandora's Box *is a terrific pot-boiler telling the age-old story of a temptress who works her way through admirers of both sexes.*

Lulu is mesmerizingly played by the great star of the time, Louise Brooks. She is viewed as highly sexual, wilful and free-spirited. Those who fall for her are unable to help themselves, and she shamelessly plays off one admirer with another: 'Alwa is my best friend,' she says with a piercing look at the Countess. 'He's the only one who wants nothing from me.' The Countess is the besotted lesbian who is given just enough encouragement by Lulu to keep her hanging on, but nothing more. She can only stand by as Lulu moves from one man to another and then into marriage. In one scene Lulu is retiring to her bridal chamber when the Countess suddenly approaches and gives her a quick, intense hug, before rushing away.

However, apart from being helplessly in love, the Countess is nevertheless seen as a balanced person. She is a respected artist and has many friends. It is Lulu who wrecks marriages, and, among other things, is tried for murder and sold as a white slave(!) before causing degradation to her friends. It is in this context that the Countess comes into her own as a true heroine. Despite knowing her preferences, Lulu asks the Countess to throw herself at a particular man to prevent him reporting her to the police. She does so reluctantly. We do not see what happens but before long a terrible altercation ensues and the Countess emerges, crawling on the floor after, we gather, rape and attack. It is implied that she dies from her wounds. Meanwhile, Lulu moves on to another man.

This presentation of lesbianism set a precedent for dozens of films which followed it (exemplified by *The Children's Hour*), in which the lesbian character, who is essentially heroic, must suffer and die. More importantly, she must never get the girl.

Pasajes 1996

Director: Daniel Calparsoro. Country: Spain. Screenplay: Daniel Calparsoro. Production company: El Deseo. Duration: 89 mins, colour, subtitled

Cast: Najwa Nimri (Gabi), Alfredo Villa (Manu), Tom Gabella (Butano), Charo Lopez (Carmina), Carla Calparsoro (Gema)

Gabi and her girlfriend Gema are members of a gang of thieves. One day they ransack an apartment, but during the getaway Gema is killed. On the run and without her partner, Gabi abandons the gang to pursue a fantasy woman who wears a perfect pair of shoes in a particular shade of green. She encounters Carmina, a woman who wears exactly the right shoes. Unexpectedly, the woman is a middle-aged, alcoholic cleaning woman. Undeterred, Gabi decides Carmina is the woman she wants.

After an amazing action-packed opening sequence, *Pasajes* settles into what it truly is: not a gangster thriller, but a reflective study of character and imagination. Gabi, like the remaining members of the gang, is a small-time loser, but with grandiose ideas. A social misfit with an overwhelming personality, she simply *decides* that Carmina will fill the void in her life, and that is that. Efforts to charm and manipulate Carmina are, after a shaky start, surprisingly quite successful. Gabi's standards are very demanding, however. As much as she seeks to mould Carmina into the woman she needs – that is, someone who will love her and give her a home – so Carmina alternately complies or resists. Soon, though, Carmina – who is being led into a life of crime by Gabi – wants to finish it all. Meanwhile, the police are getting closer and the outlook is bleak.

Curious and unusual film with some strong performances (particularly Charo Lopez as Carmina) and a moody directorial style. The lesbian relationship, unlikely as it is, is bizarrely fascinating, though it operates more like a power struggle than a love affair. Strange and idiosyncratic.

The People vs Larry Flynt 1996

Director: Milos Forman. Country: US. Screenplay: Scott Alexander and Larry Karaszewski. Production company: Phoenix Pictures. Duration: 124 mins, colour

Cast: Woody Harrelson (Larry Flynt), Courtney Love (Althea Leasure), Edward Norton (Isaacman), Brett Harrelson (Jimmy Flynt), Donna Hanover (Ruth Carter Stapleton)

From childhood on, Larry Flynt seizes every chance to make money in the spirit of free enterprise. From modest beginnings running a strip joint, Flynt's empire expands dramatically when his newsletter full of nudie pics becomes a national success. Hustler *magazine is born. Litigation and notoriety follow.*

Excellently realized biography of disreputable character Larry Flynt, exploiter of the female nude and supporter of the American right to free speech. The film follows the adventure of Flynt's life and gleefully pits him and his representation against the Christian far right via the justice system. Using the defence of free speech, Flynt manages to gain a good deal of public support for his enterprises. However, the film fights shy of examining Flynt's relentless objectification of women, which is never cross-examined in the same way that his fight for constitutional equity and fairness is.

The lesbian bit is in the form of Courtney Love, playing Althea Leasure, Flynt's wife-to-be. She tells him when they first meet that she has slept with more women in his club than he has, a claim he finds more exciting than daunting. Once married the two indulge in drug-soaked bisexual frolics with other women (mild stuff). Although she never turns down a pretty face, Althea is Larry's woman ultimately, and rather sweetly is shown to love, rather than just fancy, him.

Pepi, Luci, Bom (Pepi, Luci, Bom and the Other Girls) 1980

Director: Pedro Almodóvar. Country: Spain. Screenplay: Pedro Almodóvar. Production company: Cinearte. Duration: 77 mins, colour, subtitled

Cast: Carmen Maura (Pepi), Eva Siva (Luci), Olvido 'Alaska' Gara (Bom), Félix Rotaeta (Policeman), Diego Alvarez (Little Boy)

Pepi plans to sell her virginity, until one day a policeman takes it as a reward for

not arresting her. Discovering the policeman's wife, Luci, is a secret masochist, Pepi entices her away and into the arms of Bom, lead singer with the local punk band. Bom's first encounter with Luci, the dowdy housewife, leads to a golden shower, after which Luci is enamoured. The three women seem very happy. But the cop wants his wife back . . .

Almodóvar's first feature gives a clear insight into the interests and obsessions that dominate his later films. Transvestism, drugs and beatings are just part of everyday life for his motley group of characters. Lesbianism is simply another aspect of human interaction as far as Almodóvar is concerned, although his desire to shock some of his audience is never far away either and therefore it's all a bit disgusting. Thus there are no kisses, just the sight of one woman pissing on another. That's love in Pedro's book.

See also: **KIKA** by the same director.

Pepi, Luci, Bom and the Other Girls: see under **PEPI, LUCI, BOM**

Performance 1970

Director: Donald Cammell and Nicolas Roeg. Country: GB. Screenplay: Donald Cammell. Production company: Warner Brothers. Duration: 101 mins, colour

Cast: James Fox (Chas), Mick Jagger (Turner), Anita Pallenberg (Pherber), Michèle Breton (Lucy)

Gangland London in the 1960s. Chas heads a particularly vicious gang who commit a murder, forcing him to lie low for a while in a Notting Hill flat. There he meets the faded/jaded pop star Turner, who is whiling away his time with two young women in drug-induced reflection.

Roeg and Cammell's ultimately successful and controversial film remained on the shelves for two years after production following a twenty-minute cut by Warner Brothers. It eventually emerged in 1970 and revealed an unglamorous 1960s London, seedy, violent and unforgiving. The film itself is an exceedingly interesting blend of sex, drugs and rock 'n' roll. James Fox is marvellous as the deceptively sadistic wide boy, and Mick Jagger exploits his androgyny to the full as the sexually 'up for anything' rock god. Power games begin and slowly sexuality and gender roles begin to blur. The lesbian bit, such as it is, comes together in the latter stages of the film and is implied rather than explicit. In a house where everyone is sleeping with everyone else you just know the women are at it too, although, of course, men are the main focus of both of their attentions.

Persona (Masks)   1966

Director: Ingmar Bergman. Country: Sweden. Screenplay: Ingmar Bergman. Production company: Svensk Filmindustri. Duration: 81 mins, black and white

Cast: Liv Ullmann (Elizabeth Vogler), Bibi Andersson (Nurse Alma), Margaretha Krook (Woman Doctor), Gunnar Björnstrand (Mr Vogler), Jörgen Lindström (The Boy)

Elizabeth is an actress who, in the middle of a performance on stage, is no longer able (or willing?) to speak. She is taken to a clinic and subsequently to a deserted island, accompanied by Nurse Alma. Although their communication is without words, the two women gradually appear to assimilate and merge into each other.

This strange tale of disturbed and disturbing minds finds an expression halfway between love and hate. Nurse Alma, being of sound mind, appears at first to be the superior of the two – she is, after all, the medical one, and may hold Elizabeth's recovery in her hands. Her breezy personality means that she is able to chatter on by herself. Gradually, she begins to fill the silence with revealing secrets about her life and feelings. At first these revelations are happily given, for the silence allows Alma to believe that Elizabeth is receiving them with wise benevolence. But very soon the nurse can stand the lack of reaction to any of her conversation no longer – she demands response, and in her need she reveals her weakness. So it is Elizabeth who has true power, even within her mental breakdown, for it is she who is contained.

The film includes a scene in which the women appear to be on the verge of making love together, though this might easily be an illusion. Perhaps it is truer to say that as one personality disintegrates and merges with the other, so the bodies of the two might merge also. Interesting and significant.

See also: **THE SILENCE** by the same director.

Personal Best 1982

Director: Robert Towne. Country: US. Screenplay: Robert Towne. Production company: Geffen Company/Warner Brothers. Duration: 127 mins, colour

Cast: Mariel Hemingway (Chris Cahill), Scott Glen (Terry), Patrice Donnelly (Tori), Kenny Moore (Denny)

Female jocks sweat it out against the backdrop of the 1976 Olympic trials. Athletes Chris and Tori find themselves attracted to each other and begin a relationship. As time passes their mutual coach pits them against each other on the track and their love begins to falter.

Produced today, *Personal Best* might be laughed off the screen for being simultaneously coy and exploitative, but back in 1982, this film was an advancement of sorts for lesbians in the mainstream, although it falls apart just when it ought to be at its strongest.

Personal Best failed miserably at the box office, partly due to marketing confusion. Both the director (Robert Towne) and lead actress (Hemingway) denied that the film was about or for lesbians, presumably anxious not to alienate the potential straight audience. However, heterosexuals weren't fooled and didn't bother to go, and the lesbian audience stayed away too.

As a film about female athletes *Personal Best* is a success. The film is very textural – feel that sweat! – and the detailing of training preparation for events is interesting and well captured. Tori is a tough sporting jock. With her short black hair and assertive attitude she is clearly characterized as the 'real' lesbian. Chris, in contrast, is a blond girl/woman who needs help and guidance. She had a domineering father and in terms of her athletic performance she is a bit of a choker. The two women get together over a couple of joints and an arm-wrestling game! We have the benefit of a gentle kiss and a post-coital sex scene bathed in golden light. Later we see the woman training together, which involves lots of slow-motion running on beaches etc. They are seen to enjoy each other's company and this is probably the greatest strength of the film.

We are also given to understand that Tori and Chris are together for three years before any problems emerge, and that this relationship is accepted by other team members with no comment. Just when you believe the film is going to deliver for lesbians as well as everyone else, the plot suddenly lurches towards familiar territory along the lines of 'the blond one isn't really a lesbian, she's just experimenting/suffering arrested development, etc., but don't worry, we're going to straighten her out'.

Before you know it, Chris rather incredibly believes that Tori would deliberately try to injure her during a training session in order to prevent her competing. Suddenly, she finds a nice young man and realizes she is as straight as a die. Her new man, Denny, manfully tells her that he doesn't care about the rumours regarding her and Tori and that he will believe whatever she tells him. She says there is 'nothing to tell'. Three years ...

By the end of the movie, Tori and Chris have reconciled their friendship (nothing more) and Tori is, at least, allowed to be the sort of lesbian we can admire and who doesn't throw herself off a cliff in shame.

As a celebration of female athletes there isn't much around to rival *Personal Best*, but it constantly teeters on the brink of exploitation, with the endless close-ups and crotch-shots. Aimed at boys? You know it.

Phantom Ladies over Paris: see under CÉLINE AND JULIE GO BOATING

Picnic at Hanging Rock 1975

Director: Peter Weir. Country: Australia. Screenplay: Cliff Green (based on the novel by Joan Lindsay). Production company: Picnic Productions. Duration: 115 mins, colour

Cast: Rachel Roberts (Mrs Appleyard), Dominic Guard (Michael Fitzhubert), Helen Morse (Dianne de Portiers), Jacki Weaver (Minnie), Vivean Gray (Miss McCraw), Kirsty Child (Dora Lumley), Anne Lambert (Miranda)

On Valentine's Day in 1900, the girls of Appleyard Academy are taken to a beauty spot for a picnic. Amid the languorous heat of the afternoon, three girls and a teacher set off to explore the rock. Some of them never return ...

Deeply atmospheric film given exceptional resonance by an artful visual eye for beautiful, haunting images, and a strange lonely score echoing the emptiness of the Australian landscape. Based on a true story, the outcome of which was never resolved, Weir's film takes us on a journey of speculation. Unfortunately, as we can never know what truly happened, we are in a state of tension throughout and beyond the end of the story. Supremely confident performances from all concerned, including the estimable Rachel Roberts, give a substance to this wonderful dreamlike film.

Schoolgirl passions, of which there are several, are given an unearthly spirituality when it comes to the sublime Miranda, whom everyone loves (and of whom the much-loved teacher Mlle de Portiers herself remarks, 'She is like a Botticelli angel'). For it is Miranda who leads the trio to their presumed deaths, with a graceful inevitability that suggests premonition. Even before the girls set off for the trip Miranda tells her most passionate admirer, 'You must find someone else to love.'

It is the loss of Miranda particularly which becomes the focus for the film as far as a lesbian viewer is concerned (although the young man – Michael – who searches for the girls is besotted by another). Also of note is the likely sexuality of the teacher who disappears, Miss McCraw, the source of so much 'masculine integrity' according to the forbidding and rather butch headmistress Miss Appleyard. Beautiful, sensuous and deeply puzzling.

Note: Rachel Roberts plays another rather stern character in *Murder on the Orient Express* (1974). As Hildegarde Schmidt, Teutonic lady's maid/cook, she tells Hercule Poirot that she was 'deep friends' with Paulette, an unseen character.

See also: **BILITIS, THE GETTING OF WISDOM, MAIDENS IN UNIFORM, OLIVIA** and **SECRET PLACES** for more schoolgirl crushes.

Pink Flamingoes 1972

Director: John Waters. Country: US. Screenplay: John Waters. Production company: Dreamland Productions. Duration: 95 mins, colour

Cast: Divine (Babs Divine), David Lochary (Raymond Marble), Mary Vivian Pearce (Cotton), Mink Stole (Connie Marble), Danny Mills (Crackers)

A tabloid newspaper story forces Babs Divine, known as the 'filthiest person alive', to go into hiding. Meanwhile, Connie and Raymond Marble want the title for themselves and set about improving on Divine's record. They kidnap girls, have them impregnated by their fertile butler, and once the babies are born, sell the children to lesbian couples. The money finances an inter-city heroin ring catering to elementary school pupils.

The grotesque surreal world of John Waters once more explores his favourite themes of bad taste and disgusting personal habits. Using a hand-held camera, the production values of a home movie and ridiculous overacting from his little ensemble, Waters assaults the audience with as much awfulness as he can cram into one movie. The lesbian bit is only a tiny part of the general mélange: a couple (butch and femme) turn up at the agency to collect a baby. They seem to be by far the most balanced people around and as such make a quick exit from the picture. If lesbianism were not disgusting to Middle America, it wouldn't be in the film.

See also: **DESPERATE LIVING** by the same director.

Pit of Darkness: see under OLIVIA

The Pleasure Principle   1991

Director: David Cohen. Country: GB. Screenplay: David Cohen. Production company: Psychology News. Duration: 97 mins, colour

Cast: Peter Firth (Dick), Lynsey Baxter (Sammy), Haydn Gwynne (Judith), Lysette Anthony (Charlotte), Sara Mair-Thomas (Anne)

Dick has three women on the go, not including his ex-wife, who left him for another woman. As he faithlessly flits from one to the other he struggles to commit to one but finds he cannot resist the others. Eventually his lies and deceit catch up with him.

Low-budget drama in which Peter Firth is cast as 'Everyman', a regular, well-meaning guy whose only fault is that his namesake rules his life. The women he is involved with are not a sympathetic bunch, except for Sammy who is 'nice', a bit drippy and therefore most likely to get her man in the end.

Dick's ex-wife has the lesbian role. We see her with her girlfriend once (she does not speak and therefore makes no impression). We learn that Anne left the marriage when she discovered that she was gay, although she is not completely convinced by her own choice. Her lesbianism is twinned with her feminism (a warning to all husbands), which, in turn, is portrayed as rather tiresome. However, her ability to raise children is not questioned, her lesbianism is not an issue *per se*, and she is seen as a good, if a little stern, friend to her former husband. Passes the time.

Poison Ivy 1992

Director: Katt Shea Ruben. Country: US. Screenplay: Andy Ruben and Katt Shea Ruben. Production company: New Line Cinema. Duration: 89 mins, colour

Cast: Sara Gilbert (Sylvie Cooper), Drew Barrymore (Ivy), Tom Skerritt (Darryl Cooper), Cheryl Ladd (Georgie Cooper)

'I guess she's sort of beautiful . . . I don't know . . . those lips . . . you know lips are supposed to be a perfect reflection of another part of a woman's anatomy . . . not that I'm a lesbian, well, maybe I am . . . no, definitely not . . . I told my mother I was just for shock value . . . she said fine just so long as you don't smoke.' So begins Poison Ivy, in which Sylvie Cooper —'Coop'— tells us about a beautiful young woman she befriends and takes to live in the family home. The move is initially a success, and the whole family enjoy having Ivy around. However, it is clear that Ivy is dazzled by the wealth around her and sets her sights on becoming a replacement for Coop's mother, by whatever means necessary . . .

Drew Barrymore is unnervingly convincing as the manipulative 'poison' Ivy who insinuates herself into the Cooper household by providing each family member with the thing they most need. In Coop's case it is a friend, a close friend. Somehow, Ivy knows what Coop really wants, even before she knows it herself. Meanwhile, Ivy is giving the full works to Dad who hasn't had sex for some time because of his wife's long-term illness. The heterosexual sex is relatively graphic, with lingering shots of Ms Barrymore's body. Just a small kiss gets things going for the girls, though, and God knows that's all a lesbian needs to sustain her through an entire teenage crush.

Coop is played by Sara Gilbert, best known to British audiences as *Roseanne*'s fabulously smartass daughter Darlene in the long-running sitcom. Here she is the lonely teenager, alternately attracted to and confused by her new friend. Ivy keeps her on a string long enough to inflict considerable damage on the family, while all the time appearing sweet and innocent.

Ivy is, of course, a bad lot and has to go. Her going is preceded by an extraordinary scene in which Coop, recovering from a head injury, imagines that her (dead) mother has appeared in front of her. For the first time in her life Coop is able to tell her mother that she loves her. In a shocking moment Coop's mother steps forward and the two kiss, deeply. Coop suddenly 'comes to' and realizes she is kissing Ivy. She pulls away in horror! Incredibly perverse and probably enough to turn

Coop heterosexual or at least put her into therapy for the rest of her life. Great fun.

See also: **BOYS ON THE SIDE** for Drew in straight mode.

Preaching to the Perverted   1997

Director: Stuart Urban. Country: GB. Screenplay: Stuart Urban. Production company: Cyclops Vision. Duration: 99 mins, colour

Cast: Guinevere Turner (Tanya Cheex), Christien Anholt (Peter Emery), Tom Bell (Henry Harding MP), Julie Graham (Eugenie), Julian Wadham (M'Learned Friend), Georgina Hale (Miss Wilderspin), Ricky Tomlinson (Fibbin' Gibbins)

In order to secure his job with publicity-seeking Henry Harding MP, young Peter Emery (Christian, IT expert, virgin) agrees to infiltrate the House of Thwax fetish club to gain evidence for a prosecution. Once there he finds himself involved in a number of sinful practices at the hands of dominatrix Tanya Cheex. Will he keep to his mission, or will he find a new vocation in life?

Awful British sex 'shocker' designed to have you cheering in the aisles as the tight-assed holier-than-thou brigade are trounced by the harmless purveyors of very personal services. Revealing the hypocrisy of our elders and betters, especially over issues such as sex, is practically a national pastime, but you would be hard-pushed to enjoy this turgid (and strangely coy) exposé of the hidden world of the S&M scene. It's all been done before, many times over, but never quite as tediously as this.

The lesbian bit is all part of the general mêlée; Eugenie is in love with 'Mistress' Cheex, who occasionally indulges her but is equally at home with boys. The line that leather-clad Tanya draws is that no one is allowed to penetrate her ... Once pretty Peter is on the scene you just know what's going to happen. So does Eugenie, and she gets into a heated strop about it all. There's polymorphous sexuality all over the place, expressed in a variety of ways (except the dreaded vanilla, of course).

Lovely Guinevere Turner (writer and lead actress in **GO FISH**) – looking for all the world like Vivien Leigh – plays Tanya Cheex with as much character as the script will allow. If you are a fan of Guin's, or into leather, or S&M (or all three), you might be mildly diverted for a while. But don't bet on it.

See also: **GO FISH** and **THE WATERMELON WOMAN** for more Guin.

Le Prede Umane: see under **CAGED WOMEN**

Primary Colors 1998

Director: Mike Nichols. Country: US. Screenplay: Elaine May (based on the novel by Anonymous [Joe Klein]). Production company: Universal Pictures. Duration: 143 mins, colour

Cast: John Travolta (Jack Stanton), Emma Thompson (Susan Stanton), Billy Bob Thornton (Richard Jemmons), Adrian Lester (Henry Burton), Maura Tierney (Daisy), Paul Guilfoyle (Howard Ferguson), Kathy Bates (Libby Holden)

Governor Jack Stanton is aiming to be President of the United States. Stanton is as ambitious as his rivals, but he is basically a good man who seems to have genuine feeling for the people he wants to represent. His weakness is his womanizing ways, which force his team of campaign managers to make increasingly difficult decisions to protect him from discovery. Young idealist Henry Burton must decide if he can continue to compromise his personal morality for the sake of his man.

Very enjoyable comedy in which the real-life tribulations of a certain President and First Lady are given a fictitious airing via the characterizations of Jack and Susan Stanton. The acting is fabulous, both John Travolta and Emma Thompson are terrific, and the support is exceptional.

The lesbian character is Libby Holden, friend of the Stantons since college and supremo journalist, who is hauled on board to bring know-how to the burgeoning campaign. Exceptionally bright, foul-mouthed, slightly unstable and cynical yet visionary, Libby storms into the campaign office declaring the terms under which she will work. One of her conditions is that another office worker – whom she spots through the office window – will be her assistant. 'The one that looks like Winona Ryder. I want her,' she declares.

What Libby wants, Libby gets, it would seem. A couple of scenes later we see the young woman firmly ensconced in her new home, preparing breakfast for Libby and herself, having clearly spent the night. Which is all rather puzzling. Has the young woman been dispatched by the Stanton campaign camp to please Libby, or did it begin as a working relationship which became something more under Libby's irresistible charm? It's really not clear at all, which, oddly, makes it strangely refreshing.

Marvellous Kathy Bates enjoys this pivotal supporting role thoroughly, bullishly stampeding her way through corruption and male egos in equal measures.

See also: **DIABOLIQUE** and **FRIED GREEN TOMATOES AT THE WHISTLE STOP CAFÉ** for more Kathy (straight roles both). **SILKWOOD** is by the same director.

A Prisão: see under **BARE BEHIND BARS**

Private Benjamin 1980

Director: Howard Zieff. Country: US. Screenplay: Nancy Meyers, Charles Shyer and Harvey Miller. Production company: Warner Brothers. Duration: 110 mins, colour

Cast: Goldie Hawn (Judy Benjamin), Eileen Brennan (Captain Doreen Lewis), Armand Assante (Henri), Robert Webber (Thornbush)

American Jewish Princess Judy Benjamin's husband drops dead on their wedding night. In the confusion that follows, Judy finds she has enlisted in the army.

Popular Goldie Hawn comedy in which our heroine discovers that life in the army can be even more complicated than life outside. Lesbianism is not top of the agenda in this film but it surfaces obliquely now and again. Judy's parents tell friends that she is in a mental hospital following a collapse, to avoid explaining that she's 'living in an army barracks in Mississippi with a bunch of...' 'What?' asks Judy. 'I don't know what,' comes the reply.

But the main lesbian bit is in the form of Judy's nemesis, Captain Lewis (played by the excellent Eileen Brennan). When we first see her she is soppy over men (she is dating a male officer). Later in the film she keeps company with Helga, who is now her constant companion. Brennan is viewed as halfway good at her job, but this being a comedy and she being a figure of authority, she also becomes a figure of fun. She is characterized as devoted to the army and knowing procedure inside out, but she lacks judgement and is prone to emotional outbursts. Thus her attempts to thwart Judy and make an example of her are doomed to fail. Lesbian character as uptight, vindictive and increasingly idiotic. Amusing film, though.

Purely Legal Matter: see under **A QUESTION OF LOVE**

Pussycat: see under **FASTER, PUSSYCAT, KILL! KILL!**

Queen Christina   1933

Director: Rouben Mamoulian. Country: US. Screenplay: Salka Viertel, H. M. Harwood and S. N. Behrman. Production company: MGM. Duration: 100 mins, black and white

Cast: Greta Garbo (Queen Christina), John Gilbert (Don Antonio de la Prada), Ian Keith (Magnus), Lewis Stone (Chancellor Oxenstierna), Elizabeth Young (Ebba)

In the seventeenth century the Queen of Sweden is required to marry for both social and political reasons. During a trip away from the palace she falls for the wrong man, the Spanish Ambassador.

Hollywood treatment of the real-life Swedish Queen who would not marry. In reality she declined because she was lesbian, but in this version it's because she cannot have the man she wants. Hollywood has transformed a woman who was allegedly quite a challenge to be around (apparently she smelt rancid) and turned her into Greta Garbo at her absolute peak. Perhaps a rare example of a film making a lesbian more attractive rather than less.

Christina is a woman who has not compromised herself by conforming to female standards of dress and behaviour. In true tomboy style, she dresses in male attire, is athletic, businesslike and pragmatic. Ebba is her feminine maid/companion whom she greets with kisses on the lips and hands. Unfortunately, behind Christina's back, Ebba reveals herself to be a two-faced little straight girl who is more afraid of the Queen than enamoured of her. Nevertheless, their exchange of affection renders *Queen Christina* one of the most important early films for a lesbian audience. Her pronouncement, early on, that she will 'die a bachelor' underlines this, although it appears to be there initially as a plot device. In other words, the idea is she will be proved wrong when the film is heterosexualized a little later. But no! The subversive script, written by Salka Viertel, a woman with whom Garbo was allegedly having an affair at the time, does not disappoint.

In an interesting overnight-at-the-inn scene, charming Spaniard John Gilbert is under the impression that Christina is male. Before you can say cross-dressing comedy, we are witnessing interactions that will be copied on screen for the next hundred years. Naturally, a female serving wench also mistakes Christina for a man and makes a pass at her. Later Christina has to share a room with John Gilbert and undress in his presence, while concealing the truth from him.

By the end of the film Christina has given up her Hollywood love (John Gilbert) and everyone else, it would seem, for the sake of Her Country. After her final embrace with Ebba she exclaims out loud, 'Goodbye Sweden' (although this could be 'Goodbye Sweetie!'). It's classic stuff.

Although Garbo had many screen roles, this is the one for which she has been most remembered, particularly by lesbians. Her status as a lesbian icon also has roots outside her portrayal of Christina, and during the 1930s and 1940s people speculated wildly about her secretive private life. The media perceived the truth by and large but only dared to hint at what was going on. Garbo's string of female lovers were never named and her smokescreen short-lived affair with John Gilbert was supported by a knowing press. The truth has yet to come out properly, but the insider knowledge of Garbo's real-life preferences makes *Queen Christina* an enjoyable treat.

See also: **JUST ONE OF THE GUYS, MOROCCO, ORLANDO, SWITCH** and **YENTL** for more cross-dressing, gender-bending capers.

A Question of Love (Purely Legal Matter) 1978

Director: Jerry Thorpe. Country: US. Screenplay: William Blinn. Production company: Blinn-Thorpe Productions/Viacom. Duration: 104 mins, colour

Cast: Gena Rowlands (Linda-Rae), Jane Alexander (Barbara), Bonnie Bedelia, Ned Beatty

Linda-Rae is a nurse. She and her two sons move in with Barbara. Barbara's ex-husband Mike serves papers to sue for custody of her young son.

Based on a true story, this touching made-for-TV drama is a solid piece of pleading aimed squarely at an ignorant public. Young Billy wants to stay with his moms, but a prejudiced legal system believes it knows best. Gena Rowlands and Jane Alexander are absolutely terrific as the two women fighting a losing battle on every front. The film goes to great lengths to emphasize the women's ordinariness: they are working class, they have no money and are easily intimidated by authority. While Barbara's husband trumps up the charges with allegations of wild parties etc., the women get no help from anyone, including psychiatrists, who regard the cause as 'unpopular'. In court, the prosecutor cleverly asserts that homosexuality is of itself unnatural, so that even the most commonplace event (such as asking for a date) might 'occur in a perverse way'. Despite the husband's considerable flaws, there is really no contest and the decision goes in his favour. Heartbreakingly true to life.

See also: **LIANNA** and **LOSING CHASE** for more lesbian mothers.

Rachel, Rachel (Now I Lay Me Down; Jest of God)   1968

Director: Paul Newman. Country: US. Screenplay: Stewart Stern (based on the novel *A Jest of God* by Margaret Laurence). Production company: Kayos Productions. Duration: 101 mins, colour

Cast: Joanne Woodward (Rachel Cameron), Estelle Parsons (Calla Mackie), James Olson (Nick Kazlik), Kate Harrington (Mrs Cameron), Bernard Barrow (Leighton Siddley)

Rachel is in the 'exact middle' of her life. A teacher in a small town, she is a repressed woman who has only ever been careful and ordinary. Leading a life of dull worthiness, she takes care of her dominating mother, but she is desperate to experience love. One day Nick, an old school friend, comes into town . . .

Paul Newman's directorial debut is a beautifully realized portrait of a woman whose life, in many ways, has yet to begin. Surrounded by death as a child (her father was an undertaker), Rachel has never moved house and never travelled. Most of what life can offer has passed her by. Her mother treats her as if she was still a teenager. Rachel (Joanne Woodward, superb as ever) dreams of what she would do if she had the nerve.

The lesbian character is Calla, played by Estelle Parsons. She is another teacher, a born-again Christian who is secretly in love with Rachel and who makes a clumsy pass at her after a church service (which is not reciprocated). Calla is a good sort, dowdy but with a heart of gold. She is as lonely as Rachel but faces an even emptier future. By the end of the film the two are reconciled. Rachel, remarkably, says to Calla in a touching exchange, 'I wish I could have been different for you.' 'Not to worry. I'll survive,' replies Calla, displaying immense personal dignity. She is dealt with sympathetically and can be viewed as a sad, tragic, but heroic type. Therefore, although by no means ideal, Calla was a new cinema lesbian for the time and the audience was expected to be understanding.

The Rainbow 1988

Director: Ken Russell. Country: GB. Screenplay: Ken Russell and Vivian Russell. Production company: Vestron Pictures. Duration: 106 mins, colour

Cast: Sammi Davis (Ursula Brangwen), Paul McGann (Anton Skrebensky), Amanda Donohoe (Winifred Inger), Christopher Gable (Will Brangwen), David Hemmings (Uncle Henry), Glenda Jackson (Anna Brangwen)

Ursula searches for the spiritual and earthly meaning of life within her Midlands home town.

In the same year as he made **THE LAIR OF THE WHITE WORM**, Ken Russell put together this adaptation of D. H. Lawrence's classic novel. Featuring two of the same actresses (Sammi Davis and Amanda Donohoe), the film traces the social and sexual development of intense young woman Ursula Brangwen via a number of romantic attachments. The lesbian interlude is significant enough (although transient naturally).

Sammi Davis is very good as the wide-eyed young woman, interested in all life has to offer. Amanda Donohoe, however, is really far too knowing and modern to be a turn-of-the-century teacher! From the moment she meets Ursula, Winifred goes straight for her. In the swimming pool she gives her particular (physical) attention before she even knows her name. A true predator and too forward by half... Her seduction of Ursula occurs without hesitation. In fact, neither she nor Ursula experiences a moment's doubt about their actions. This kind of sexual confidence is enjoyable to watch, but it is doubtful in its veracity. Maybe things should have happened like that, but in real life they surely did not...

See also: **THE LAIR OF THE WHITE WORM**, by the same director, in which Amanda Donohoe vamps it up with boys and girls.

Rebecca   1940

Director: Alfred Hitchcock. Country: US. Screenplay: Robert E. Sherwood and Joan Harrison (based on the novel by Daphne du Maurier). Production company: David Selznick Productions. Duration: 130 mins, black and white

Cast: Laurence Olivier (Maxim), Joan Fontaine (Narrator), George Sanders (Jack Favell), Judith Anderson (Mrs Danvers), Leo G. Carroll (Dr Baker), Florence Bates (Mrs Van Hopper)

A young woman accompanies rich snob Mrs Van Hopper on her travels around the world. While in Monte Carlo she meets the rich and dashing Maxim De Winter. The two fall in love, marry and return to England to the family estate of Manderley. But no one, including Maxim, seems able to forget Rebecca, the first Mrs De Winter, who died in a mysterious boating accident.

'Last night I dreamed I went to Manderley again.' So begins *Rebecca*, a thriller of the highest order, Hitchcock's first for Hollywood and winner of the Best Film Oscar for 1940. It is within the brooding magnificence of the Manderley estate that Joan Fontaine, scared and overwhelmed, is terrorized by the hard and unforgiving housekeeper Mrs Danvers.

'Danny's' devotion to the first Mrs De Winter means that she will never welcome the childlike (unnamed) heroine into the house. Instead, she contrives to control her by reminding her that she cannot hope to match the sophistication and beauty of Rebecca. In one memorable scene, Mrs Danvers shows the new wife around the dead woman's bedroom, holding items of underclothing close to her face and pointing out the transparency of her nightwear. Mrs Danvers is an archetypal screen lesbian – brutal, slightly unhinged, and nursing perverse, unrealized desires for a dead woman whom she continues to love beyond the grave. However, nothing to fear: truth, justice and heterosexuality will prevail.

Note: Judith Anderson was apparently lesbian in real life, although she never came out publicly. Her real-life antipathy towards Joan Fontaine was occasionally noted, however. Recently, it has been suggested that Daphne du Maurier was herself lesbian.

Red Sonja 1985

Director: Richard Fleischer. Country: US. Screenplay: Clive Exton and George MacDonald Fraser. Production company: Dino de Laurentiis Corporation. Duration: 89 mins, colour

Cast: Brigitte Nielsen (Red Sonja), Arnold Schwarzenegger (Kalidor), Sandahl Bergman (Queen Gedren), Paul Smith (Falkon), Ernie Rayes, Jr (Prince Tarn), Ronald Lacey (Ikol), Pat Roach (Brytag)

Queen Gedren wants to rule the land and imprisons her enemies in a pit, the key to which is a special talisman. The talisman can only be touched by women.

Hilarious 'medieval legend' story in which Brigitte Nielson plays Red Sonja, fighter warrior. She decides that her mission is to overcome the Queen, who just happens to be a true lesbian – mad, bad and dangerous to know. Gedren has a soft spot for Sonja but Sonja rejects her advances. The Queen is not pleased to be refused, and in anger kills Sonja's parents, thus proving she wasn't a good bet relationship-wise. Sonja begins a quest for revenge.

For some reason Sonja has an aversion to men, which is noted by one of her tutors. 'Hatred of men in a lovely young woman ... it could be your downfall.' Well, possibly. Anyway, Sonja decides that she will only give herself to a man who can beat her in a fair sword fight (she seems fairly certain this won't happen). Enter Arnie, so to speak, who gives her a sword fighting seeing-to.

Back at the plot, Sonja finds the Queen and they have a final stand off. 'We could have ruled the world together,' Gedren tells Sonja just before they have a great sword fight and most of the country apparently suffers an earthquake.

See also: **CHAINED HEAT II** for more Brigitte, and **THE BOSTON STRANGLER** by the same director.

Rescuing Desire 1996

Director: Adam Rogers. Country: US. Screenplay: Catherine May Levin. Production company: Pilgrims 4 Corporation. Duration: 115 mins, colour

Cast: Melinda Mullins (Toni), Tamara Tunie (Van), Caitlin Dulany (Evonne), Bruce Atman (Ralph), Barton Heyman (Willard)

Toni's life seems straightforward. As a nurse she is outstanding, and is about to be married. Then she decides she might be a lesbian.

'A gay romantic comedy. Get Engaged, Get Married, Have Children. She never realized there was another choice.' So says the poster, above an airbrushed picture of two women dancing, one in jeans and a shapeless T-shirt, the other looking like an extra from **SHOWGIRLS**. So what is going on? Not much, unfortunately. Toni realizes that marriage is not for her, although she doesn't know quite what is.

Just-out young lesbians will enjoy this bewildering comedy the most, as Toni capers about investigating the lesbian scene while trying not to jeopardize her career.

In keeping with society's expectations of lesbians generally, once Toni decides she might be gay her IQ drops dramatically, she begins to dress soft butch, and she goes off to a club helpfully named Dykes Way. Actually, this bar scene is quite good. It's crowded, with an interesting mix of people. A world away from **LIANNA** or even **BAR GIRLS** (where there only ever seemed to be ten people out on a Friday night). Lea De Laria cameos as a formidable stone butch.

Some strange adventures later Toni decides she fancies Evonne, who turns out to be a stripper. She visits a sex shop and buys a dildo and long black fisting gloves (and she hasn't gotten laid yet). That's preparation for you.

See also: **THE FIRST WIVES CLUB** for more Lea.

Roma, Città Aperta: see under OPEN CITY

Rome, Open City: see under OPEN CITY

The Rose   1979

Director: Mark Rydell. Country: US. Screenplay: Bill Kerby and Bo Goldman. Production company: Twentieth Century Fox. Duration: 134 mins, colour

Cast: Bette Midler (Rose), Alan Bates (Rudge), Frederic Forrest (Houston Dyer), Harry Dean Stanton (Billy Ray).

Story loosely based on the life of Janis Joplin.

Bette Midler's first starring role is an over-the-top affair, although Midler herself is sensational in the role of the rock star with an action-filled private life. Charting her rise to fame and her rather sudden departure, *The Rose* is a musical biopic with a coy sentimentality at its core.

The lesbian bit is kept to a minimum, considering this is a thinly disguised portrait of Janis Joplin. A long-lost friend turns up to see Rose. Their embrace suggests more than a platonic relationship and Rose's boyfriend looks slightly awkward, but within seconds the friend is expressing envy rather than love for Rose, and a moment later she has left the film for ever. It would be a mistake to expect too much, though, this is the director who gave us one of the most homophobic films of all time, **THE FOX**.

See also: **THE FOX** by the same director.

Le Rouge aux Lèvres: see under DAUGHTERS OF DARKNESS
Salmonberries   1991

Director: Percy Adlon. Country: US and Germany. Screenplay: Percy Adlon and Felix Adlon. Production company: PeleMele Film. Duration: 94 mins, colour

Cast: kd lang (Kotzebue), Rosel Zech (Roswitha), Chuck Connors (Bingo Chuck)

Kotzebue, a lonely androgynous woman, leads a tough life in a remote Alaskan town. She becomes infatuated with the local librarian Roswitha, an attractive older woman, who initially mistakes Kotz for an aggressive boy. Kotzebue is a tormented soul in search of her past and wants the resistant librarian to help her find it. It transpires that Roswitha too has old ghosts to find and lay to rest.

Percy Adlon's drama, mostly narrative but punctuated with little surreal scenes, was written especially for kd lang, she of the extraordinary voice and, lately, lesbian icon. Interestingly, kd had not come out when the film was made (although everybody *knew*), so this tantalizing foray into lesbian infatuation was perhaps rather unexpected.

Kotzebue is a sad creature who frequently behaves like the foundling she is, as if barely touched by civilization. She is unable to communicate very well verbally, and expresses herself largely through tangible gestures. As a sign of her burgeoning love for the librarian she brings Roswitha an enormous fish. In return Kotz is offered some berries – Roswitha seems to have a million of them bottled and stored in a room filled with golden light. This exchange of gifts gets things going a little as our heroine tries to endear the frosty older woman to

SALMONBERRIES

Snowgirl: kd lang stars in *Salmonberries*. Courtesy of Electric Pictures.

her. Kotzebue's persistence and earnestness gradually wear her down and the two begin to reach a weary understanding.

As far as the lesbian element is concerned, *Salmonberries* is one big tease and provides us with one of those maddeningly frustrating 'nearly' scenes we've experienced so many times before, in which two women are close to some sort of consummation, and yet it doesn't quite happen. The scene is beautifully paced and Kotzebue's expressions of love are endearing and sweet, but Roswitha is straight and can only decline. Suddenly we're back where we have been in a hundred movies, wherein the lesbian character has fallen for the wrong woman and will not be fulfilled.

As far as the film itself is concerned, *Salmonberries* delivers in a most unexpected way. As the closing credits roll you may be surprised to reflect how densely packed the apparently slight story has been. The desolate beauty of the Alaskan wasteland is breathtaking. Rosel Zech, an experienced German actress who worked frequently for Fassbinder, is first-rate as Roswitha. kd lang, too, is rather good in her first screen role. The pudding-basin haircut may do little for kd's appearance, but this will put off her fans not one jot. There's a nude scene, brief and surprising. And as if all of that were not enough, she sings the haunting theme song, too.

The Satin Spider (L'Araignée de Satin)   1984

Director: Jacques Baratier. Country: France. Screenplay: Jacques Baratier (based on *Les Détraquées* by P. L. Palau). Production company: Baraka Productions. Duration: 79 mins, colour

Cast: Catherine Jourdan, Ingrid Caven, Alexander Sycluna, Michel Albertini, Daniel Mesguich

Solange, a former teacher at a select girls' school, has an obsession with silk. She is prepared to steal in order to get it, and after being arrested is the subject of psychiatric examination. She escapes and returns to her old school, perhaps to rekindle her special relationship with the headmistress.

Dreamlike experimental drama in which schoolgirls do little schoolwork, but seem engaged in life of flirting, dancing and discussions on sex, all under the gaze of the hypnotic headmistress. Solange, now a morphine addict, wanders through the film picking up her friend Lucienne on the way. The two discuss various experiences while Solange appears to be having some sort of mild existential crisis.

For all its introspection and analysis on the part of various characters, *The Satin Spider* does not reveal very much to the viewer. As far as lesbian content goes, there is of course a continuous undercurrent of Sapphic desire wherever you look, although the only fervent embraces occur between Solange and Lucienne. Unfortunately, this is while Lucienne is reliving an assault by a man she experienced on a train a few years before and which she admits to having enjoyed.

Pretty to look at and the perverse headmistress is worth an hour of anyone's time.

Score   1972

Director: Radley Metzger. Country: US and Yugoslavia. Screenplay: Jerry Douglas. Production company: Audubon Films. Duration: 89 mins, colour

Cast: Claire Wilbur (Elvira), Calvin Culver (Eddie), Lynn Lowry (Betsy), Gerald Grant (Jack), Carl Parker (Mike)

Sophisticated swingers Elvira and Jack live happily in gay – and straight – abandon, seducing whoever takes their fancy. They set their sights on a sweetly naive couple who live nearby . . .

Inasmuch as a very soft porn film can be truly wonderful, *Score* is up there with the best. It has everything you could ever hope for: a European setting (beautiful small town), the longest seduction on screen (it's the only thing the film is about after all), great camera angles (shots *through* wine glasses, reflections in mirrors, all that stuff) and hilarious dialogue (it's written that way, a proper comedy for modern types). But if that wasn't enough, the men wear beige slacks at all times (well, not *all* the time), Elvira sashays around sporting her diaphanous, flimsy dresses low and her hair high, high, high! Lynn Lowry twinkles about playing the innocent waiting for her lesbian predator to get the better of her (which she does of course, eventually). The sex is inventive – lots of dressing up and a variety of toys are involved in the proceedings. But clever photography means that the film always appears to be much more explicit than it is. Never a dull moment!

See also: **THERESE AND ISABELLE** by the same director.

Screaming Mimi 1958

Director: Gerd Oswald. Country: US. Screenplay: Robert Blees (based on the novel by Frederic Brown). Production company: Sage Productions. Duration: 71 mins, black and white

Cast: Anita Ekberg (Virginia Wilson), Phil Carey (Bill Sweeney), Gypsy Rose Lee (Joann Mapes), Harry Townes (Dr Greenwood), Linda Cherney (Ketti), Romney Brent (Charlie Wilson), Alan Gifford (Captain Bline)

Yolanda works at a strip club, El Madhouse, performing a fetishistic dance to the club regulars. One night a dancer is murdered. She is found clutching a figurine of a woman screaming. Shortly afterwards a 'Screaming Mimi' is delivered to Yolanda . . .

Very strange 1950s film, half thriller, half psychoanalytic drama. The very pneumatic Anita Ekberg plays the enigmatic Yolanda (or should that be Virginia?), a woman with a past and a diverting, 'classy' (if perverse) strip routine. Journalist Bill Sweeney tries to get to the bottom of things, but waters are very muddy down at El Madhouse, and indeed Yolanda seems her own worst enemy.

The lesbian in the film is the club's owner/manager, Joann Mapes. She's a likable character, wise-cracking, glamorous and sassy (although don't forget she is engaged in a dubious profession and is not meant to be admired). She is having a relationship with one of her female dancers. This fact is revealed when Bill comes to Joann's home to ask questions and finds the two women spending the afternoon together. Finally, the penny drops and he realizes he's interrupting. 'Sorry, girls, I didn't realize it was tea for two,' he says, and makes a sharp exit.

Scrubbers 1982

Director: Mai Zetterling. Country: GB. Screenplay: Roy Minton, Jeremy Watt and Mai Zetterling. Production company: Handmade Films. Duration: 93 mins, colour

Cast: Amanda York (Carol Howden), Chrissie Cotterill (Annetta Brady), Kate Ingram (Eddie), Imogen Bain (Sandy), Elizabeth Edmonds (Kathleen)

Petty criminals Carol and Annetta are caught by the police and sent to the borstal from which Carol has only recently been released. In her absence Carol's inmate girlfriend has found another lover and the two taunt her at every opportunity. Meanwhile, Annetta, a young mother desperate to see her child, blames Carol for their capture and determines to make her life hell.

Almost unwatchably grim British drama, deeply depressing on many levels, revealing life in a grimy, brutal prison. This may be a 'girls behind bars' film, but it is a million miles away from the better-known soft-core exploitation films of the genre. Uncompromising viciousness, both verbal and physical, are the order of the day, in which the warders are either too blind, too complicit or too uncaring to intervene. Lesbianism is rife, and as such is not an issue. The consequences of betrayal, whether towards a mate or a lover, are terrible, for this is a world where bullies rule and others cower in terror.

Zetterling's film captures its mood with a noisy, clanging resonance, though there are scenes of contemplation, too. Moments of kindness, particularly between Carol and her new admirer Eddie, are few and far between, however, and in the end *Scrubbers* may be too harrowing for some. Look out for a youthful Kathy Burke as one of the inmates.

Secret Ceremony   1968

Director: Joseph Losey. Country: GB. Screenplay: George Tabori (based on a short story by Marco Denevi). Production company: Universal Pictures. Duration: 109 mins, colour

Cast: Elizabeth Taylor (Leonora), Mia Farrow (Cenci), Robert Mitchum (Albert), Pamela Brown (Aunt Hilda), Peggy Ashcroft (Aunt Hanna)

Leonora, a middle-aged prostitute, is 'adopted' one day by a young, very rich, waif-like girl in need of a mother. With nothing better to do, Leonora willingly moves into the child-woman's mansion.

It's Extremely Strange Relationship time as Elizabeth Taylor and Mia Farrow act out increasingly bizarre rituals with each other in a lonely (but fabulous) house. Cenci, a very disturbed young thing, seems to half believe that Leonora is in fact her dead mother. Oddly, Cenci bears more than a passing resemblance to Leonora's daughter who drowned some years previously. On this rather unpromising, not to say distinctly unsettling, basis, the two engage in a series of mind games and it becomes increasingly unclear who is in control.

Of course, this is not a lesbian film at all, but there are undercurrents flowing about all over the place. A hair-brushing sequence, a back massage and a near-kiss are what we get, but why we get them remains a mystery. *Secret Ceremony* behaves like the intense psycho-drama that it is, inviting the viewer to guess how unhinged each character really is and what will happen to ensure that it all ends in tears.

See also: ZEE & CO, in which Elizabeth Taylor appears in another ambiguous role.

Secret Places   1984

Director: Zelda Barron. Country: GB. Screenplay: Zelda Barron. Production company: Skreba Films. Duration: 98 mins, colour

Cast: Marie-Therese Relin (Laura Meister), Tara MacGowran (Patience), Claudine Auger (Sophy Meister), Jenny Agutter (Miss Laurie), Cassie Stuart (Nina)

Laura arrives at an English boarding-school during World War II. She is 'from abroad', a beautiful, solemn girl whom the other girls speculate about endlessly. Patience, a popular girl who is idolized by younger pupils, becomes a friend to Laura.

When Laura arrives at the school, Patience is instantly taken. 'Patience is obviously going to have a pash on her' decide the others. Indeed, we are in the realm of the schoolgirl crush set against the dramatic backdrop of an unfolding war. A gentle tale, with a few harsh moments thrown in, as the girls do not always react positively to the refugee. As an observation of 1940s boarding-school life, the film is restrained and polite. The girls spend their time in the usual ways, smoking, gossiping, experimenting with sex and struggling with adolescence. But Laura herself is largely excluded from these adventures, and leads a difficult life at home.

There is a genuine potential for a loving relationship between the two girls which is stifled before it can be properly realized. Talk between the two girls of the 'have you ever been kissed' variety leads Laura to tell Patience that she has been kissed by a boy, a friend of her brother's. Rather more interestingly, she has also been kissed by her governess, who embraced her 'like a man would' while they were dancing. Patience is appalled and comments, 'There are women like that. I think they're often lonely.' She makes a hasty exit.

Later the two, predictably enough, fall out over a boy they are both keen on. However, once reconciled they dance together one evening, then get into bed and hold hands. Patience asks if Laura ever did this with her governess. Laura says no. Patience then asks if she thinks it's wrong. Laura says, rather amazingly, that all love is good, so if God forbids it, God must be wrong. With that they hug. And there it ends, Sapphically speaking, although there is more heartbreak on the way for the unfortunate Laura.

As sweet and innocent as the girls themselves.

See also: **BILITIS, THE GETTING OF WISDOM, MAIDENS IN UNIFORM, OLIVIA** and **PICNIC AT HANGING ROCK** for more schoolgirl crushes.

Seduction, the Cruel Woman   1985

Director: Monika Treut. Country: Germany. Screenplay: Elfi Mikesch and Monika Treut. Production company: Hyäne Filmproduktion. Duration: 84 mins, colour

Cast: Mechthild Grossmann (Wanda), Odo Kier (Gregor), Sheila McLaughlin (Justine), Carola Regnier (Caren), Peter Weibel (Herr Mahrsch)

Dominatrix Wanda is a businesswoman who stages sado-masochistic fantasies for select audiences in her 'gallery'. One of her cast, Gregor, is obsessed with Wanda, and resents the intrusion of an American woman, Justine, into their lives. Wanda, however, is conducting relationships with most of her cast and friends, and doesn't see why she should change.

Very daring for its time, *Seduction, the Cruel Woman* is a sophisticated examination of various sexual games and perversions, including S&M, bondage and humiliation. Gorgeous, classy costumes, minimalist surroundings and an intense performance from Mechthild Grossmann make this a highly stylized foray into a rarely seen world.

It would be a push to describe this as entertainment, however (although it does have one or two engaging moments). Really, this is a visual exploration of certain sexual taboos, observed via the liberating tool of performance art. When a journalist comes to interview Wanda, he becomes enthralled by the opportunity to act out his personal fantasy. He doesn't want to do it for her audience, though, he wants to play-act for real, so to speak, and it is this blurring of theatre and 'reality' that is of particular interest in *Seduction, the Cruel Woman*.

See also: **MY FATHER IS COMING** by the same director.

See Here My Love: see under ÉCOUTE VOIR

The Sentinel   1976

Director: Michael Winner. Country: US. Screenplay: Michael Winner and Jeffrey Konvitz. Production company: Universal Pictures. Duration: 92 mins, colour

Cast: Chris Sarandon (Michael Lerman), Cristina Raines (Alison Parker), Martin Balsam (Professor), John Carradine (Father Halliran)

New York model discovers that her rented flat is, in fact, the gateway to Hell.

Dreary horror flick with a stupendously unbelievable plot. This is Michael Winner territory, so the shock elements are full on, unsubtle and always link sex with evil. The presence of newcomers Jeff Goldblum, Christopher Walken and Tom Berenger in minor supporting roles just goes to show that some people will do anything when they're starting out. However, Winner must have used every ounce of his personal charm to persuade the galaxy of established stars to perform in this piece.

Sylvia Miles has the unlucky role of disgusting lesbian neighbour, with Beverley D'Angelo as her equally revolting girlfriend. Meeting them for the first time, Alison innocently enquires what they do for a living. 'We fondle each other,' replies Gerde, thrusting her hand down Sandra's bodysuit onto her breasts. (Why are they both wearing leotards and bodysuits? Perhaps it's standard uniform for lesbians from Hell.) The lesbians turn out to have been murderers in their previous lives (as do the other ghostly neighbours), and have a proclivity for human flesh which they have maintained from beyond the grave. Nearly hilarious, *The Sentinel* unfortunately takes itself far too seriously, which severely undermines the potential for camp sleaze. It was justifiably pilloried on release because Winner used people with disfigurements in the film's climactic scene to suggest overwhelming evil.

Serving in Silence: The Margarethe Cammermeyer Story 1994

Director: Jeff Bleckner. Country: US. Screenplay: Alison Cross. Production company: Barwood Films. Duration: 88 mins, colour

Cast: Glenn Close (Colonel Margarethe Cammermeyer), Judy Davis (Diane), Jan Rubes, Wendy Makkena, Susan Barnes, William Converse-Roberts

True story of Colonel Margarethe Cammermeyer, the highest-ranking officer ever to be discharged from the United States Army for 'immoral behaviour'.

After twenty-three years in the army Margarethe Cammermeyer, an army colonel already showered with honours and plaudits, decides she is going for the very top: she wants to be a general. In order to advance further she must obtain top secret clearance. During the security assessment she calmly tells the interviewer that she is a lesbian (rationalizing later to her partner Diane that the whole point of the assessment was to tell the truth).

The simple statement has a cataclysmic effect on her career and her personal life. Almost despite itself the army machine moves into court martial mode and Margarethe finds herself in the centre of a moral dilemma. Her colleagues and superiors are for the most part horrified that she should be in this position and Margarethe is given much verbal support. She is repeatedly given the opportunity to retract the statement in order to escape the trial, but ironically it is her personal moral principles that prevent her from recanting. Offered the option of retiring with honours, she decides, remarkably, to face the charges. Friends beg her to change her mind. As one fellow officer tells her, 'You could commit murder and have a better chance of staying in.'

This is a superb made-for-TV drama starring the brilliant Glenn Close, who gives another peerless performance, this time as a woman facing a searching test of character and belief. Close always manages to convey both intensity and depth, and here she communicates massive personal integrity too, while allowing Cammermeyer her one weakness: an extraordinary blind faith in the army and its 'reasonableness'.

Set in contrast with the army goings-on is Margarethe's personal life. We see her as the mother to her three Mormon sons, and as the daughter to her distant father. We also see her meet and fall in love with artist Diane (an excellent supporting role from Judy Davis). There's a little romance, some hesitancy, humour, and then suddenly the two are domestically entwined. There's just one kiss – very tender – right at the end.

The outcome of the trial is inevitably damaging, but Cammermeyer emerges morally victorious and the tone is upbeat. The family are weary but proud. As Diane puts it, 'I had to fall in love with a hero!'

Note: This film was produced by Glenn Close and Barbra Streisand.

See also: **THE HOUSE OF THE SPIRITS**, in which Glenn Close plays another lesbian character.

Set It Off 1997

Director: F. Gary Gray. Country: US. Screenplay: Takashi Bufford and Kate Lanier. Production company: New Line Cinema. Duration: 119 mins, colour

Cast: Jada Pinkett (Stoney), Queen Latifah (Cleo), Viveca A. Fox (Frankie), John C. McGinley (Detective Strode), Kimberly Elise (Tisean), Blair Underwood (Keith)

Four black women find that life deals them no favours, and out of a sense of injustice and desperation begin to rob banks. Successfully.

Terrific female-led shoot 'em up action movie in which our heroines, as much by accident as design, pull off an amazing string of robberies before the law and destiny catch up. Unsubtle and sometimes heavy-handed, with several plot twists that surely stretch credibility to breaking point (Stoney's unbelievably wonderful boyfriend for one), *Set It Off* goes for the emotional jugular every time.

Our sympathies are with the women right from the very opening scene when Frankie is unfairly dismissed from her job as a bank teller. Without a reference, her only option is to join her old friends working as a cleaner. One of these is the big butch Cleo, played with much stomping about by Queen Latifah. Cleo is a lesbian with attitude as well as a useful – hitherto unappreciated – ability to shoot two guns at once. She has a girlfriend, and the two enjoy a bit of a sexy scene, but their encounters are sleazy compared to the heterosexual romance. Still, Cleo is quite a woman, and a brave, self-sacrificing one, too. On the wrong side of the law, naturally.

Seven Women   1965

Director: John Ford. Country: US. Screenplay: John McCormick and Janet Green. Production company: John Ford Productions. Duration: 87 mins, colour

Cast: Anne Bancroft (Dr Cartwright), Margaret Leighton (Agatha Andrews), Sue Lyon (Emma Clark), Flora Robson (Miss Binns)

China, 1935. A group of Western missionaries are under attack by nearby Mongols.

After casting almost no women in starring roles in his films during his long career, western specialist John Ford made up for it in one fell swoop with his very last movie, a classy psychological drama set in a Christian mission. A marvellous film, except for the unpleasant streak of racism running all the way through it.

Six of the seven women in the title are a predictable bunch, all religious morals and repressed desires. Strong lesbian undercurrents are the order of the day for Miss Andrews, an older woman and unofficial leader of the group. While she is strong and capable with the other members of the group, she completely collapses, metaphorically speaking, in the presence of the glorious young Miss Emma Clark (Sue Lyon, the same 'object of desire' as in **THE NIGHT OF THE IGUANA**). Miss Andrews cannot express her longing, of course, and her religious convictions would not permit such things either. In any case, Emma is not interested and does not return the compliment.

Enter Dr Cartwright (Anne Bancroft, as alluringly handsome as ever), who throws everyone off balance with her trousers, short hair and attitude. She smokes, is terrific at her job and is both butch and cute. Within thirty seconds she is established as straight. 'It's a woman,' exclaims Mrs Pether when they first meet. 'Unless a lot of men have been kidding me,' remarks our heroine drily.

Emma takes an immediate shine to Dr Cartwight, leaving Miss Andrews bereft and jealous. 'I've always searched for something that isn't there. God isn't enough,' she says sadly. As Miss Andrews is essentially a 'real lesbian' (albeit unconscious) she is doomed to frustration and bitterness. Emma's crush on the good doctor is forgiven, though, because her interest is not carnal and her youth suggests a temporary phase.

See also: **THE NIGHT OF THE IGUANA**, in which Sue Lyon is once more the object of desire for an older woman.

Shades of Fear: see under GREAT MOMENTS IN AVIATION

She Must Be Seeing Things   1987

Director: Sheila McLaughlin. Country: US. Screenplay: Sheila McLaughlin. Production company: Sheila McLaughlin. Duration: 90 mins, colour

Cast: Sheila Dabney (Agatha), Lois Weaver (Jo), Kyle DiCamp (Catalina), John Erdman (Eric), Ed Bowes (Richard)

Agatha, a lawyer, and Jo, a film-maker, live together as a couple. When Agatha reads Jo's diary and discovers that her past is filled with a number of heterosexual encounters (some illustrated with photographs), she is filled with jealousy and suspects that Jo might be being unfaithful to her with a man.

Deeply controversial film on release, *She Must Be Seeing Things* managed to upset a wide section of the lesbian community by being a lesbian film largely concerned with heterosexuality. Many were so offended by the way that the female characters were treated that the film was dismissed outright by some as pornography. Clearly, the director made some serious errors of judgement in the way in which certain scenes were filmed, a fact that was not helped by what was obviously a very small budget. Although its main objective may have been to provoke the audience with some interesting explorations on voyeurism and role-playing, the result is more depressing than challenging. Its relatively ground-breaking examination of sexual play between women, including the use of sex toys and lingerie, is lost amid the more memorable images of, as many saw it, female degradation.

When Agatha decides to follow Jo to see if her instincts are true, she does so disguised as a man. We discover that Jo does indeed have sexual encounters with men, some of which are shown relatively graphically. Adding to the general confusion is the fact that Jo is herself making a film, the subject of which is a repressed nun. Generally, films within films rarely add much to storylines, and in this case the blurring of reality with fiction seems the result of poor editing rather than being in itself deeply symbolic. Somehow one is left with the impression that *She Must Be Seeing Things* is telling us that most lesbians do indeed fantasize about sleeping with men and that, caught at the right moment, they might be up for it for real. Not so much an issue these days, perhaps, but a molten-hot topic back in the 1980s.

She's Gotta Have It 1986

Director: Spike Lee. Country: US. Screenplay: Spike Lee. Production company: Forty Acres and a Mule Filmworks. Duration: 85 mins, black and white

Cast: Tracy Camila Johns (Nola Darling), Tommy Redmond Hicks (Jamie), John Canada Terrell (Greer), Spike Lee (Mars), Raye Dowell (Opal)

Nola is going out with three men and trying to decide which one is the man for her. All three know about the others, all three are in love, and each individually addresses both Nola and the audience with the various reasons why he, above the others, should be chosen.

Spike Lee's first feature, a domestic comedy with charisma and attitude, sees good-time girl Nola Darling keep all her men in a spin while she chooses between them. The men are contrasted in terms of jobs, aspirations and degrees of self-obsession. Of the three it is Jamie, sweet and steady, who would be the most loving and is perhaps the most in love. It is therefore very disappointing to have him articulating the homophobia of the film, brought into focus by the presence of lesbian predator opportunist Opal. He remarks, 'It was bad enough Nola and all her male friends, but there was also this one particular female who was after her and that was a bit much.'

Opal is not the most endearing screen lesbian ever to be invented. We know little and care much less about her than any of Nola's male suitors. And besides which, she's so damn *pushy*. She says of herself, 'At a young age I knew where my preference was and I pursued it. Nola may have been straight as an arrow, I just wanted her to be open-minded, check it out, then decide. That's all.'

When Nola asks her what it's like to sleep with a woman, Opal can only reply in the negative. 'I can tell you what it's not,' she says. 'It's not some musty man pounding away inside of you a mile a minute.' Nola is perhaps understandably unimpressed by this description, although Opal insists it's only a matter of time before she comes round. (She doesn't.)

Maybe Lee introduced the character of Opal to be modern and up to date, and to show that Nola has been given every option before making her choice. But Opal is no contender. She isn't even very nice. Perfunctory.

Shisheng Huamei: see under **THE SILENT THRUSH**

Showgirls 1995

Director: Paul Verhoeven. Country: US. Screenplay: Joe Eszterhas. Production company: MGM/UA. Duration: 131 mins, colour

Cast: Elizabeth Berkley (Nomi), Kyle MacLachlan (Zack), Gina Gershon (Cristal), Glenn Plummer (James), Robert Davi (Al Torres)

Nomi hitches a ride to Las Vegas with dreams of becoming a dancer. Tricked out of her possessions within seconds of her arrival, she falls upon the charitable assistance of Molly, a young wardrobe mistress for the biggest show in town. Nomi aims to progress from lap dancer at The Cheetah nightclub and get to the very top, whatever it takes.

Serious adult entertainment or glossy semi-pornographic provocation? The jury weren't out for long on this one and *Showgirls* was lambasted from every side as being a disastrous overblown failure. The film might aspire to lofty heights, and certainly writer Joe Eszterhas had stated his intention to write a morality tale, but in the end sleaze wins out and what we have here is possibly – at $40 million – the most expensive exploitation film in cinema history. The team that brought you the seamy **BASIC INSTINCT** excelled themselves with this nudie-fest, which manages to be completely about sex without being erotic. At all.

Showgirls is a paean to the less tasteful side of heterosexuality, and perhaps (to give it more credit than it's due) an amusing examination of male sexuality generally. The lesbian side of things exists as another indication of the glamorous sexual free-for-all going on, but is not completely sidelined, as it involves the two female leads (who are both essentially straight). 'Leave Your Inhibitions at the Door' advised the *Showgirls* publicity. If you are also able to leave your feminist sensibility, your cynicism and the uneasy feeling that you are being taken for a ride, you may find many aspects of the film diverting, including the spectacle of the Vegas shows and the backstage frolics. Best fun is had by Gina Gershon as Cristal, the current big thing in Vegas, who purrs her way through the most laughable of scenes with admirable delicacy. It is the stormy relationship between herself and the up-and-coming Nomi that provides the lesbian frisson, such as it is.

The two are first introduced in Cristal's dressing room, where Nomi tells her that she, too, is a dancer. As Cristal observes, 'I don't know what it is you do darlin', but if it's at The Cheetah, it ain't dancing.' Nomi is wounded by this remark and walks out. Indeed, one of the most amazing aspects of the film is Nomi's reaction – affronted astonishment usually – whenever anyone suggests that she is doing something overtly sexual or presenting herself in a sexual way. Cristal is intrigued by this walk-out, though, and arranges for Nomi to be auditioned for something slightly more artistic than sliding over men's crotches. (Not before paying for her own private lap dance for her boyfriend, however.) The two women have a few verbal ding-dongs and there is a rehearsal scene between them which verges on the exciting before, guess what, Nomi has a strop and walks out. Fortunately we are treated to a kiss at the very end which does contain some erotic oomph, but then it's over and the two go their separate ways (not that you could ever quite imagine them setting up home together).

Despite some extravagant on-stage dance routines (with music by Dave Stewart), *Showgirls* was remorselessly panned by the critics. Not for being sordid (it's not realistic enough for that), but for being an empty vessel, gift-wrapped sleaze. As well as being a critical failure, crowds stayed away in droves and the film sank badly at the box office (although it has picked up a little since, as audiences have become curious to know how just bad it really is). This failure was rather ungallantly attributed to the young lead actress Elizabeth Berkley. This apportioning of blame was ridiculously unfair, unless both director and writer feel they play little part in the success of a film these days. Moreover, no one could accuse Ms Berkley of not giving (and revealing) her *all* for this movie. The main problem with *Showgirls* as a film is not the demeaning of the characters and the reduction of any kind of sexuality to a kind of bump-and-grind vacuousness; it's the lack of an emotional core that would have given the film something to hold on to. Perhaps significantly, the only character who might be considered the template for any real integrity – Molly – is well and truly punished for her naivety.

If you see it, be prepared to go with it. Or don't go at all.

See also: **BASIC INSTINCT** by the same director and, for more Gina Gershon, don't miss **BOUND**.

The Silence (Tystnaden)   1963

Director: Ingmar Bergman. Country: Sweden. Screenplay: Ingmar Bergman. Production company: Svensk Filmindustri. Duration: 96 mins (GB 84 mins), black and white

Cast: Ingrid Thulin (Ester), Gunnel Lindblom (Anna), Jörgen Lindström (Johan)

Ester, beautiful, severe and elegant, is on a trip through Europe with her sister Anna and Anna's ten-year-old son. Ester becomes more and more ill and the trio have to book into a hotel.

The last part of Bergman's trilogy (which began with *Through a Glass Darkly* [1961] and continued with *Winter Light* [1962]) explores the human need for both physical as well as spiritual satisfaction, and the difficulty of obtaining both, or even one, of those things.

As a director Ingmar Bergman has never been accused of superficiality. The intensity of his characters and the complexity of their relationships have always been his trademark. In *The Silence* we learn that Ester is the dominant sister, within whose grip the younger sister Anna feels trapped even when Ester is immobile with illness. In an effort to break away, Anna goes into the town looking for men to pick up. Ester remains in the hotel, drinking, smoking and masturbating in a state of neurotic depression.

Ester is deeply jealous of Anna. She has barely repressed lesbian feelings for her sister, which Anna senses, and uses as a stick to beat her with. Her feelings of loneliness and despair are compounded when Anna brings back a man to the hotel, partly motivated by a desire to hurt Ester even further. The cruelties involved depress the sombre mood of the film even more than is at first apparent. One feels more than a degree of sympathy for the tormented sister whose careless, selfish sibling does nothing to ease her feelings, but rather enjoys inflaming them. In the end, however, the audience is unlikely to warm to either sister, both of whom are fixated by the other in various ways. The lesbianism seems more situational than purposeful. In other words, it is neither a cause of Ester's problems nor a solution to them. It is simply there.

Too cold to be sad, but fascinating all the same.

See also: **PERSONA** by the same director.

The Silent Thrush (Shisheng Huamei)   1992

Director: Sheng-Fu Cheng. Country: Taiwan. Screenplay: Chi-Wei Yu, K'ang-Nien Li and Sheng-Fu Cheng (based on the novel by Yen Ling). Production company: San Pen Enterprises. Duration: 100 mins, colour

Cast: Li Yu-Shan (Ah-Yun), Lu Yi-Ch'an (Chia-Feng), Chang Ying-Chen (Ai-Ch'ing), Yuan Chia-P'ei (Tou-Yu)

A travelling opera troupe makes its way around Taiwan. Ah-Yun, a young graduate who has been devoted to the art of travelling opera since she was a child, realizes a dream in joining the troupe. However, things are not what they were in the world of opera. The public are turning away from traditional forms of entertainment and desperate measures are needed to attract an audience.

Interesting, if incredibly noisy, film (everyone shouts all the time), with the story of the troupe at its centre but a strong lesbian sub-theme involving the central character. Ah-Yun is the nice, relatively innocent, feminine girl who is attracted to the rather butch Chia-Feng. The two have an affair and there is a brief, fairly explicit, love scene. The film takes no particular position on the relationship, which is to say that it neither condemns nor celebrates it. Improves the film, though.

Silkwood (Chain Reaction)   1983

Director: Mike Nichols. Country: US. Screenplay: Nora Ephron and Alice Arlen. Production company: ABC Motion Pictures. Duration: 131 mins, colour

Cast: Meryl Streep (Karen Silkwood), Kurt Russell (Drew Stephens), Cher (Dolly Pelliker), Craig T. Nelson (Winston), Diana Scarwid (Angela)

Karen Silkwood, a technician at a local nuclear power plant, stumbles on information which reveals that she and her co-workers are in serious danger of plutonium contamination. As she tries to alert others to what is happening, those in charge take action to prevent her speaking out.

Compelling true story of a working-class heroine, starring Meryl Streep in one of her greatest roles. *Silkwood* is less of a thriller and more of an examination of the background to a complex woman who had many personal difficulties before she discovered her political consciousness.

The lesbian character in *Silkwood* is an important one. Cher plays Dolly Pelliker, close friend to Karen, who in fact lives with Karen and her boyfriend Drew. Dolly is an attractive figure, and fairly normal, in that she is not neurotic or pathological in any obvious way. She is also physically attractive (even though Cher at the time made much of the fact that she was 'dressing down' for the part). However, Dolly is unrequitedly in love with heterosexual Karen (though the real-life Karen Silkwood was bisexual and apparently had several female lovers), which tends to position her as a loser in the love-stakes. This impression is compounded when later in the film Dolly finds a lover in the form of Angela, a mortuary beautician, who is on vacation from her husband. Unlike the character of Dolly, who was based on two of Silkwood's real-life friends, Angela is an invention, and her profession – a source of amusement – seems intended to inject some bizarre light relief at Dolly's expense into the middle of the film.

Nevertheless, the character of Dolly Pelliker was an important step forward for lesbians on film in 1983. She does not perish or become miraculously heterosexual, and she is right up there in the co-starring role. But she is still a symbol of unrealized desire and Karen has to 'deal with' her unwanted advances.

See also: **MANHATTAN**, in which Meryl Streep plays a lesbian character, and **HOUSE OF THE SPIRITS**, in which she is the object of desire. Also **BAR GIRLS**, in which Cher's real-life lesbian daughter

Chastity Bono makes a (very) brief appearance. Mike Nichols also directed **PRIMARY COLORS**.

Sister My Sister   1994

Director: Nancy Meckler. Country: GB. Screenplay: Wendy Kesselman. Production company: NFH Productions. Duration: 89 mins, colour

Cast: Julie Walters (Mme Danzard), Joely Richardson (Christine), Jodhi May (Lea), Sophie Thursfield (Isabelle Danzard), Amelda Brown (Visitor), Lucita Pope (Visitor)

Mme Danzard and her daughter Isabelle engage Christine to work as their housemaid. Before long Christine's younger sister Lea joins the household too, and the Danzards could not be happier with their diligent servants. As time passes, the two young women turn increasingly inward, and a passionate incestuous relationship develops.

Remarkably powerful drama, based on a true story of a murder which occurred in France in 1933. Nancy Meckler's feature deals with themes of incest, power, oppression and isolation, and combines them to create an intense and disturbing film experience.

When we first see the introverted but immaculate Christine, she is the epitome of the perfect servant. Quiet, discreet and uncomplaining, she works from dawn till dusk and expects no thanks. Once Lea arrives she continues to serve perfectly, but her motivation is now the love of her little sister. The film's drama then develops the young women's relationship against the backdrop of endless subjugation and drudgery. In stark contrast to the airless atmosphere in the main house, the two sisters find escape in each other's arms. The scenes are fervent and sexy, particularly the first seduction of the desperate Christine by the younger, knowing Lea. (Humorously, Meckler simultaneously compares the eroticism going on in the attic with Mme Danzard's uninhibited excitement at winning at cards downstairs.)

The tension develops when the maids' exemplary work falls slightly below par, partly as a result of Lea's distracted thoughts. Mme Danzard knows exactly the threat to use to put things right – she tells the sisters she will have them separated. The fear that the threat inspires creates an anxiety in the sisters which they can barely contain. Strained to the limit, they exact a terrible revenge.

Sister My Sister is a remarkable debut feature from theatre director

Mother's Pride. Jodhi May and Joely Richardson star in *Sister My Sister*. Photo credit: Jill Furmanovsky. Courtesy of British Film Institute: Stills, Posters and Designs.

Meckler, and she receives some excellent support all round, particularly from the fine script. The acting is excellent in what is basically a four-hander, with Julie Walters frighteningly convincing as the cruel and dominant Mme Danzard. Bourgeois and snobbish but basically unsophisticated, she is interestingly compared to her rather more down-to-earth daughter Isabelle. Sophie Thursfield is first-rate in the less 'showy' role, as the bored and sulky daughter longing for excitement and with a great line in deflating sarcasm. Joely Richardson and Jodhi May both excel as the oppressed sisters.

See also: **LES ABYSSES** and **THE MAIDS** for different versions of the same story. Joely Richardson's real-life mother, Vanessa Redgrave, appears in **THE BOSTONIANS, GREAT MOMENTS IN AVIATION, JULIA** and **MRS DALLOWAY**.

Skin Deep   1995

Director: Midi Onodera. Country: Canada. Screenplay: Midi Onodera and Barbara O'Kelly. Production company: Daruma Pictures Inc. Duration: 81 mins, colour

Cast: Natsuko Ohama (Alex), Keram Malicki-Sanchez (Chris), Dana Brooks (Penny), Melanie Nicholls-King (Montana), David Crean (Stephen)

Film director Alex, assisted by her partner Montana, has the resources and the determination to make a film about love, tattoos, pleasure, pain and obsession. An advert for suitable participants in the movie attracts transgendered Chris, young, disturbed and impressionable . . .

Onodera's film looks at the way we preconceive gender and sexuality and tries to break down some of society's limiting notions of what it is to be female or male. There are some interesting aspects to the film, and the dialogue is occasionally insightful and thought-provoking. The drama itself gets going when Alex decides to deceive Chris by offering her the opportunity to become her production assistant, all the better to study her more closely for the benefit of her film. Despite warnings from Montana, who sees clearly that Chris is becoming infatuated as well as increasingly volatile, Alex presses ahead. It is only a matter of time before Chris realizes she is being used and the consequences are predictably destructive. Keram Malicki-Sanchez is quite good as the troubled Chris, and Melanie Nicholls-King makes a sexy on-screen presence. Natsuko Ohama is rather flat as Alex, however, and the performance lacks variation, which means, in turn, that the film loses out when it ought to be at its strongest. Nevertheless, it's an unusual movie, with some intriguing comments to make about appearance and identity (particularly in the shape of a most unusual drag queen!).

Slaves to the Underground   1997

Director: Kristine Peterson. Country: US. Screenplay: Bill Cody. Production company: Overseas Film Group, First Look Pictures and NEO Motion Pictures. Duration: 92 mins, colour

Cast: Molly Gross (Shelly), Jason Bortz (Jim), Marisa Ryan (Suzy), Bob Neuwirth (Big Phil), Natacha LaFerriere (Zoe), Claudia Rossi (Brenda), James Garver (Brian), Peter Szumlas (Dale)

SLAVES TO THE UNDERGROUND

Shelly is raped by her boyfriend Jimmy's best friend. In reaction she leaves Jimmy, joins an all-girl band and begins a relationship with Suzy, the lead singer.

Modern and occasionally edgy coming-of-age story centring around a triangular relationship, set against the hip and groovy world of underground girl bands in slackerville Seattle.

Suzy is confidently gay and Jim is straightforwardly heterosexual. Between them is Shelly, exploring her sexuality and causing both her lovers pain and confusion with her selfishness and pursuit of her own identity. One moment she wants Suzy, the next she is back with her ex-boyfriend Jim.

Suzy is an attractive character, a resourceful riot girl of the first order, organizing spontaneous attacks on shops selling porn mags through some judicious and unscrupulous chatting-up of the owners. Jimmy is a decent man, an idealist who produces his own [maga]'zine', and is definitely the most likable person in the film. He genuinely cares for Shelly but feels sidelined by her on-off attitude.

Set against the tangle of relationships, and interspersed throughout the film, are a series of amusing tirades against popular culture, voiced by the main protagonists. Each reveals more about the character speaking than the thing or person being criticized, but they're all witty and occasionally bizarrely accurate: most memorably a critique of the film *The Graduate* (1967), "a film about a stalker..." according to one disenchanted contributor, and a diatribe against Cindy Crawford's tyrannical bodyshape.

Director Kristine Peterson is an accomplished film-maker – this is no debut feature and it shows. Musically it's very interesting – almost all of it was written as original material for the film. Be warned, however, that the music is central to the film and if it's not your style you may find *Slaves to the Underground* a little hard going. Overcome this reaction if you can and give it a try, you might be surprised how much grunge you can take!

Some Prefer Cake   1997

Director: Heidi Arnesen. Country: US. Screenplay: Jeannie R. Kahaney. Production company: Up All Night Productions. Duration: 90 mins, colour

Cast: Kathleen Fontaine (Kira Bergen), Tara Howley (Sydney Korel), Desi Del Valle (Robin), Machiko Saito (Katie), Leon Acord (Devon McCormack), Tammy Dubose (Susie Fielding), Mimi Gonzalez (Cory Bergen)

Kira is an aspiring stand-up lesbian comic with stage fright. She is more successful in the bedroom, however, and routinely picks up a different woman every night. Kira's best friend is Sydney, who is stuck in a rut writing copy for the Bay Guardian, *but longing to be their restaurant critic. Sydney causes concern among her friends for preferring chocolate cake to sex with her boyfriend Greg. One day Kira meets someone who might really count for her. Sydney is not too pleased.*

Heidi Arnesen's romantic comedy, a bright and breezy œuvre set in San Francisco's gay district, is all about friendship. It is this singular feature that makes *Some Prefer Cake* different, and therefore more beguiling than many modern lesbian fables, which are mainly based on the joining of two souls against various odds. The comings and goings of a group of friends are amusingly explored, and the film is populated with a series of unusual and occasionally offbeat characters. Of these, none is more terrifying than Katie (Machiko Saito), one of Kira's discarded one-night stands, who decides, à la *Fatal Attraction* (1987), to stalk her fickle lover.

Kira and Sydney may be on different sexual wavelengths, but straight or gay, their friendship appears destined to survive all complications. Both women suffer with insecurity, jealousy, lust and love, and both struggle to achieve their career ambitions, but through it all their relationship with each other is the thing that endures. The fact that sexuality is a given rather than a theme is another refreshing aspect of the story. The San Francisco setting provides full novelty value, too, and brilliantly demonstrates the breadth of its lesbian social scene when Kira attends a – wait for it – Lesbian Sushi Group outing!

Shot on a shoestring, the film holds together technically better than most. It flounders a little here and there, but perhaps the only serious criticism would be that Kira's comedy routines are not, in fact, very funny, which might explain why she's not making much headway in that department.

See also: **COSTA BRAVA**, in which Desi Del Valle co-stars.

The Sticky Fingers of Time 1997

Director: Hilary Brougher. Country: US. Screenplay: Hilary Brougher. Production company: Crystal Pictures. Duration: 81 mins, colour

Cast: Terumi Matthews (Tucker Harding), Nicole Zaray (Drew), Belinda Becker (Ofelia), James Urbaniak (Isaac), Leo Marks (Dex), Samantha Buck (Gorge), Thomas Pasley (JL)

New York City 1953. When Tucker Harding, a writer of hard-boiled fiction, leaves her apartment to buy some coffee, she finds herself transported into the year 1997. Here she meets Drew, a suicidal young woman wandering the city, and the two form a wary alliance. Pursuing Tucker into 1997 is friend Isaac, who tells her that both she and Drew have a rare condition caused by the post H-bomb mutation of their souls. As a result, they are able to travel in time, often against their will. The problem is, there are others like them, and they're not very friendly . . .

This is a first for lesbian films: two women who meet across time, suffer love, confusion and violence, meet and separate through complex twists and turns before solving the riddle of their own existences via the unexpected pages of pulp fiction. Hilary Brougher's film is a debut feature, made with earnest conviction and a detailed imagination. Brougher, clearly a bit of a sci-fi geek as much as a film director, goes to enormous pains to explain the conceptual notion of time travel without paralysing the audience with boredom. By and large she achieves her aim.

Unlike almost every other sci-fi film ever made, *The Sticky Fingers of Time* relies entirely on the viewer's imagination to convey time travel. There are no overt special effects here, the budget of $250,000 did not allow for such luxuries. The result is a thoughtful, if complicated, foray into parallel universes, rather than a feast of sensational visual tricks.

Ultimately, the film doesn't quite come together, because it lacks thrilling emotional engagement and the ending is too low key to allow anyone to jump for joy. But it's a fascinating, unusual movie with an ambitious and complex plot. It's probably insufficiently lesbian to be called a lesbian film (yet if a version of this film had turned up in the mainstream, we would be falling over ourselves to claim it).

The Stolen Diary (Le Cahier Volé) 1992

Director: Christine Lipinska. Country: France and Italy. Screenplay: Christine Lipinska and Bernard Revon (based on the novel by Régine Deforges). Production company: Providence Films. Duration: 95 mins, colour

Cast: Elodie Bouchez (Virginie), Edwige Navarro (Anne), Benoit Magimel (Maurice), Malcolm Conrath (Jacques), Serge Avedikian (Virginie's Father), Laurence Calame (Anne's Mother), Marie Riviere (Lucie), Anne-Marie Pisani (Georgette)

At the close of World War II in France, two village schoolgirls Virginie and Anne await the return of Jacques, released from internment in a concentration camp. Deeply traumatized and physically weak, Jacques reveals that his survival was due to his love for Virginie. But Virginie is in love with Anne, something she confides to her secret diary . . .

Wonderful romantic drama in which the two young girls engage in a gentle, tender relationship, unaffected by others until the day the diary is 'stolen' and the secret threatens to come out. Virginie is very much the centre of the film as well as being the centre of attraction for Anne, the broken Jacques and Anne's brother Maurice. Somehow she inspires the jealous devotion of all three friends, and so intertwined are they that later she speculates as to whether it was not three loves but one single love, experienced by her simultaneously.

When Virginie, at the request of Anne (but a little reluctantly), refuses Jacques on the grounds that there is 'someone else', he becomes desperately unhappy. Maurice, similarly hurt under the surface, but presenting a façade of wishing to protect his friend, decides to steal the diary and find out who the 'other man' really is. When the truth comes out, the village and Virginie's father are less than amused.

Although the relationship between the two girls is presented as sweet and loving, it is interesting that we are allowed no glimpse into the life of the sensitive and beautiful Anne, outside of her interaction with her girlfriend. Indeed, the intensity of her feelings is only properly illustrated at the end of the film. When the girls are separated we do not see her for some time and we do not see her distress or pain until later. However, we do gain considerable insight into Jacques's predicament and, indeed, one cannot help but be moved by his simple passion. Similarly, we see much of Maurice and his agonies and longings. Parents are portrayed as tunnel-visioned and cruel, with the exception of Virginie's lovely step-mother. Most surprising of all, though, is the way that Virginie simply does not match, or perhaps even deserve, the depth of feeling the three young friends express for her. Although she is the subject of the drama, it is they who are truly experiencing it.

Strangers in Good Company: see under THE COMPANY OF STRANGERS

Switch   1991

Director: Blake Edwards. Country: US. Screenplay: Blake Edwards. Production company: Cinema Plus LP. Duration: 99 mins, colour

Cast: Ellen Barkin (Amanda), Jimmy Smits (Walter), JoBeth Williams (Margo), Perry King (Steve), Lorraine Bracco (Sheila)

Steve uses and abuses women without a second thought. When one of his many lovers murders him, he ends up in a kind of purgatory. He is told that he can only get to heaven if he returns to earth in a new body and locates one single woman who genuinely liked him. The only catch is, he must return in the body of a woman . . .

Woefully underrated sex-reversal comedy with some brilliantly hilarious moments and a fascinating lesbian scene. When Steve returns to mortal guise in the form of Amanda (the excellent Ellen Barkin), 'he' realizes 'she' must quickly learn what it is to be female. Being none too bright she constantly forgets herself and, initially, continues to behave just as she did when she was a he. She eyes up women, comments on them and stomps around in a butch fashion, while using crude, 'manly' language. Somehow this behaviour is misinterpreted and she is assumed to be some kind of Madonna-style new feminist. Back at work, Amanda takes over Steve's sales job and in an effort to gain an account she dates Sheila, an important client. And here's the surprise – Sheila (Lorraine Bracco, on good form) is a lesbian who accepts Amanda's flirtation very happily. First there is a come-on in the office, then a party and finally a bedroom scene. So just when we're set for a real humdinger of a lesbian sex scene (and straight man Steve gets to find out what lesbians do in bed), Amanda suffers a crisis of guilt (or something similar) and can't go through with it. Oh no! It's the only unbelievable bit in the whole film (which is really saying something, all things considered). Ultimately, all ends well for everyone, and importantly, our lesbian is not belittled. Very funny, very clever.

See also: **JUST ONE OF THE GUYS, MOROCCO, ORLANDO, QUEEN CHRISTINA** and **YENTL** for more cross-dressing, gender-bending capers. Lorraine Bracco appears as a woman-identified cowgirl in **EVEN COWGIRLS GET THE BLUES**.

Therese and Isabelle 1968

Director: Radley Metzger. Country: US. Screenplay: Jesse Vogel (based on the novel by Violette Leduc). Production company: Amsterdam Film Corporation. Duration: 118 mins (GB 111 mins), black and white

Cast: Essy Persson (Therese), Anna Gael (Isabelle), Barbara Laage (Therese's Mother), Anna Vernon (Mme Leblanc)

Schoolgirl love story based on the autobiographical novel by French writer Violette Leduc.

Soft-core exploitation movie directed with a gloss and panache usually absent from this type of film. Told in flashback, we learn that Therese and Isabelle met at that well-known hotbed of lesbian desire, the Catholic girls' boarding school, where they had a tender and passionate affair. Emotional anxiety and sexual longing lead to some scenes of lovemaking which are genuinely exciting and erotic. Although the women themselves are clearly old enough to be teachers rather than pupils, this is probably a plus rather than a weakness for most viewers. Definitely worth a look.

See also: **SCORE** by the same director.

Thin Ice 1994

Director: Fiona Cunningham Reid. Country: GB. Screenplay: Geraldine Sherman and Fiona Cunningham Reid. Production company: Thin Ice Productions. Duration: 92 mins, colour

Cast: Charlotte Avery (Natalie), Sabra Williams (Steffi), James Dreyfuss (Greg), Clare Higgins (Fiona), Cathryn Harrison (Vandy), Suzanne Bertish (Lotte), Ian McKellen (Himself)

Black ice-skater Steffi is all set to enter the 1994 Gay Games in New York, when her partner walks out just weeks before the start. The only available alternative is Natalie, a young white woman, shy, middle-class and straight.

Enjoyable romantic comedy in which two unlikely women find love (eventually) against the backdrop of the Gay Games. The characters are interestingly drawn (although Steffi seems to have no family or friends at all beyond journalist pal Greg) and there is strong support from assorted theatrical thespians (Clare Higgins and Suzanne Bertish). Considering the low budget the film is remarkably ambitious in terms of the scope of the story and the extensive use of some great locations. It moves well between the drama of the unfolding romance and the sporting event. Once we reach New York the film takes on an almost documentary feel, as we see the – real – Gay Games taking place before us.

The love story is pleasant and both leads give charming, convincing performances. The moment when Natalie falls for Steffi's charm is gentle and understated, and the subsequent misunderstandings add the essential romantic tension. The dialogue wavers a little and one or two details may make you cringe, but overall it's not bad at all. The theme tune is likeable too.

See also: Clare Higgins in **NINETEEN NINETEEN**.

Three of Hearts 1993

Director: Yurek Bogayevicz. Country: US. Screenplay: Adam Greenman and Mitch Glazer. Production company: New Line Cinema. Duration: 102 mins, colour

Cast: William Baldwin (Joe), Kelly Lynch (Connie), Sherilyn Fenn (Ellen), Joe Pantoliano, Gail Strickland

Tall, modish, hippy Connie is in love with short, literary, Laura Ashley-type Ellen. They split up because Ellen needs her space and wants to be by herself for a while. Connie hires Joe, a male prostitute, to get Ellen back for her by breaking her heart, thus returning her to Connie's arms. Instead, Joe finds himself falling for Ellen, and he starts to question his lifestyle.

First the good news: This *is* a comedy, just about, therefore the offensive plotline is treated with a light touch. The bad news? Everything else. Time and time again the film so nearly gets it right, only to let itself down by continuously compromising everybody and every situation.

Baldwin plays a tart with a heart who helps out at the local sex phone-line service. He's on the run from a gangster type and just waiting to be saved. Along comes Connie who needs a male companion for a wedding (now that Ellen won't come out to play). Connie hires Joe, takes him to the wedding, whereupon he is a great success and everyone loves him. When Joe's apartment is trashed by the aforementioned heavy, he moves in with Connie (who is obviously used to rescuing pretty people in distress).

That night he comes up with the idea that if Ellen is fucked over by some man she's bound to come running back to the woman who really loves her. Amazingly, Connie thinks this is a really bright idea, and hires Joe to do the dirty deed. He joins Ellen's literature class, charms her and takes her out, all the while reporting his progress back to Connie, who spends her time weeping over home videos of happier times. Still watching? Joe falls for Ellen and starts to wonder if sex should be restricted to people who love each other and not done for, gasp!, money. Suddenly he doesn't want to be a callboy any more. His career is over because he's in lurve!

On and on it goes until the inevitable point when Ellen finds out what's been happening and makes the only believable decision in the entire film: she leaves both of them. Groan. Actually, the best jokes *are* at the end, so if you make it that far you could see it as a kind of reward. But this is not the modern, risky, screwball comedy it would like to be and should have been. The lesbian relationship is not presented in any way as enthusiastically or as warmly as the heterosexual ones are. The greatest expressions of love are reserved for the straights: the best music, the tenderest love scene, the romantic 'moment of realization' dash through the streets. The lesbians are seen separating or arguing from beginning to end. Still, it's good to see significant Hollywood actresses playing it gay and all three leads are strong performers.

See also: **TWO MOON JUNCTION**, in which Sherilyn Fenn flirts a bit, and also **JUST ONE OF THE GUYS**, in which she falls for a girl in drag.

Times Square 1980

Director: Alan Moyle. Country: US. Screenplay: Jacob Brackman. Production company: RSO Films. Duration: 111 mins, colour

Cast: Tim Curry (Johnny LaGuardia), Trini Alvarado (Pamela Pearl), Robin Johnson (Nicky Marotta), Peter Coffield (David Pearl)

Rich, misunderstood Pamela and poor, antisocial Nicky meet in a mental institution and form a close friendship. They escape the hospital into the city, set up a grungy home in a deserted warehouse and try to form a rock band. With the assistance of DJ Johnny LaGuardia they become a cult success and the future begins to look promising.

It's music all the way for this girl/buddy picture that should have been a bit more on the edge as far as the girls' relationship is concerned. Somehow, though, the lesbian theme was submerged and although scenes were filmed that confirmed their more-than-platonic love, some deft editing left them out. What remains is the butch(ish) Nicky and the femme(ish) Pamela embarking on a teenage odyssey for freedom and understanding that begins and ends with the duo metaphorically holding hands, if nothing else. Energetic in a way that usually only boys' films manage.

To Forget Venice (Dimenticare Venezia)   1979

Director: Franco Brusati. **Country:** Italy and France. **Screenplay:** Franco Brusati and Jaja Fiastri. **Production company:** Rizzoli Films. **Duration:** 110 mins, colour

Cast: Erland Josephson (Nicky), Mariangela Melato (Anna), Eleonora Giorgi (Claudia), David Pontremoli (Picchio)

A family reunion on an old country estate is cause for introspection and reflection. One male couple and one female couple think back over their childhoods in an atmosphere of repression and refinement.

Venezia is the beautiful Italian province in which Nicky is compelled to visit his sister Marta, a fading opera singer. He is accompanied by a handsome young man and the two can be assumed to be a couple, although it is not made explicit. They meet up with a lesbian couple who live with Marta. The older woman is Marta's adopted niece, and she lives with her schoolteacher 'friend'. Four gay people in one film does not a party make, however, and the older man and the older lesbian contemplate their partners, and wonder if they are merely younger versions of themselves. They also think back to the moments in their lives which they believe made them gay. Very contentious on that level but otherwise rather like a walk in a forest: relaxing, not life-changing.

To Live and Die in LA   1985

Director: William Friedkin. Country: US. Screenplay: William Friedkin and Gerald Petievich. Production company: New Century Entertainment Corporation. Duration: 116 mins, colour

Cast: William Petersen (Richard Chance), Willem Dafoe (Eric Masters), John Pankow (John Vukovich), Debra Feuer (Bianca Torres), John Turturro (Carl Cody), Darlanne Fluegel (Ruth Lanier)

Masters is a super-crook and expert forger. The LA cops are on his trail, and when he kills a policeman his partner decides on revenge no matter what.

Violent crime film which resists the viewer's attempt to engage with any of the characters. No one is very likable and those you don't despise you will probably pity. Deeply cynical in tone, the film paints a bleak picture of the LA underworld where everyone is in it for the money, everyone has a price, and any breath may be your last. The excursion into lesbianism is extremely brief. Masters, pleased with his girlfriend, arranges a 'surprise' for her, consisting of another woman. The two women look at each other meaningfully, and that's all. Later, when just about everyone is dead, they are seen driving off into the sunset together. We know nothing about these women. Lesbianism is there merely to underline the chaos and delinquency of the game.

Too Much Sun   1990

Director: Robert Downey. Country: US. Screenplay: Robert Downey, Laura Ernst and Al Schwartz. Production company: Too Much Sun Productions. Duration: 110 mins, colour

Cast: Robert Downey, Jr (Reed), Eric Idle (Sonny), Andrea Martin (Bitsy), Leo Rossi (George), Jim Haynie (Father Kelly), Laura Ernst (Susan)

Middle-aged brother and sister, Sonny and Bitsy, are outed to their elderly father by a conniving priest. When dad has a heart attack at the news, Father Kelly alters the will so that neither Sonny nor Bitsy will inherit unless one of them produces an offspring, via heterosexual sex. Bitsy rushes away to find the son she gave up for adoption, while Sonny tries very hard to do the right thing ...

Hilarious, crude, rude and very underrated, *Too Much Sun* is one of those straight-to-video comedies that really should have been given a wider release – more chance to offend more people. The gay men are stereotyped – lots of pink and lace – whereas the lesbian Bitsy is less obvious in terms of her appearance (on the other hand, she's halfway crazy). Most of the film's humour is based around sex, and the problem of having to do it with someone of the wrong gender. Sonny's efforts to be briefly heterosexual are truly comical, especially the moment when he tries to bed Bitsy's girlfriend Susan, who has accommodatingly dressed as a boy to help him out. He, meanwhile, has done the same thing in reverse, although his appearance as a girl is rather less convincing, to put it kindly. The film has a strongly British feel about it, despite being set in glamorous California. The humour is very reminiscent of Joe Orton (religion, sex and death inextricably linked), particularly a scene where Bitsy's long-lost adult son Reed masturbates under the bedclothes while his mother sings him lullabies (it's funnier than it sounds). All the gay people in the film are more honest, straightforward and nicer than their hetero counterparts, who just want money or sex. Lesbianism as completely normal in a mad, mad world. Laura Ernst, who stars as Susan, co-wrote the screenplay.

Touch of Evil   1958

Director: Orson Welles. Country: US. Screenplay: Orson Welles (based on the novel *Badge of Evil* by Whit Masterson). Production company: Universal Pictures. Duration: 108 mins, black and white

Cast: Charlton Heston (Ramon Miguel Vargas), Janet Leigh (Susan Vargas), Orson Welles (Hank Quinlan), Joseph Calleia (Pete Menzies), Akim Tamiroff (Joe Grandi), Joanna Moore (Marcia Linnekar), Ray Collins (Adair)

Hank Quinlan, a corrupt detective, attempts to frame Mexican cop (Charlton Heston) in a small border town filled with death and decay.

When celluloid lesbians hadn't been invented, it was the butch woman who conveyed *that* sort of thing. Although she was in disguise, the butch knew what she was there for, and straight audiences secretly knew as well. In *Touch of Evil*, Mercedes McCambridge makes a fleeting but memorable appearance as the only girl in a group of thugs. At one stage this gang intimidate and frighten Susan Vargas (Janet Leigh), and there is even the suggestion of rape. Far from wanting nothing to do with the situation, our leather-bound dyke identifies totally with the men and insists on staying. 'I wanna watch,' she says. Nasty.

See also: **JOHNNY GUITAR** for Mercedes in another ambiguous role.

Twins of Evil 1971

Director: John Hough. Country: GB. Screenplay: Tudor Gates. Production company: Hammer. Duration: 87 mins, colour

Cast: Madeleine Collinson (Frieda), Mary Collinson (Maria), Peter Cushing (Gustav Weil), Kathleen Byron (Katy Weil), Dennis Price (Dietrich)

Young orphaned twins Frieda and Maria arrive at the home of their nearest relative, the fearsome Gustav Weil. Mr Weil is a witch-burner, misogynist and all-round despot. This doesn't stop the naughty twin seeking a bit of excitement with the local vampire.

Amusing vampire flick featuring real-life twins Madeleine and Mary Collinson as the good and evil protagonists. Not as lesbian as many a vampire film and indeed there is only one very brief scene in which a Sapphic frisson occurs. The 'bad' twin, i.e. the undead one, is celebrating her recent conversion in the castle of her male vampire lover. He tells her to bite into an unfortunate peasant girl who happens to be chained up to a nearby wall. She does so, but instead of going for her neck she aims squarely for the breast instead. Otherwise it's straight all the way.

See also: **DRACULA'S DAUGHTER, THE HUNGER** and **LUST FOR A VAMPIRE** for more gratifying vampire experiences.

Two Moon Junction 1988

Director: Zalman King. Country: US. Screenplay: Zalman King. Production company: Samuel Goldwyn Company. Duration: 105 mins, colour

Cast: Sherilyn Fenn (April), Richard Tyson (Perry), Louise Fletcher (Belle), Kristy McNichol (Patti-Jean), Martin Hewitt (Chad)

Rich all-American April is about to be married to her longtime sweetheart. Two weeks before the big day she meets and beds hunky fairground attendant Perry, who (naturally) shows her what real sex is all about.

Soft-porn flick given minor respectability through its cast. The plot merely serves to offer up one sex scene after another, all of which are heterosexual. The only lesbian moment occurs between Perry's former girlfriend Patti-Jean and April. They swap clothing in one scene and have a little dance together in another. Hardly earth-shattering and not worth enduring the entire movie for. Extremely tedious. Builds to a tremendous climax – will she, won't she marry good old Chad? Watch it if you care.

See also: **JUST ONE OF THE GUYS**, in which Sherilyn Fenn plays straight to a dragged-up girl. She also plays bisexual in **THREE OF HEARTS**.

Tystnaden: see under **THE SILENCE**

The Unbearable Lightness of Being 1988

Director: Philip Kaufman. Country: US. Screenplay: Jean-Claude Carrière. Production company: Saul Zaentz Company. Duration: 171 mins, colour

Cast: Daniel Day-Lewis (Tomas), Juliette Binoche (Tereza), Lena Olin (Sabina), Erland Josephson (The Ambassador), Daniel Olbrychski (Interior Ministry Official)

Prague 1968. Tomas is an arrogant young doctor who seduces women with his easy charm. His most frequent female companion is Sabina until he meets the naive Tereza, who falls in love with him. As the Russians invade, all three leave for Geneva, and Tomas is forced to consider his position in relation to love, communism and work.

The lesbian frisson in this film is exactly that: a quiver and nothing more. Tereza is required to produce a portfolio of nude photos in order to secure a job. Sabina acquiesces and the two have a drink to steady their nerves. About three hundred photos later the two are on the floor together, but alas! Sabina's current lover appears and the moment is lost. The scene is infused with eroticism and potential. Or so the director would like to think.

See also: **HENRY & JUNE** by the same director.

Vixen 1968

Director: Russ Meyer. Country: US. Screenplay: Russ Meyer and Anthony James Ryan. Production company: Eve/Coldstream Productions. Duration: 72 mins, colour

Cast: Erica Gavin (Vixen Palmer), Harrison Page (Niles), Garth Pillsbury (Tom Palmer), Michael Donovan O'Donnell (O'Bannion), Vincene Wallace (Janet King), Jon Evans (Jud), Robert Aiken (Dave King)

Vixen has sex.

Russ Meyer is known entirely for his skin-flicks, most of them made throughout the Swinging Sixties and all of them demonstrating a worshipful interest in women's bodies. Depending on your point of view, his films are either shameless, offensive exploitation movies or hilarious satires on the genre. *Vixen* is typical of his style. The film opens with shots of rugged Canadian forest and quickly gets down to business as Vixen seduces a Mountie in a glade. With a style reminiscent of a surreal travelogue, we move from one attractive setting to another as Vixen makes her way through all-comers. The lesbian scene has many of the familiar prerequisites we have come to know and love: both women get drunk, one is currently sex-starved (not Vixen, needless to say), no men are currently available, the episode is one of accidental discovery rather than premeditation and, once over, both women go back to men with even greater vigour. Compared to the heterosexual counterparts the lesbian scene – all lip-gloss and heavy breathing – has definite erotic impact. Erica Gavin plays Vixen with tireless professionalism. She also features in **BEYOND THE VALLEY OF THE DOLLS** as the lesbian seductress.

See also: **BEYOND THE VALLEY OF THE DOLLS** and **FASTER, PUSSYCAT, KILL! KILL!** by the same director. Erica Gavin appears in **BEYOND THE VALLEY OF THE DOLLS** and **CAGED HEAT**.

Les Voleurs 1996

Director: André Téchiné. Country: France. Screenplay: André Téchiné and Gilles Taurand. Production company: Films Alain Sarde. Duration: 116 mins, colour, subtitled

Cast: Daniel Auteuil (Alex), Catherine Deneuve (Marie), Laurence Côte (Juliette), Fabienne Babe (Mireille), Ivan Desny (Victor), Julien Rivière (Justin), Benoît Magimel (Jimmy), Didier Bezace (Ivan)

Alex, a remote and reserved cop, is trailing a gang of car thieves who may or may not be working for his brother Ivan. During the investigation Alex becomes involved with a withdrawn young woman, Juliette, who is in turn involved with her philosophy professor Marie.

Téchiné's film is less a police thriller than a psychological study of dysfunctional families and mismatched lovers. While it has some tense moments – in keeping with the heist theme – much of the movie is

LES VOLEURS

Bathtime. Laurence Côte and Catherine Deneuve star in *Les Voleurs*. Courtesy of Metro Tartan Distribution.

more concerned with the intense relationships between the main four protagonists, particularly the furious rage that exists between the two brothers.

Catherine Deneuve plays Marie, and it is her relationship with the bisexual student Juliette that forms the secondary lesbian sub-plot. Marie is a college professor with a grown-up family somewhere in a distant background, but this one fact aside we know frustratingly little about her. Her infatuation with Juliette seems unlikely somehow and is rather puzzling for that reason. Relationships do, of course, form between professional women and wayward youths, but this particular pairing looks implausible at best. We are given no insight as to why Marie should feel so deeply for Juliette and her reaction to their separation later in the film appears bizarre and extreme.

Laurence Côte's Juliette moves between her male and female lovers with ease. She is characterized as a lost child trying to find herself within the unpromising mêlée of the criminal underworld. She speaks of idolizing Marie, but has the arrogance and self-absorption of youth, and thus unwittingly generates potent emotions in those who love her and cares little about it.

Catherine Deneuve develops the character of Marie as far as the limited script will allow. She looks as lovely as ever, and would doubtless fulfil the dreams of any twenty-year-old student lucky enough to catch her eye. But the Deneuve star quality – and the characteristics she brings to all her films, including a certain class, intelligence, mental strength and sophistication – is compromised in *Les Voleurs* with no explanation. While the Marie and Juliette relationship might be believable – just – Catherine Deneuve's position as victim is so improbable as to seem absurd.

See also: **BELLE DE JOUR, ÉCOUTE VOIR** and **THE HUNGER** for more Catherine.

Walk on the Wild Side   1962

Director: Edward Dmytryk. Country: US. Screenplay: John Fante and Edmund Morris (based on the book by Nelson Algren). Production company: Famous Artists Productions. Duration: 114 mins, black and white

Cast: Laurence Harvey (Dove Linkhorn), Capucine (Hallie), Jane Fonda (Kitty Twist), Barbara Stanwyck (Jo Courtney), Anne Baxter (Teresina Vidaverri), Richard Rust (Oliver), Joanna Moore (Miss Precious)

New Orleans in the Depression-hit 1930s. Dove hitches there looking for his true love Hallie. Unknown to Dove, Hallie is now a fallen woman and living in a local bordello (in some comfort). When they finally meet he offers marriage and Hallie is torn between telling him the truth and risking rejection, or remaining where she is.

This highly entertaining, moralistic melodrama has at its core not just the relationship between Dove and Hallie but the far more interesting dynamic between Hallie and Jo (Barbara Stanwyck), owner of the bordello. The two women are characterized in very different ways. Capucine, as Hallie, is glamorous and beautiful, a talented sculptress who is now, as she puts it, 'at the bottom of the well'. She is high-class and only selling herself because she has no other option. She has been 'saved' from total poverty by Jo, who claimed her interest was only in art. Jo is portrayed quite differently to Hallie. She displays many of the required traits of the cinema lesbian: attractive but severe. She is also butch, manipulative, hard and rich from immoral earnings. The two women have an unspecified relationship, although they are very close. Jo has the air of a woman who is biding her time, 'Oh you know me, Hallie. Sometimes I've waited years for what I want.' When Jo tells Hallie to forget Dove, on the grounds that he will never accept her past, she is perceived by the audience as selfish and malicious. Clearly, like all sly dykes, she doesn't really care about her girlfriend, she just wants to keep her at any cost.

As it happens, Jo's assessment of Dove turns out to be correct: he rejects her when he discovers the truth. However, since he is still in love, he somehow persuades himself that Hallie must be a prostitute because she can't resist men. He decides to take her away from temptation, and for reasons unknown, Hallie agrees. Jo has a fit of anger which she directs mainly at her disabled husband. 'Don't talk to me about love . . .' she says. 'What does any man know?' She also tells him, 'Love is understanding and sharing and enjoying the beauty of life without the reek of lust!' This cleverly confirms a commonly held belief that lesbians are frigid, and that their relationships with women are safely spiritual rather than basely carnal. The fact that Jo's husband is wheelchair-bound tends to underline this idea.

The final reel concerns itself with the showdown. Who will win Hallie? Will it be the good man who has learned to forgive or the ruthless twisted madam? Well, it's not quite so straightforward as all that but there are no surprises . . .

Barbara Stanwyck was – and still is – a lesbian favourite, and in dozens of her films she played the strong female lead with a touch of sexual ambivalence. In real life she had several lesbian relationships, although married more than once. Joan Crawford also had lesbian relationships and Capucine, too, was bisexual. Capucine is less well known to modern audiences but she was an important star for many years, bringing a Continental glamour to several American films.

See also: **JOHNNY GUITAR** for more Joan Crawford.

The Watermelon Woman 1997

Director: Cheryl Dunye. Country: US. Screenplay: Cheryl Dunye. Production company: Dancing Girl Productions. Duration: 80 mins, colour

Cast: Cheryl Dunye (Cheryl), Guinevere Turner (Diana), Valarie Walker (Tamara), Lisa Marie Bronson (Fae 'The Watermelon Woman' Richards), Irene Dunye (Herself), Brian Freeman (Lee Edwards), Ira Jeffries (Shirley Hamilton)

Cheryl works in a video store by day and spends her spare time endeavouring to make a documentary about forgotten black Hollywood actress Fae Richards (the Watermelon Woman).

Low-budget, independent first feature from Cheryl Dunye heralds an amusing introspective view into the world of the film-maker herself. Twenty-five-year-old Cheryl's professional and personal life is fraught with difficulties, including the search for archive material, suitable interviewees and, coincidently, a girlfriend. All are forthcoming eventually, the latter in the form of the attractive Diana (Guin Turner, as comely as ever). That the film is concerned with a black lesbian's search for a (fake) black Hollywood actress is interesting in itself, for the personal is political throughout *The Watermelon Woman*. But the film is also informed with interesting, gossipy interviews featuring, among others, the erudite Camille Paglia (tongue firmly in cheek). Stylistically the film takes the familiar 'indie first feature' route, which is to say the quality is as variable as the enthusiasm is infectious. The acting is fair, the direction not bad and the editing could have been tighter. Seven hundred people are credited with assisting the film's production, and it would be a hard heart who said it wasn't worth it.

See also: **GO FISH** and **PREACHING TO THE PERVERTED** for more Guin.

When Night Is Falling   1994

Director: Patricia Rozema. Country: Canada. Screenplay: Patricia Rozema. Production company: Crucial Pictures. Duration: 93 mins, colour

Cast: Pascale Bussières (Camille), Rachel Crawford (Petra), Henry Czerny (Martin), David Fox (Reverend DeBoer), Don McKellar (Timothy)

Romance is in the air *When Night Is Falling*. Rachel Crawford and Pascale Bussières star. Courtesy of Metro Tartan Distribution.

WHEN NIGHT IS FALLING

Camille is a professor of mythology engaged to be married to theologian Martin, and their future together at a Protestant college looks secure. By chance she meets Petra, a circus performer, at the local launderette. Petra flirts with Camille and forces another meeting by switching their washing. Camille is drawn to Petra, but torn between her conventional, safe life and one of risk and uncertainty.

Transformation is the keynote to this wonderful film, in which two dissimilar women meet by chance and a wavering romance develops. Petra, an intriguing circus performance artist, knows her own sexuality, feels instantly attracted to Camille and has no hesitation in making a clever move towards her. Camille is scarcely aware of Petra's interest, but is forced to seek her out in order to retrieve her clothes. Her search leads her to the mysterious travelling circus 'Sirkus of Sorts', a world of shadowy figures, flame-throwers, magic and reverie.

When the women meet up, Petra flirts outrageously, and Camille flees, feeling 'out of her element'. Petra is apologetic but undeterred. A single, unexpected and blissfully sexy kiss gives her the encouragement she needs and she begins a persistent, one-sided courtship. Camille is interested but fearful. 'Fear is what you pay for adventure,' advises Petra. Camille faces a conflict. Martin, the man she has loved, is a good soul and still wants her. But she is no longer the woman she was. A new self is emerging with a desire focused on the engagingly spirited Petra. For Camille there is really no choice. Being true to herself must be her only destiny.

When Night Is Falling was made for the sum of $2 million and, after fourteen written drafts, took thirty days to shoot. Director Rozema has said that her Calvinist background partly inspired the movie, as well as her own teenage interest in the sensuous and the conflict therein.

Superb, captivating, tender, often funny and frequently beautiful, *When Night Is Falling* is like a lyrical poem, deeply felt and perfectly formed. Rich, vibrant colours, romantic images – naked women swimming in clear blue water – a dusting of snow, a half-moon and always the night just a moment away. First-rate performances all round – particularly the wide emotional range endearingly demonstrated by Pascale Bussières – and a gifted director with a painterly eye. Unmissable.

See also: **I'VE HEARD THE MERMAIDS SINGING** by the same director.

Wild Flowers 1989

Director: Robert Smith. Country: GB. Screenplay: Sharman MacDonald. Production company: Front Room Productions. Duration: 80 mins, colour

Cast: Beatie Edney (Sadie), Colette O'Neil (Annie), Stevan Rimkus (Angus), Sheila Keith (Marguerite)

Annie MacFarlan is dead and Sadie prepares to attend her funeral. Sadie remembers the first time she met Annie, the mother of her former fiancé Angus. On visiting the small Scottish village some years before, Sadie learned that Annie bore the burden of disapproving gossip from the local people. Most disapproving of all was Annie's own mother.

Beautiful tale, told largely in flashback, of a middle-aged woman who, in her own words, has 'dreamed her life away'. Annie is the subject of endless speculation among the locals, particularly two old women who regard her with scornful fascination. For Annie is not behaving herself and growing old gracefully. She is allowing herself to experience 'passion', as one of the women notes with regretful envy. Annie's passion, such as it is, is modest enough, and seems to consist mainly of answering her mother back and dressing to please herself. Sadie's arrival allows for an expression of something more.

When Angus introduces his intended future wife to Annie, the two immediately get along and begin to spend time together. Ever watchful is Annie's tyrannical mother, who sees a great deal happening below the surface. Eventually, she cannot hold her tongue any longer and in a shocking outburst made in front of Sadie, she tells Annie that she is wicked. When Annie boldly retorts 'I'm one of God's chosen', her mother is contemptuous and brutal: 'God will not forgive you,' she says, 'that's your *son's* girlfriend there.'

In the aftermath, Annie tells Sadie of the time when she was nineteen and fell in love with another woman. Physically it amounted to merely a kiss, but her mother caught them and has never let her forget it. Sadie's response to this revelation is low-key but intense. Her view is modern, less repressed. 'It's all allowed is it, in this world of yours?' asks Annie, as the two sit regarding the empty Scottish countryside (observed as always, for they are never completely alone).

Lesbianism thwarted in this instance is seen as harsh and cruel. By disallowing Annie the fulfilment of the real passion in her life her spirit has been nearly quelled, but not quite. The attempts by the village and her mother to render Annie harmless by smothering her have just about worked. But somehow a flame keeps burning. A gentle film about an exceptional woman.

Note: Beatie Edney's real-life mother, Sylvia Syms, plays a lesbian in **THE WORLD TEN TIMES OVER**.

The Wild Party   1974

Director: James Ivory. Country: US. Screenplay: Walter Marks. Production company: Wild Party. Duration: 91 mins, colour

Cast: James Coco (Jolly Grimm), Raquel Welch (Queenie), Perry King (Dale Sword), Tiffany Bolling (Kate), Royal Dano (Tex), Jennifer Lee (Madeline True), Marya Small (Bertha)

Fading silent film star Jolly Grimm throws a big Hollywood party in an attempt to rekindle his career. As the night progresses, things go very wrong and the debauchery ends in murder. Based on the Fatty Arbuckle scandal.

Mostly heterosexual goings-on in this entertaining soapy drama, but with a couple of exciting, brief scenes in which a glamorous lesbian seduces an innocent (but interested) young woman. When the young woman's sister discovers them later asleep on a bed she screams the place down. Great fun.

See also: **THE BOSTONIANS** by the same director.

The Women's Club (Club de Femmes)   1936

Director: Jacques Deval. Country: France. Screenplay: Jacques Deval. Production company: Ccb Jacques Deval. Duration: 105 mins, black and white

Cast: Danielle Darrieux (Claire), Betty Stockfeld (Greta), Else Argal (Alice), Raymond Galle (Robert), Eve Francis (Mme Fargeton), Valentine Tessier (Dr Aubry), Josette Day (Juliette)

Comedy set in an all-female hotel in Paris.

Wonderful French comedy, years ahead of its time, whose main characters include a dancer who wants sex as often as she can get it, another who is involved in procuring for a prostitution ring, a man in drag and a beautiful non-stereotypical lesbian in love with her close, but uncomprehending, friend.

Living in a hotel so gorgeous most of us would happily move into it for the rest of our lives, the various protagonists come and go with a refreshing *joie de vivre*, even in the face of misfortune. Our lesbian is the highly moral and chivalrous Alice, whose desperately restrained love for Juliette is galvanized into action when the innocent girl is badly treated by the hotel's lounge lizard.

Effervescent and exuberant, the film is clever, funny and wise. See it if you get the chance.

Work   1996

Director: Rachel Reichman. Country: US. Screenplay: Rachel Reichman. Production company: District Pictures. Duration: 93 mins, colour

Cast: Cynthia Kaplan (Jennie), Sonia Sohn (June), Peter Sprague (Will), Patt Franklin (Winnie)

Jennie searches for work in her small dead-end mill town, but despite making up different CVs to suit the job, she cannot get employment. Her husband tries to hold on to his job at the local factory. With no money and no future and feeling trapped in a loveless marriage, Jennie escapes into an affair with her neighbour's African-American granddaughter.

Jennie's small-town life and lack of prospects are honestly conveyed in this slice-of-life feature. Slow paced, gentle and non-judgemental, *Work* is an insightful glimpse into a dead-end world, where an affair is the difference between living and existing, at least for Jennie. The scenes where the two women make love are surprisingly explicit and filmed in an extraordinarily frank way, without a romantic gloss.

A less than upbeat ending and an arthouse feel means that *Work* has never reached the mainstream audiences who would benefit from seeing it. The narrative may fail to satisfy – it somehow promises more than it delivers – but the acting is superb.

The World Ten Times Over   1963

Director: Wolf Rilla. Country: GB. Screenplay: Wolf Rilla. Production company: Cyclops Film Productions. Duration: 93 mins, black and white

Cast: Sylvia Syms (Billa), Edward Judd (Bob), June Ritchie (Ginnie), William Hartnell (Dad)

Sixties London. Billa and Ginnie share a flat together and work as nightclub hostesses. While Ginnie, flighty and fun-loving, tries to decide whether to

commit herself to Bob, Billa attempts to sort out her relationship with her father. Billa is also watchful of Ginnie.

Sylvia Syms, one of Britain's greatest actresses, plays Billa, in a performance of considerable depth. She is practical, pragmatic and silently in love with the wayward Ginnie. Her tenderness towards her flatmate and her anger towards her father are both carefully controlled beneath an inscrutable visage. June Ritchie, as Ginnie, is suitably oblivious to the unexpressed feelings surrounding her, fretting only about whether or not married suitor Bob really loves her. With the swinging sixties all around them, the two women live in relative contentment, fending off disruptions as best they can.

While this film is an indication of how little one could show of a lesbian relationship (or potential one) in 1963, it also works very well as a study of unrealized love. Nothing *happens* between the two women, in the way a lesbian viewer would expect or hope for these days. But the strong, silent Billa is an attractive character and her love is crystal clear to anyone caring to look.

Note: Sylvia Syms's real-life daughter, Beatie Edney, plays a burgeoning lesbian in **WILD FLOWERS**.

X, Y & Zee: see under ZEE & CO

Yentl   1983

Director: Barbra Streisand. Country: US. Screenplay: Barbra Streisand and Jack Rosenthal (based on Yentl, the Yeshiva Boy by Isaac Bashevis Singer). Production company: United Artists. Duration: 133 mins, colour

Cast: Barbra Streisand (Yentl), Mandy Patinkin (Avigdor), Amy Irving (Hadass)

Eastern Europe 1904. At a time when only males are taught the Talmud, Yentl disguises herself as a man in order to get an education.

Ambitious drama/musical which saw Barbra Streisand not only take the leading role, direct and produce but also accomplish a credit as screenwriter. As an indictment against the subservience of women in Jewish culture at the time, the film works very well, particularly as the tone is light and the direction deft. As with most cross-dressing films, the switch from girl to boy is the source of much of the comedy.

When Yentl moves to the city to study she strikes up a friendship with Avigdor, in whom she finds an intellectual match. This being that sort of story, Yentl soon falls in love with the manly Avigdor, and spends as much time as possible with the chap, while at the same time hiding her true feelings as well as her gender. Normally, this tension alone would be enough for the purposes of confusion, but the film follows an interesting line. Avigdor is madly in love with Hadass (the very feminine Amy Irving), but he cannot marry her as his family has a history of melancholia. In desperation he tells Yentl that since they are like brothers, (s)he must marry her instead. Being head over heels in love, and wanting to please her man, Yentl somehow agrees to this doubtful idea. Meanwhile, Hadass has rather taken to the young and cute Yentl, who behaves like no other man she has ever met (by 'noticing' her cooking, for one thing).

So the two agree to marry despite Yentl's half-hearted protests. Come the wedding night – the anticipation of which is much drawn out – Yentl avoids sex by initiating a pillow fight instead. A kiss cannot be evaded, however, and their lips meet against a gentle twilight. ('Just pretend it's an arm,' Ms Streisand allegedly told the – presumably apprehensive – Ms Irving prior to the scene.)

Well, all good things come to an end and Yentl soon reveals her true self and sorts everything out. Lots of fun. Ms Streisand displays a good deal of endearing boyish charm throughout and her comic timing is, as ever, impeccable.

Note: Barbra also co-produced **SERVING IN SILENCE**.

See also: **JUST ONE OF THE GUYS, MOROCCO, ORLANDO, QUEEN CHRISTINA** and **SWITCH** for other cross-dressing, gender-bending capers.

Yo, la Peor de Todas: see under **I, THE WORST OF ALL**

Young Man with a Horn (Young Man of Music)   1950

Director: Michael Curtiz. Country: US. Screenplay: Carl Foreman and Edmund H. North (based on the Dorothy Baker novel). Production company: Warner Brothers. Duration: 112 mins, black and white

Cast: Kirk Douglas (Rick Martin), Lauren Bacall (Amy North), Doris Day (Jo Jordan), Hoagy Carmichael (Smoke Willoughby), Juano Hernandez (Art Hazzard), Jerome Cowan (Phil Morrison), Mary Beth Hughes (Marge Martin)

Hollywood biopic based on the jazz legend Bix Beiderbecke.

Kirk Douglas plays Rick, sensational trumpet player but no judge of women. He initially overlooks nice girl Doris Day in favour of the coolly sophisticated Amy (the glorious Lauren Bacall). One marriage-in-haste later, Rick realizes that he made a mistake and Amy cares little for him. Amy's implicit lesbianism is indicated only very slightly (although it was quite intense in the novel). Amy is seen as having flamboyant friends, and, rather more significantly, arranges to go to Europe with an attractive, young – female – art student. Rick is at a loss. 'You're a sick girl, Amy – you'd better see a doctor,' he tells her.

Young Man of Music: see under YOUNG MAN WITH A HORN

Yuwakusha: see under THE ENCHANTMENT

Zee & Co (X, Y & Zee) 1971

Director: Brian G. Hutton. Country: GB. Screenplay: Edna O'Brien. Production company: Zee Films. Duration: 109 mins, colour

Cast: Elizabeth Taylor (Zee Blakeley), Michael Caine (Robert Blakeley), Susannah York (Stella)

Modern couple Zee and Robert fight and bicker their way through their relationship, but their mutual understanding runs deep. Robert meets Stella, a sensitive fashion designer, and decides to leave his wife. But Zee won't let it happen, and will go to any lengths to retrieve him.

Very dated, but clever and complex, and shocking too, in the end (which is when the lesbian bit is realized). Elizabeth Taylor is one of those women you can't really imagine having a lesbian relationship, yet for her to do it in order to 'get her man back' seems entirely plausible – for she always seems capable of such ruthlessness when she plays a blousy broad. Zee is such a character and her ability to discover others' weaknesses makes this film much more than just a slanging match (although it's that, too). Lesbianism used as a means to an end then, which must have caused one or two gasps in the audience back in 1971. As always, Taylor's watchability factor is so great you hardly notice anyone else, although Michael Caine and Susannah York are very good, too. Camp, funny and very noisy.

See also: **SECRET CEREMONY**, in which Elizabeth Taylor plays a very strange woman, and **THE KILLING OF SISTER GEORGE**, in which Susannah York plays a lesbian opposite Beryl Reid. She also stars in **THE MAIDS**.

Index of Directors

Aaron, Paul *A Different Story*
Adlon, Percy *Salmonberries*
Akerman, Chantal *Je, Tu, Il, Elle*
Aldrich, Robert *The Killing of Sister George; The Legend of Lylah Clare*
Allen, Woody *Manhattan*
Almodóvar, Pedro *Kika; Pepi, Luci, Bom*
Anders, Allison *Grace of My Heart*
Appleby, Daniel *Bound and Gagged: A Love Story*
Aranda, Vincente *The Girl with the Golden Panties*
Arcand, Denys *Love and Human Remains*
Arnesen, Heidi *Some Prefer Cake*
Audry, Jacqueline *Olivia*
August, Bille *The House of the Spirits*
Avakian, Aram *11 Harrowhouse*
Avnet, Jon *Fried Green Tomatoes at the Whistle Stop Café*

Bacon, Kevin *Losing Chase*
Balasko, Josiane *Gazon Maudit*
Balletbo-Coll, Marta *Costa Brava*
Baratier, Jacques *The Satin Spider*
Barron, Zelda *Secret Places*
Bashore, Juliet *Kamikaze Hearts*
Bemberg, Maria Luisa *I, the Worst of All*
Beresford, Bruce *The Getting of Wisdom*
Bergman, Ingmar *Persona; The Silence*
Bertolucci, Bernardo *The Conformist; The Last Emperor*
Bleckner, Jeff *Serving in Silence: The Margarethe Cammermeyer Story*
Bogayevicz, Yurek *Three of Hearts*
Borden, Lizzie *Born in Flames*
Bown, John *Monique*
Brody, Hugh *Nineteen Nineteen*
Brougher, Hilary *The Sticky Fingers of Time*
Brusati, Franco *To Forget Venice*
Buck, Jeannette *Out of Season*
Buñuel, Luis *Belle de Jour*

Cahn, Edward L. *Girls in Prison* (1956)
Calparsoro, Daniel *Pasajes*
Cammell, Donald *Performance*
Casaril, Guy *Emilienne*
Chabrol, Claude *Les Biches*
Chamberlain, Joy *Domestic Bliss; Nocturne*
Chechik, Jeremiah *Diabolique*
Cheng, Sheng-Fu *The Silent Thrush*
Clouzot, Henri-Georges *Les Diaboliques*
Cohen, David *The Pleasure Principle*
Conn, Nicole *Claire of the Moon*
Cox, Paul *Man of Flowers*
Croghan, Emma-Kate *Love and Other Catastrophes*
Cromwell, John *Caged; The Goddess*
Cunningham Reid, Fiona *Thin Ice*

INDEX OF DIRECTORS

Curtiz, Michael *Young Man with a Horn*

Danielewski, Tad Z. *No Exit*
Deitch, Donna *Desert Hearts*
Demme, Jonathan *Caged Heat*
De Oliveira, Oswaldo *Bare Behind Bars*
Deval, Jacques *The Women's Club*
Dmytryk, Edward *Walk on the Wild Side*
Downey, Robert *Too Much Sun*
Duckworth, Jacqui *Homemade Melodrama*
Dunye, Cheryl *The Watermelon Woman*
Dyer, Julia *Late Bloomers*

Edwards, Blake *Switch*
Eisenman, Rafael *Lake Consequence*

Fassbinder, Rainer Werner *The Bitter Tears of Petra von Kant*
Faucon, Philippe *Muriel's Parents Have Had It Up to Here*
Figgis, Mike *Internal Affairs*
Fleischer, Richard *The Boston Strangler; Red Sonja*
Forbes, Bryan *The L-Shaped Room*
Ford, John *Seven Women*
Forman, Milos *The People vs Larry Flint*
Fosse, Bob *Lenny*
Friedkin, William *To Live and Die in LA*

Gilbert, Lewis *The Greengage Summer*
Giovanni, Marita *Bar Girls*
Gorris, Marleen *Antonia's Line*; *Mrs Dalloway*
Gottlieb, Lisa *Just One of the Guys*
Gray, F. Gary *Set It Off*

Hamilton, David *Bilitis*
Hamilton, Guy *Goldfinger*
Harmon, Jeff B. *Isle of Lesbos*
Harrington, Raquel Cecilia *Entwined*
Harron, Mary *I Shot Andy Warhol*
Hillyer, Lambert *Dracula's Daughter*
Hippolyte, Alexander Gregory *Mirror Images; Mirror Images II; Night Rhythms*
Hitchcock, Alfred *Rebecca*
Hough, John *Twins of Evil*
Hughes, Terry *The Butcher's Wife*
Hurd, Kelli *It's in the Water*
Huston, Danny *Becoming Colette*
Huston, John *The Night of the Iguana*
Hutton, Brian G. *Zee & Co*

Ivory, James *The Bostonians; The Wild Party*

Jackson, Peter *Heavenly Creatures*
Jaeckin, Just *Emmanuelle*
Jeunet, Jean-Pierre *Alien: Resurrection*
Jordan, Neil *Mona Lisa*

Kaufman, Philip *Henry & June; The Unbearable Lightness of Being*
Kidron, Biban *Great Moments in Aviation*
King, Zalman *Two Moon Junction*
Kokkinos, Ana *Only the Brave*
Kümel, Harry *Daughters of Darkness*
Kurys, Diane *At First Sight*

Lee, Spike *She's Gotta Have It*
Lipinska, Christine *The Stolen Diary*
Losey, Joseph *Secret Ceremony*
Lucchetti, Leandro *Caged Women*
Lumet, Sydney *The Group*
Luna, Bigas *Golden Balls*

INDEX OF DIRECTORS

McLaughlin, Sheila *She Must Be Seeing Things*
Maclean, Alison *Crush*
McNaughton, John *Girls in Prison (1994)*
Maggenti, Maria *The Incredibly True Adventure of Two Girls in Love*
Main, Stewart *Desperate Remedies*
Makk, Karoly *Another Way*
Malle, Louis *May Fools*
Mamoulian, Rouben *Queen Christina*
Margolin, Stuart *The Glitter Dome*
Meckler, Nancy *Sister My Sister*
Mehta, Deepa *Fire*
Merzbacher, Charles *Jane Street*
Metzger, Radley *Score; Therese and Isabelle*
Meyer, Russ *Beyond the Valley of the Dolls; Faster, Pussycat, Kill! Kill!; Vixen*
Miles, Christopher *The Maids*
Montes, Eduardo *Double Obsession*
Moyle, Allan *Times Square*

Nagasaki, Shunichi *The Enchantment*
Newell, Mike *The Good Father*
Newman, Paul *Rachel, Rachel*
Nichols, Mike *Primary Colors; Silkwood*

Onodera, Midi *Skin Deep*
Oswald, Gerd *Screaming Mimi*

Pabst, G. W. *Pandora's Box*
Papatakis, Nico *Les Abysses*
Peterson, Kristine *Slaves to the Underground*
Polanski, Roman *Bitter Moon*
Pool, Lea *Anne Trister*
Potter, Sally *Orlando*

Rafelson, Bob *Black Widow; Five Easy Pieces*
Ray, Nicholas *In a Lonely Place; Johnny Guitar*
Reichman, Rachel *Work*
Richardson, Tony *The Hotel New Hampshire*
Rilla, Wolf *The World Ten Times Over*
Rivette, Jacques *Céline and Julie Go Boating*
Roeg, Nicholas *Performance*
Rogers, Adam *Rescuing Desire*
Ross, Herbert *Boys on the Side*
Rossellini, Roberto *Open City*
Rossen, Robert *Lilith*
Rozema, Patricia *I've Heard the Mermaids Singing; When Night Is Falling*
Ruben, Katt Shea *Poison Ivy*
Russell, Ken *The Lair of the White Worm; The Rainbow*
Rydell, Mark *The Fox; The Rose*

Sagan, Leontine *Maidens in Uniform*
Sangster, Jimmy *Lust for a Vampire*
Santiago, Hugo *Écoute Voir*
Sayles, John *Lianna*
Schlöndorff, Volker *The Handmaid's Tale*
Scott, Cynthia *The Company of Strangers*
Scott, Tony *The Hunger*
Sichel, Alex *All Over Me*
Simandl, Lloyd *Chained Heat 2*
Singleton, John *Higher Learning*
Smith, Kevin *Chasing Amy*
Smith, Robert *Wild Flowers*
Spielberg, Steven *The Color Purple*
Starrett, Jack *Cleopatra Jones*
Streisand, Barbra *Yentl*
Streitfeld, Susan *Female Perversions*

Téchiné, André *Les Voleurs*
Thomas, Betty *The Brady Bunch Movie*

INDEX OF DIRECTORS

Thorpe, Jerry *A Question of Love*
Towne, Robert *Personal Best*
Treut, Monika *My Father Is Coming; Seduction, the Cruel Woman*
Troche, Rose *Go Fish*
Trueba, Fernando *Belle Époque*
Tsukerman, Slava *Liquid Sky*
Turner, Ann *Dallas Doll*

Urban, Stuart *Preaching to the Perverted*

Vadim, Roger *Barbarella*
Van Sant, Gus *Even Cowgirls Get the Blues*
Verhoeven, Paul *Basic Instinct; Showgirls*
von Grote, Alexandra *Novembermoon*
von Sternberg, Josef *Morocco*

Wachowski Brothers *Bound*

Waters, John *Desperate Living; Pink Flamingoes*
Weill, Claudia *Girlfriends*
Weir, Peter *Picnic at Hanging Rock*
Welles, Orson *Touch of Evil*
Wells, Peter *Desperate Remedies*
Wilson, Hugh *The First Wives Club*
Winner, Michael *The Sentinel*
Winterbottom, Michael *Butterfly Kiss*
Wise, Robert *The Haunting*
Wyler, William *The Children's Hour*

Yazaki, Hitoshi *Afternoon Breezes*
Young, Terence *From Russia with Love*
Yuan, Chu *Intimate Confessions of a Chinese Courtesan*

Zetterling, Mai *Scrubbers*
Zieff, Howard *Private Benjamin*
Zielinski, Rafal *Fun*
Zinnemann, Fred *Julia*

Index of Countries of Origin

Argentina

I, the Worst of All

No Exit (with USA)

Australia

Dallas Doll
The Getting of Wisdom
Love and Other Catastrophes

Man of Flowers
Only the Brave
Picnic at Hanging Rock

Belgium

Antonia's Line (with GB and the Netherlands)
Daughters of Darkness (with France, Germany and Italy)

Je, Tu, Il, Elle

Brazil

Bare Behind Bars

Canada

Anne Trister
The Company of Strangers
Fire
Fun (with USA)
I've Heard the Mermaids Singing

Love and Human Remains
The Maids (with GB)
Skin Deep
When Night Is Falling

Denmark

The Hotel New Hampshire (with Germany, Portugal and USA)

The House of the Spirits (with Germany, Portugal and USA)

INDEX OF COUNTRIES OF ORIGIN

France

Les Abysses
At First Sight
Barbarella (with Italy)
Becoming Colette (with USA and Germany)
Belle de Jour (with Italy)
Belle Époque (with Spain)
Les Biches (with Italy)
Bilitis
Bitter Moon (with GB)
Céline and Julie Go Boating
The Conformist (with Germany and Italy)
Daughters of Darkness (with Belgium, Germany and Italy)
Les Diaboliques
Écoute Voir
Emilienne
Emmanuelle
Gazon Maudit
May Fools (with Italy)
Muriel's Parents Have Had It Up to Here
Novembermoon (with Germany)
Olivia
Orlando (with GB, Russia, Italy and the Netherlands)
The Satin Spider
The Stolen Diary (with Italy)
To Forget Venice (with Italy)
Les Voleurs
The Women's Club

Germany

Becoming Colette (with USA and France)
The Bitter Tears of Petra von Kant
The Conformist (with France and Italy)
Daughters of Darkness (with Belgium, France and Italy)
The Handmaid's Tale (with USA)
The Hotel New Hampshire (with Denmark, Portugal and USA)
The House of the Spirits (with Denmark, Portugal and USA)
Maidens in Uniform
My Father Is Coming (with USA)
Novembermoon (with France)
Pandora's Box
Salmonberries (with USA)
Seduction, the Cruel Woman

Great Britain and Northern Ireland

Antonia's Line (with Belgium and the Netherlands)
Bitter Moon (with France)
The Bostonians
Butterfly Kiss
Domestic Bliss
11 Harrowhouse
From Russia with Love
Goldfinger
The Good Father
Great Moments in Aviation
The Greengage Summer
The Haunting
Homemade Melodrama
I Shot Andy Warhol (with USA)
The Lair of the White Worm
The Last Emperor (with Italy)
The L-Shaped Room
Lust for a Vampire
The Maids (with Canada)

INDEX OF COUNTRIES OF ORIGIN

Mona Lisa
Monique
Mrs Dalloway (with the Netherlands and USA)
Nineteen Nineteen
Nocturne
Orlando (with Russia, France, Italy and the Netherlands)
Performance
The Pleasure Principle
Preaching to the Perverted
The Rainbow
Scrubbers
Secret Ceremony
Secret Places
Sister My Sister
Thin Ice
Twins of Evil
Wild Flowers
The World Ten Times Over
Zee & Co

Hong Kong

Intimate Confessions of a Chinese Courtesan

Hungary

Another Way

Italy

Barbarella (with France)
Belle de Jour (with France)
Les Biches (with France)
The Conformist (with France and Germany)
Daughters of Darkness (with Belgium, France and Germany)
The Last Emperor (with GB)
May Fools (with France)
Open City
Orlando (with GB, Russia, France and the Netherlands)
The Stolen Diary (with France)
To Forget Venice (with France)

Japan

Afternoon Breezes
The Enchantment

Netherlands

Antonia's Line (with Belgium and GB)
Mrs Dalloway (with GB and USA)
Orlando (with GB, Russia, France and Italy)

233

INDEX OF COUNTRIES OF ORIGIN

New Zealand

Crush
Desperate Remedies

Heavenly Creatures

Portugal

Caged Women

The Hotel New Hampshire (with Denmark, Germany and USA)

Russia

Orlando (with GB, France, Italy and the Netherlands)

Spain

Belle Époque (with France)
Costa Brava
The Girl with the Golden Panties (with Venezuela)

Golden Balls
Kika
Pasajes
Pepi, Luci, Bom

Sweden

Persona

The Silence

Taiwan

The Silent Thrush

United States

Alien: Resurrection
All Over Me
Bar Girls
Basic Instinct
Becoming Colette (with France and Germany)
Beyond the Valley of the Dolls
Black Widow
Born in Flames
The Boston Strangler
Bound
Bound and Gagged: A Love Story

Boys on the Side
The Brady Bunch Movie
The Butcher's Wife
Caged
Caged Heat
Chained Heat 2
Chasing Amy
The Children's Hour
Claire of the Moon
Cleopatra Jones
The Color Purple
Desert Hearts

INDEX OF COUNTRIES OF ORIGIN

Desperate Living
Diabolique
A Different Story
Double Obsession
Dracula's Daughter
Entwined
Even Cowgirls Get the Blues
Faster, Pussycat, Kill! Kill!
Female Perversions
The First Wives Club
Five Easy Pieces
The Fox
Fried Green Tomatoes at the Whistle Stop Café
Fun (with Canada)
Girlfriends
Girls in Prison (1956)
Girls in Prison (1994)
The Glitter Dome
The Goddess
Go Fish
Grace of My Heart
The Group
The Handmaid's Tale (with Germany)
Henry & June
Higher Learning
The Hotel New Hampshire (with Denmark, Portugal and Germany)
The House of the Spirits (with Germany, Denmark and Portugal)
The Hunger
In a Lonely Place
The Incredibly True Adventure of Two Girls in Love
Internal Affairs
I Shot Andy Warhol (with GB)
Isle of Lesbos
It's in the Water
Jane Street
Johnny Guitar
Julia
Just One of the Guys
Kamikaze Hearts
The Killing of Sister George
Lake Consequence
Late Bloomers
The Legend of Lylah Clare
Lenny
Lianna
Lilith
Liquid Sky
Losing Chase
Manhattan
Mirror Images
Mirror Images Ii
Morocco
Mrs Dalloway (with GB and the Netherlands)
My Father Is Coming (with Germany)
The Night of the Iguana
Night Rhythms
No Exit (with Argentina)
Out of Season
The People vs Larry Flynt
Personal Best
Pink Flamingos
Poison Ivy
Primary Colors
Private Benjamin
Queen Christina
A Question of Love
Rachel, Rachel
Rebecca
Red Sonja
Rescuing Desire
The Rose
Salmonberries (with Germany)
Score (with Yugoslavia)
Screaming Mimi
The Sentinel
Serving in Silence: The Margarethe Cammermeyer Story
Set It Off
Seven Women
She Must Be Seeing Things
She's Gotta Have It

235

INDEX OF COUNTRIES OF ORIGIN

Showgirls
Silkwood
Slaves to the Underground
Some Prefer Cake
The Sticky Fingers of Time
Switch
Therese and Isabelle
Three of Hearts
Times Square
To Live and Die in LA
Too Much Sun

Touch of Evil
Two Moon Junction
The Unbearable Lightness of Being
Vixen
Walk on the Wild Side
The Watermelon Woman
The Wild Party
Work
Yentl
Young Man with a Horn

Venezuela

The Girl with the Golden Panties (with Spain)

Yugoslavia

Score (with USA)

Index of Actors

Abrahms, Jerry 120
Abril, Victoria 83, 84, 85, 121
Acord, Leon 202
Adams, Joey Lauren 42
Adjani, Isabelle 60, 61
Affleck, Ben 42
Agutter, Jenny 185
Aiken, Robert 213
Akerman, Chantal 117
Akers, Andra 56
Akiyoshi, Kumiko 69
Albertini, Michel 182
Alcorn, Joan 145
Alexander, Jane 174
Allen, Ginger Lynn 33
Allen, Woody 141
Alterio, Hector 107
Alvarado, Trini 208
Alvarez, Diego 162
Anderson, Judith 177
Anderson, Martha 17
Andersson, Bibi 164
Anholt, Christien 170
Anspach, Susan 76
Anthony, Lysette 168
Araujo, Graciela 107
Arbolino, Richard 143
Arestrup, Niels 117
Argal, Else 221
Armstrong, Kerry 84
Arndt, Denis 18
Artel, Sabrina 109
Ashcroft, Peggy 185
Asher, Jane 96
Assante, Armand 172
Atake, Mari 8

Atman, Bruce 178
Attal, Henri 22
Audran, Stéphane 22, 23
Auger, Claudine 185
Auteuil, Daniel 214
Avedikian, Serge 204
Avery, Charlotte 206
Avery, Margaret 49
Aya, Setsuko 8
Ayola, Rakie 94
Azmi, Shabana 74

Babe, Fabienne 214
Bacall, Lauren 224, 225
Bacri, Jean-Pierre 15
Badel, Sarah 146
Baillargeon, Paule 115
Bain, Imogen 184
Bainter, Fay 44
Balasko, Josiane 83
Baldwin, William 110, 207, 208
Balkin, Karen 44
Balletbo-Coll, Marta 52
Balsam, Martin 187
Bancroft, Anne 190, 191
Bancroft, Cameron 135
Banderas, Antonio 104
Banes, Lisa 103
Banks, Tyra 102
Bardem, Javier 90
Barkin, Ellen 205
Barnes, Christopher

Daniel 35
Barnes, Susan 188
Barr, Roseanne 71
Barrow, Bernard 175
Barrymore, Drew 34, 35, 169, 170
Basil, Toni 76
Bates, Alan 179
Bates, Florence 177
Bates, Kathy 60, 61,79, 171, 172
Bates, Ralph 137
Bauchau, Patrick 15
Baxter, Anne 216
Baxter, Lynsey 168
Beatty, Ned 174
Beatty, Warren 132
Beck, Stanley 130
Becker, Belinda 203
Bedelia, Bonnie 174
Bell, Tom 124, 170
Benes, Lucie 41
Berge, Colette 7
Berge, Francine 7
Bergen, Candice 66, 97, 98
Bergman, Sandahl 177
Berkeley, Elizabeth 193, 195
Berkin, Sandra 150
Berlin, Mark 116
Bernard, Susan 71
Bernhard, Sandra 54, 55
Berry, Stephanie 109
Bertei, Adele 28
Bertish, Suzanne 206, 207

INDEX OF ACTORS

Berto, Juliet 40
Best, Alyson 140
Betty 111
Bezace, Didier 214
Bianca, Raquel 90
Bianchi, Daniela 80
Bigiaoui, David 147
Binoche, Juliette 213
Björnstrand,
　Gunnar 164
Black, Karen 33, 76
Blackman, Honor 91,
　92, 93
Blake, Julia 140
Blanc, Dominique 142
Blodgett, Michael 20
Bloom, Claire 99
Blundell, Jake 54
Bluteau, Lothaire 106,
　158
Bogart, Humphrey
　108, 109
Boling, Alex 112
Bolling, Tiffany 221
Bond, Ward 117
Bonifas, Paul 7
Bono, Chastity 16,
　198
Borgnine, Ernest 129
Bories, Marcel 142
Bortz, Jason 200
Bossley, Caitlin 53
Bouchez, Elodie 204
Bowes, Ed 191
Bowie, David 105
Bown, Nicola 145
Bown, Paul 37
Bracco, Lorraine 71,
　205, 206
Bradford, Richard 110
Brady, Scott 117
Brandauer, Klaus
　Maria 19
Bream, Cass 103
Brennan, Eileen 172
Brent, Romney 183
Breton, Michèle 163
Bridges, Beau 103,
　134

Bridges, Lloyd 89
Briggs, Pat 10
Bright, Bob 156
Broadbent, Jim 93
Brodie, V. S. 88, 89
Bronson, Lisa
　Marie 217
Brooks, Dana 200
Brooks, Louise 160
Brown, Amelda 198
Brown, Clancy 72
Brown, Juanita 39
Brown, Pamela 185
Browne, Coral 122,
　123
Bruno, Nando 157
Buck, Samantha 203
Bull, Richard 62
Bunnage, Avis 124
Burns, Mark 139
Burton, Richard 149
Busch, Dennis 71
Bush, Billy 'Green' 76
Busia, Akosua 49
Bussemaker,
　Reinout 14
Bussières, Pascale 218,
　219
Butler, Dean 56
Byrne, Anne 141
Byrne, Rose 54
Byron, Kathleen 212

Caicedo, Franklin 107
Caillat, Jean-Louis 147
Caine, Michael 144,
　225
Calame, Laurence 204
Calleia, Joseph 211
Callow, Simon 93
Calparsoro, Carla 161
Capaldi, Peter 125
Capucine 216, 217
Carey, Phil 183
Carlisle, Anne 133
Carmichael,
　Hoagy 224
Caron, Leslie 124
Carradine, John 187

Carroll, Kevin 116
Carroll, Leo G. 177
Carstensen, Margit 25,
　26
Carter, Gary 127
Cartwright,
　Veronica 44
Casanovas, Alex 121
Casey, Bernie 49
Caven, Ingrid 182
Chabat, Alain 83
Chamberlain, Joy 103
Chang Ying-
　Chen 196
Chapman, Keri
　Jo 113, 114
Chappell, Lisa 59
Charbonneau,
　Patricia 56, 57
Charter, Nancy 113
Chen, Joan 126
Cher 197
Cherney, Linda 183
Cherry, Helen 66
Child, Kirsty 166
Chong, Rae Dawn 49
Chowdhry, Ranjit 74
Christie, Helen 137
Churchill,
　Marguerite 65
Clauss, Rusty 159
Clémenti, Pierre 20,
　51
Close, Glenn 104,
　105, 188, 189
Clouzot, Vera 61
Coco, James 221
Coffield, Peter 208
Cohen, Adam 85
Cole, Gary 35
Colin, Margaret 37
Collentine, Barbara 62
Colletin, Jeanne 68
Collins, Ray 211
Collins, Roberta 39
Collinson,
　Madeleine 212
Collinson, Mary 212
Collyer, Eve 30

238

INDEX OF ACTORS

Coltrane, Robbie   144
Compton, Fay   99
Compton, Juliette   146
Conaway, Jeff   143
Connelly, Jennifer   102
Connery, Sean   80, 91, 92
Connors, Chuck   180
Conrath, Malcolm   204
Converse-Roberts, William   188
Cooper, Ben   117
Cooper, Gary   146
Copeland, Joan   89
Corby, Ellen   38
Cortese, Valentina   129
Côte, Laurence   214
Cotterill, Chrissie   184
Courtneidge, Cicely   124
Cowan, Jerome   224
Cox, Alan   146
Coyote, Peter   24, 121
Crawford, Joan   117, 118
Crawford, Rachel   218
Crean, David   200
Crider, Missy   87
Crisp, Quentin   158
Crutchley, Rosalie   99
Cruz, Pénelope   20
Cruz, Wilson   10
Culver, Calvin   182
Cuny, Alain   68
Curry, Tim   208
Curtin, Valerie   62
Curtis, Cliff   59
Curtis, Tony   29
Cushing, Peter   212
Czerny, Henry   218

D'Abo, Maryam   64
D'Agostino, Liza   16
D'Angelo, Beverley   188
D'Arbanville, Patti   23, 24
Dabney, Sheila   191

Dafoe, Willem   210
Daly, Nancy   159
Daniels, Jeff   37
Dano, Royal   221
Darrieux, Danielle   96, 221
Darwell, Jane   86
Das, Nandita   74
Davey, Maude   156
Davi, Robert   193
Davis, Judy   188, 189
Davis, Sammi   125, 176
Day, Doris   224, 225
Day, Josette   221
Day, Matt   136
Day-Lewis, Daniel   213
de Baer, Jean   85
de Berg, Marina   155
de Boysson, Pascale   7
De Brauw, Elsie   14
de Bray, Yvonne   155
De Medeiros, Maria   90, 91, 101, 102
de Palma, Rossy   121
de Young, Cliff   105
Dear, Elizabeth   96
Decleir, Jan   14
Dehelly, Suzanne   155
Del Valle, Desi   52, 202
Delay, Florence   65
Delevanti, Cyril   149
Delgado, Iris   69
Delorme, Danièle   154
Deneuve, Catherine   20, 65, 66, 105, 214, 215, 216
Denning, Richard   86
Dennis, Sandy   76, 78
Denton, Christopher   33
Denton, Lucas   134
Desny, Ivan   214
DeVries, Jon   131
Diabo, Alice   50
Díaz-Aroca, Miriam   20

DiCamp, Kyle   191
Dickenson, Sheila   46
Dickey, Dale   109
Dietrich, Marlene   146
Dillon, Matt   94
Divine   167
Dobson, Tamara   49
Donat, Peter   62
Donhowe, Gwyda   30
Donnell, Jeff   109
Donnelly, Patrice   165
Donohoe, Amanda   125, 176
Dorff, Stephen   106
Dotson, Michael   112
Dottermans, Els   14
Dougherty, Suzi   136
Douglas, Illeana   94
Douglas, Kirk   224, 225
Douglas, Michael   18
Doukas, Susan   133
Dourdan, Gary   9
Dowd, Ann   10
Dowell, Raye   192
Dowie, Freda   37
Downey, Robert, Jr   210
Dreyfuss, James   206
Dubose, Tammy   202
Duchaussoy, Michel   142
Dulany, Caitlin   178
Dullea, Kier   76
Dunaway, Faye   98
Dundas, Jennie   103
Dundas, Jennifer   75
Dunye, Cheryl   217
Dunye, Irene   217
Duvall, Robert   98
Dyktynski, Matthew   136
Dzundza, George   18, 37

Eaton, Shirley   91
Ecoffey, Jean-Philippe   101
Edel, Alfred   148

239

INDEX OF ACTORS

Edmonds, Elizabeth 184
Edney, Beatie 220, 221
Ehlers, Beth 105
Eichhorn, Lisa 152, 153
Ekberg, Anita 183
Ekers, Jackie 152
Elise, Kimberly 189
Emerson, Hope 38
Epps, Omar 102
Erdman, John 191
Ernst, Laura 210, 211
Evans, John 115
Evans, Jon 213
Ewell, Dwight 42

Fabrizi, Aldo 157
Fackeldey, Gisela 25
Falk, Rossella 129
Fargas, Antonio 49
Farrow, Mia 185
Fecteau, Dennis 159
Feist, Harry 157
Fenn, Sherilyn 119, 120, 207, 208, 212, 213
Ferriti, Danielle 17
Feuer, Debra 210
Feuillère, Edwige 155, 156
Finch, Peter 129
Finlay, Frank 150
Firth, Colin 150
Firth, Peter 168
Fishburne, Laurence 102
Fisher, Beth 64
Fisher, Frances 72
Fitz-Jones, Jacob 145
Flagg, Fannie 76
Fletcher, Louise 212
Flowers, Kim 9
Fluegel, Darlanne 210
Folland, Alison 10, 11
Fonda, Bridget 94
Fonda, Henry 29
Fonda, Jane 17, 118, 216

Fonda, Peter 132
Fontaine, Joan 177
Fontaine, Kathleen 202
Forqué, Veronica 121
Forrest, Frederic 64, 179
Foster, Jodie 103, 104
Foster, Meg 62, 63
Fowle, Susannah 84
Fox, David 218
Fox, James 163
Fox, Viveca A. 189
Francis, Eve 221
Franklin, Patt 222
Fraser, Ronald 122
Freeman, Brian 217
Frey, Sami 27, 65
Frobe, Gert 91
Fuller, Lance 86

Gabella, Tom 161
Gable, Christopher 176
Gael, Anna 206
Gallacher, Frank 54
Galle, Raymond 221
Galletti, Giovanna 157
Gam, Rita 152
Gara, Olvido 'Alaska' 162
Garbo, Greta 173, 174
Garcia, Andy 110
Garcin, Stéphane 154
Gardner, Ava 149
Garneau, Constance 50
Garner, Alice 136
Garner, James 44, 46, 88
Garrett, Teresa 113, 114
Garver, James 200
Gaspar, Flora 148
Gassmann, Alessandro 90
Gavin, Erica 20, 39, 213, 214
Gere, Richard 110

Germany, Serge 147
Germon, Nane 22
Gershon, Gina 31, 32, 33, 193, 194, 195
Gibson, Thomas 135
Gidden, Yvonne 63
Gielgud, John 66
Gifford, Alan 183
Gil, Ariadna 20
Gilbert, Helen 86
Gilbert, John 173, 174
Gilbert, Sara 169
Gillette, Ruth 109
Giorgi, Eleonora 209
Giraudeau, Bernard 23
Glen, Scott 165
Glover, Danny 49
Glover, John 119
Gold, Lynda 39
Goldberg, Whoopi 34, 35, 49
Gomes, Marliane 17
Gómez, Fernando Fernán 20
Gonzalez, Mimi 202
Götz, Carl 160
Graham, Caren 46
Graham, Heather 71
Graham, Julie 170
Grahame, Gloria 108, 109
Grant, Gerald 182
Grant, Hugh 24, 125
Grant, Richard E. 101
Gray, Vivean 166
Green, Marika 68
Grey, Nan 65
Griffiths, Linda 131
Griggs, Camilla 16
Grodin, Charles 66, 67
Gross, Molly 200
Grossmann, Mechthild 186
Guard, Dominic 166
Guerin, Nathalie 67
Guest, Christopher 85
Guilfoyle, Paul 171
Guilhe, Albane 11
Gwynne, Haydn 168

240

INDEX OF ACTORS

Gyngell, Kim   136

Hackett, Joan   97
Hailey, Leisha   10
Haji   71
Hale, Georgina   170
Hall, Grayson   149
Hallaren, Jane   131
Hallum, John   113
Han, Maggie   127
Hanover, Donna   161
Harada, Kiwako   69
Harden, Marcia Gay   53, 75
Hardie, Kate   144
Harmon, Jeff B.   112, 113
Harrelson, Brett   161
Harrelson, Woody   161
Harrington, Kate   175
Harris, Jared   106
Harris, Julie   99
Harrison, Cathryn   206
Hartman, Elizabeth   97
Hartnell, William   222
Harvey, Laurence   216
Haupt, Ulrich   146
Hauser, Cole   10
Hawn, Goldie   75, 172
Hayden, Sterling   117
Haynie, Jim   210
Haywood, Chris   140
Headley, Lena   146
Heche, Anne   87
Heckart, Eileen   75
Hedaya, Dan   75, 105
Hemingway, Margaux   64
Hemingway, Mariel   141, 165
Hemmings, David   17, 176
Henderson, Jo   131
Hennigan, Dee   127, 128, 129
Hensley, Sonya   112
Hepburn, Audrey   44
Hermann, Irm   25

Hernandez, Juano   224
Heston, Charlton   211
Hewitt, Martin   150, 212
Heyman, Barton   178
Heywood, Anne   76
Hicks, Tommy Redmond   192
Hiegel, Catherine   83
Higgins, Clare   150, 151, 206, 207
Hiken, Gerald   89
Hill, Jean   58
Hill, Steve   89
Ho, Lily   111
Hoffman, Dustin   130
Holbrook, Hal   118
Holden, Gloria   65
Holden, Winifred   50
Holgado, Ticky   83
Holland, Betty Lou   89
Holloman, Laurel   109, 110
Honey   28, 29
Hong, James   27
Hope, Leslie   81
Hopkins, Anthony   93
Hopkins, Miriam   44
Hopper, Dennis   27
Hoskins, Bob   144
Howard, Trevor   66
Howley, Tara   202
Hudson, Toni   119
Hughes, Mary Beth   224
Humphrey, Renee   81, 82
Humphries, Barry   84
Hunter, Kim   132
Huppert, Isabelle   15
Hurst, Michael   59
Hurt, John   71, 94
Hyser, Joyce   119

Ice Cube   102
Idle, Eric   210
Ingram, Kate   184
Irons, Jeremy   104
Irving, Amy   223, 224

Ito, Naomi   8

Jaaferi, Jaaved   74
Jackson, Glenda   139, 140, 176
Jacoby, Billy   119
Jagger, Mick   163
Jankowska-Cieslak, Jadwiga   12, 13
Jefford, Barbara   137
Jeffries, Ira   217
Jenson, Jane   116
Jergens, Adele   86
Johns, Tracy Camilla   192
Johnson, Michael   137
Johnson, Richard   99
Johnson, Robin   208
Jones, Karen   152
Josephson, Erland   209, 213
Jourdan, Catherine   182
Judd, Edward   222

Kamino, Brenda   115
Kaplan, Cynthia   222
Karasun, May   126
Karlen, John   55
Kaskanis, Dora   156
Kästner, Shelly   148
Kates, Kimberley   41
Kay, Sibylla   145
Kaye, Norman   140
Keaton, Diane   75, 141
Keith, Ian   173
Keith, Sheila   220
Kelly, Joy   159
Kelly, Kristine   143
Kennedy, Flo   28
Kennedy, George   29
Kensit, Patsy   94
Kent, Diana   100
Kerr, Deborah   149
Kharbanda, Kulbushan   74
Kidder, Margot   88
Kier, Odo   186
King, Perry   62, 63, 205, 206, 221

241

INDEX OF ACTORS

Kinski, Natassia 103, 104
Kirby, Christa 116
Kirshner, Mia 135
Kitchen, Michael 146
Klein, Catherine 147
Knight, Shirley 97
Kohler, Gilles 23
Kortner, Fritz 160
Koslo, Paul 41
Krajeski, Janet 112
Kristel, Sylvia 68
Kristensen, Mona 23
Kroner, Josef 12
Krook, Margaretha 164
Kruger, Otto 65
Kusakari, Masao 69

La Zar, John 20
Laage, Barbara 206
Labourier, Dominique 40
Lacey, Ronald 177
Ladd, Cheryl 169
LaFerriere, Natacha 200
Lambert, Anne 166
Lancaster, Stuart 71
lang, kd 71, 180, 181
Lasater, Barbara 113
Latifah, Queen 189, 190
Laurier, Lucie 11
Law, John Phillip 17
Le Tallec, Rozenn 142
Lederer, Franz 160
Lee, Bernard 124
Lee, Gypsy Rose 183
Lee, Jason 42
Lee, Jennifer 221
Lee, Spike 192
Leigh, Janet 211
Leigh, Suzannah 137
Leighton, Margaret 190
Leitch, Donovan 106
Lenya, Lotte 80
Lester, Adrian 171

Li Yu-Shan 196
Libossart, Isabel 39
Lindblom, Gunnel 195
Lindfors, Viveca 152
Lindley, Audra 56
Lindström, Jörgen 164, 195
Lisano, Sarah 69
Lithgow, John 88
Lochary, David 167
Lone, John 126
Long, Jenny 152
Long, Shelley 35
Longley, Victoria 54
Longman, Alix 84
Lopez, Charo 161
Lorenz, Cristian 39
Love, Courtney 161
Lovejoy, Frank 108
Lowe, Rob 103, 104
Lowe, Susan 58
Lowry, Lynn 182
Lu Yi-Ch'an 196
Ludwig, Karen 141
Lynch, Kelly 207
Lynskey, Melanie 100
Lyon, Sue 149, 190, 191

McBroom, Marcia 20
McCambridge, Mercedes 117
McCarthy, Helena 152
McCarthy, Sheila 115
McConaughey, Matthew 34
McCrane, Paul 103
McDevitt, Faith 46, 48
MacDonald, Ann-Marie 115
McDonald, Francis 146
McDonald, Jessica Wight 131
McDormand, Frances 37
McElhone, Natascha 146, 147

McGann, Paul 176
McGinley, John C. 189
McGovern, Elizabeth 98
MacGowran, Tara 185
McKean, Michael 35
McKellar, Don 218
McKellen, Ian 206
McKenna, Robert 120
McKinney, Bill 49
MacLaclan, Kyle 193
MacLaine, Shirley 44, 46
McLaughlin, Sheila 186
McMillan, T. Wendy 88
McNamara, Madelaine 103
McNichol, Kristy 212
Madigan, Amy 72
Madsen, Virginia 19
Magimel, Benoît 204, 214
Magnani, Anna 157
Mair-Thomas, Sara 168
Makkena, Wendy 188
Malaret, Montserrat 52
Malicki-Sanchez, Keram 200
Mallett, Tania 91
Malone, Dorothy 18
Mandalis, Elena 156
Mantel, Henriette 35
Marchand, Guy 15
Margolin, Stuart 88
Margolyes, Miriam 93
Marks, Leo 203
Marleau, Louise 11
Marley, John 88
Mars, Betty 67
Marshall, Ruth 135
Martin, Andrea 210
Martin, Jon 120
Mason, James 66, 67
Massee, Michael 148

INDEX OF ACTORS

Massey, Edith 58
Masterson, Mary Stuart 79
Mattes, Eva 25
Matthews, Terumi 203
Maura, Carmen 162
Maxwell, Lois 99
May, Jodhi 198, 199
May, Mathilda 19
Mayron, Melanie 85, 86
Meacham, Anne 132
Meddings, Cissy 50
Medina, Patricia 122
Meigs, Mary 50, 51
Melato, Mariangela 209
Melendez, Migdalia 88
Meloni, Christopher 31
Menjou, Adolphe 146
Mennett, Tigr 120
Merchant, Vivien 139
Merrison, Clive 100
Mesguich, Daniel 182
Mestres, Isabel 85
Metcalf, Laurie 110, 111
Mette, Nancy 85
Meurisse, Paul 61
Mewes, Jason 42
Michi, Maria 157
Midler, Bette 75, 179
Miles, Sylvia 188
Miller, Warren 39
Millet, Christiane 154
Mills, Danny 167
Mills, Kiri 59
Miner, Jan 130
Mink Stole 58, 167
Miou-Miou 15, 142
Mirren, Helen 134
Mitchell, Melissa 46
Mitchell, Rahda 136
Mitchell, Sharon 120
Mitchum, Robert 185
Monda, Carol 159
Monette, Richard 115

Moore, Demi 37
Moore, Joanna 211, 216
Moore, Kenny 165
Moore, Maggie 109, 110
Moorehead, Agnes 38
More, Kenneth 96
More, Mandy 63
Morse, Helen 166
Morton, Gary 130
Moschin, Gastone 51
Moses, William R. 81
Mullins, Melinda 178
Murphy, Michael 141
Murphy, Rosemary 118
Murua, Lautaro 85, 107
Myers, Cynthia 20

Navarro, Edwige 204
Nelson, Connie 127, 128
Nelson, Craig T. 197
Neuwirth, Bob 200
Nice, Penny 63
Nicholls-King, Melanie 200
Nicholson, Jack 76
Nielsen, Brigitte 41, 177
Nimri, Najwa 161
Nollier, Claude 96
Norton, Edward 161
Novak, Kim 129
Novikoff, Rashel 130

O'Brien, Maureen 152
O'Connor, Frances 136
O'Connor, Simon 100
O'Donnell, Chris 79
O'Donnell, Michael Donovan 213
O'Neil, Colette 220
O'Quinn, Terry 27
O'Shea, Milo 17
O'Toole, Peter 126

Ogier, Bulle 40
Ogilvy, Pierre 67
Ohama, Natsuko 200
Olbrychski, Daniel 213
Olin, Lena 213
Olivia, Claire 155, 156
Olivier, Laurence 177
Olson, James 175
Orive, Pilar 39
Osburg, Gabriele 154
Ostrenko, Kim 69
Ouimet, Danièle 55
Oxenberg, Catherine 125
Ozdogru, Nuvit 11

Page, Genevieve 20
Page, Harrison 213
Pagliero, Marcello 157
Pallenberg, Anita 17, 163
Palminteri, Chazz 60
Pankow, John 210
Pantoliano, Joe 31, 207
Parillaud, Anne 65
Parker, Carl 182
Parker, Eleanor 38
Parker, Lisa 16
Parker, Mary Louise 34, 79
Parker, Nicole 109, 110
Parker, Sarah Jessica 75
Parsey, Martha 63
Parsons, Estelle 175
Pasley, Thomas 203
Patinkin, Mandy 223
Patterson, Caroline 152, 153
Pearce, Mary Vivian 58, 167
Peirse, Sarah 100
Perlman, Ron 9
Perrier, Dominique 147
Perrine, Valerie 130
Persson, Essy 206

243

INDEX OF ACTORS

Peters, Brock   124
Peters, Clarke   144
Peterson, Lisa   127
Peterson, William   210
Pettet, Joanna   97
Phoenix, Pat   124
Phoenix, Rain   71
Piccoli, Michel   20, 142
Pichel, Irving   65
Pillsbury, Garth   213
Pinchot, Bronson   75
Pinkett, Jada   189
Pinon, Dominique   9
Pisani, Anne-Marie   204
Pisier, Marie-France   40, 41
Plimpton, Martha   106
Plummer, Amanda   37
Plummer, Glenn   193
Pontremoli, David   209
Pope, Lucita   198
Potter, Madeleine   30
Powell, Esteben   127
Pradal, Bruno   154
Price, Dennis   212
Pryce, Jonathan   94
Pugh, Willard E.   49

Quester, Hugues   11
Quick, Diana   150
Quinn, Aidan   98

Rabal, Francisco   20
Raines, Cristina   187
Rau, Andréa   55
Rayes, Ernie, Jr   178
Read, Dolly   20
Redgrave, Vanessa   30, 31, 94, 95, 118, 119, 146
Rees, Donogh   53
Reeve, Christopher   30
Reeves, Keanu   71
Reeves, Saskia   37
Regina, Sonia   17
Regis, Colette   7

Regnier, Carola   186
Reid, Beryl   122, 123, 124
Reid, Carl Benton   108
Reid, Ella   39
Reid, Gregory A., Jr   159
Rekhi, Kushal   74
Relin, Marie-Therese   185
Renay, Liz   58
Renucci, Robin   15
Reviczky, Gabor   12
Rhys, Paul   19
Ribeiro, Neide   17
Richardson, Joely   198, 199
Richardson, Natasha   98
Richie, June   222, 223
Rimkus, Stevan   220
Rivière, Julien   214
Riviere, Marie   147, 204
Roach, Pat   177
Robards, Jason   118
Roberts, Alice   160
Roberts, Rachel   166, 167
Robins, Laila   72
Robson, Flora   190
Roche, Catherine   50
Rohner, Clayton   119
Romero, Marilyn   69
Rossi, Claudia   200
Rossi, Leo   210
Rotaeta, Félix   162
Rowlands, Gena   174
Rubes, Jan   188
Russell, Kurt   197
Russell, Theresa   27
Russo, Ronald   39
Rust, Richard   216
Ryan, Hilary   84
Ryan, John P.   30
Ryan, Marisa   200
Ryder, Winona   9, 10, 104

Saito, Machiko   202
Sakata, Harold   91
Saltarrelli, Elizabeth   33
Sambrell, Aldo   39
Sanchez, Veronica   69
Sanda, Dominique   51, 107, 108
Sanders, Derrick   113
Sanders, George   177
Sandrelli, Stefania   51
Sanz, Jorge   20
Sarandon, Chris   187
Sarandon, Susan   105, 106
Sarelle, Leilani   18
Sarky, Daniel   68
Sartain, Gailard   79
Sassard, Jacqueline   22
Satana, Tura   71
Satterfield, Jeanne   28
Sayles, John   131
Scarwid, Diana   197
Schaake, Katrin   25
Schell, Maria   150, 151
Schell, Maximilian   118
Schlichter, Hedwig   138
Schroeder, Barbet   40
Schwannecke, Ellen   138
Schwarzenegger, Arnold   177
Schygulla, Hanna   25
Scofield, Paul   150
Scorsese, Nicolette   87
Scott-Thomas, Kristin   24, 25
Seberg, Jean   132
Sedgwick, Kyra   134
Segado, Alberto   107
Seghers, Mil   14
Seigner, Emmanuelle   24
Selzer, Milton   129
Serna, Assumpta   107, 108
Serrano, Nestor   87
Severance, Joan   126
Seyrig, Delphine   55

INDEX OF ACTORS

Sharp, Anastasia 88
Shaver, Helen 56, 57
Shaw, Robert 80
Shaw, Stan 79
Sheppard, Delia 143, 150
Sheppard, Paula E. 133
Sheridan, Danica 112
Signoret, Simone 61
Sillas, Karen 72
Simon, Simone 155
Siva, Eva 162
Skerritt, Tom 169
Skinner, Anita 85
Skye, Ione 87
Slater, Justine 16
Small, Marya 221
Smart, Jean 35
Smith, Art 108–9
Smith, Kevin 42, 59
Smith, Kirsten Holly 112
Smith, Lois 76
Smith, Maggie 75
Smith, Paul 177
Smith, Pete 53
Smits, Jimmy 205, 206
Sohn, Sonia 222
Soloman, Jesse 131
Sorel, Jean 20
Spacey, Kevin 101
Splendore, Marie Stella 17
Sprague, Peter 222
Sprinkle, Annie 148
Stafford, Kate 109
Stanley, Kim 89
Stanley, Lyndey 103
Stanton, Harry Dean 179
Stanwyck, Barbara 216, 217
Steele, Barbara 39
Steenburgen, Mary 37
Stensgaard, Yutte 137
Sterne, Morgan 152
Stewart, Martha 108
Stockfeld, Betty 221

Stolz, Eric 94
Stone, Lewis 173
Stone, Sharon 18, 19, 60, 61
Streep, Meryl 104, 105, 118, 141, 142, 197
Streisand, Barbra 223, 224
Strickland, Gail 207
Stuart, Cassie 185
Subkoff, Tara 10
Sugita, Hiroshi 8
Suli, Ania 81
Sumner, David 145
Sutton, Dudley 158
Swanson, Kristy 102
Sweeney, Michelle 50
Swinton, Tilda 72, 73, 158, 159
Sycluna, Alexander 182
Sykes, Brenda 49
Syms, Sylvia 222, 223
Szapolowska, Grazyna 12, 13
Szumlas, Peter 200

Tamblyn, Russ 99
Tamiroff, Akim 211
Tandy, Jessica 30, 79
Taroscio, Enzo 51
Taylor, Christine 35
Taylor, Elizabeth 185, 225, 226
Taylor, Joan 86
Taylor, Lili 106, 107
Tennant, Victoria 98
Terrell, John Canada 192
Tessier, Valentine 221
Thauvette, Guy 11
Thiele, Hertha 138
Thompson, Emma 171
Thornton, Billy Bob 171
Thulin, Ingrid 195
Thurman, Uma 71, 101, 102

Thursfield, Sophie 198, 199
Tierney, Maura 171
Tilly, Jennifer 31, 32, 33
Tinti, Gabriele 129
Todd, Trisha 46, 47
Tomlinson, Ricky 170
Touati, Elisa 90
Townes, Harry 183
Travis, Nancy 110
Travolta, John 171
Trinka, Paul 71
Trintignant, Jean-Louis 22, 51
Tripplehorn, Jeanne 18
Trumbo, Karen 46, 47
Tung Lin 111
Tunie, Tamara 178
Turner, Guinevere 42, 88, 89, 170, 217, 218
Turpin, Bahni 87
Turturro, John 94, 210
Tutin, Dorothy 94, 95
Tweed, Tracey 150
Tyson, Cathy 144, 145
Tyson, Cicely 79
Tyson, Richard 212

Ubach, Alanna 35
Ullmann, Liv 164
Unde, Emilia 138
Underwood, Blair 189
Urbaniak, James 203

Vahle, Timothy 113
Valandrey, Charlotte 158
Valentine, Scott 64
Van Ammelrooy, Willeke 14
Van Der Groen, Dora 14
Van Overloop, Veerle 14
Van Sloan, Edward 65

245

INDEX OF ACTORS

Vanel, Charles   61
Vannicola, Joanne   135
Vasque, Sparky   120
Vaughan, Peter   66
Vellani, Luca   24
Vera, Hilda   85
Verdi, Dominique   22
Verdú, Maribel   20, 90
Vernon, Anna   206
Vidal, Albert   90
Villa, Alfredo   161
Viner, Frances   93
Von Wernherr, Otto   133
Vonasek, Perla   85

Wadham, Julian   170
Walker, Valarie   217
Walker, Sarah   140
Wallace, Vincene   213
Wallach, Eli   85
Walter, Harriet   93, 142
Walters, Julie   198, 199
Wan Chung-shan   111
Ward, Fred   101
Ward, Skip   149
Ward-Lealand, Jennifer   59
Waters, John   84
Wauthion, Claire   117
Weaver, Jacki   166
Weaver, Lois   191
Weaver, Sigourney   9
Webber, Beth   50
Webber, Robert   172
Weibel, Peter   186
Welch, Racquel   221
Welles, Orson   211
Whalley, Joanne   93
Whirry, Shannon   143
Whitman, Kari   41
Wieck, Dorothea   138
Wiedermann, Elena   39
Wilbur, Claire   182
Williams, Heathcote   158
Williams, JoBeth   205, 206
Williams, Lori   71
Williams, Richard   96
Williams, Sabra   206
Williamson, Nicol   27
Wilson, Elizabeth   89
Wincott, Michael   9
Winfrey, Oprah   49
Winger, Debra   27
Winslet, Kate   100
Winters, Shelley   49
Witt, Alicia   81, 82
Wolfe, Nancy Allison   16
Woodward, Joanne   175
Wright, Amy   86

Yarmush, Michael   134
Yaroshevskaya, Kim   11
Ying Ruocheng   126
York, Amanda   184
York, Susannah   96, 97, 122, 123, 139, 140, 225, 226
Young, Elizabeth   173
Yuan Chia-P'ei   196
Yueh Hua   111

Zabka, William   119
Zane, Billy   126, 158
Zappa, William   53
Zaray, Nicole   203
Zech, Rosel   180, 181